# RUSSIAN ENERGY STRATEGY IN THE ASIA-PACIFIC

## IMPLICATIONS FOR AUSTRALIA

# RUSSIAN ENERGY STRATEGY IN THE ASIA-PACIFIC

## IMPLICATIONS FOR AUSTRALIA

**EDITED BY
ELIZABETH BUCHANAN**

Australian
National
University

PRESS

**ANU PRESS**

Published by ANU Press
The Australian National University
Acton ACT 2601, Australia
Email: anupress@anu.edu.au

Available to download for free at press.anu.edu.au

ISBN (print): 9781760463380
ISBN (online): 9781760463397

WorldCat (print): 1246214161
WorldCat (online): 1246214035

DOI: 10.22459/RESAP.2021

Cover design and layout by ANU Press

# Contents

## Part 1: An Asia-Pacific Energy Outlook

## Part 2: Russian Foreign Energy Strategy

## Part 3: Australia's Asia-Pacific Energy Interests

## Part 4: Russian Energy Strategy and the Future Ahead

# Acronyms

| | |
|---|---|
| ADF | Australian Defence Force |
| ANU | The Australian National University |
| APC | African, Caribbean and Pacific Group |
| APEC | Asia-Pacific Economic Cooperation |
| APR | Asia-Pacific region |
| ASEAN | Association of South-East Asian Nations |
| BAM | Baikal–Amur Mainline |
| BGG | Beijing Gas Group |
| BRI | Belt and Road Initiative |
| CAATSA | *Countering America's Adversaries through Sanctions Act* |
| CAGP | Central Asian Gas Pipeline |
| CBR | Central Bank of Russia |
| CDB | China Development Bank |
| CDU | Central Dispatching Unit |
| CNOOC | China National Offshore Oil Corporation |
| CNPC | China National Petroleum Corporation |
| COOEC | China Offshore Oil Engineering Company |
| COSCO | China Ocean Shipping Company |
| DSME | Daewoo Shipbuilding & Marine Engineering |
| ECT | Energy Charter Treaty |
| EIA | Energy Information Administration |
| EPC | engineering, procurement and construction |
| ESD | Energy Security Doctrine |
| ESPO | Eastern Siberia – Pacific Ocean |

| ETRI | Economic and Technology Research Institute |
| EWP | Energy White Paper |
| FID | financial institutions duty |
| IDF | Industrial Development Fund |
| IEA | International Energy Agency |
| IEEJ | Institute of Energy Economics, Japan |
| IR | International relations |
| JBIC | Japan Bank for International Cooperation |
| JOGMEC | Japan Oil, Gas and Metals National Corporation |
| LNG | liquefied natural gas |
| MOL | Mitsui OSK Lines |
| NATO | North Atlantic Treaty Organization |
| NDRC | National Development and Reform Commission |
| NERA | National Energy Resources Australia |
| NESA | National Energy Security Assessment |
| NPS | new policies scenario |
| NSR | Northern Sea Route |
| OECD | Organisation for Economic Cooperation and Development |
| OPEC | Organization of the Petroleum Exporting Countries |
| POS | Power of Siberia |
| PRRT | Petroleum Resources Rent Tax |
| RDIF | Russian Direct Investment Fund |
| RFE | Russian Far East |
| RPR | Reserves–Production Ratio |
| SOE | State-Owned Enterprise |
| SWIFT | Society for Worldwide Interbank Financial Telecommunication |
| VGK | Vostochnaia gornorudnaia kompaniia |

## Measurement

| | |
|---|---|
| bcf | billion cubic feet |
| bcf/d | billion cubic feet per day |
| bcm | billion cubic metres |
| bcm/y | billion cubic metres per year |
| b/d | barrels per day |
| km | kilometre |
| mb/d | million barrels per day |
| mmbtu | million metric British thermal units |
| mmt | million metric tons (tonnes) |
| mmt/y | million metric tons (tonnes) per year |
| mt | million tons |
| mtoe | million tons of oil equivalent |
| mt/y | million tons per year |
| MW | megawatt |
| tcm | trillion cubic metres |
| tmt | thousand metric tons (tonnes) |

# Figures

# Tables

# Introduction

## Elizabeth Buchanan

Given Australia's lack of energy security strategy, it is not surprising that the country is void of institutional knowledge and know-how of Russian foreign energy strategy. The 'lucky country' as it were, relies entirely on sea lines of communication to the north to supply fuel and to export Australian coal and natural gas. Australia has entered the 2020s as the world's largest liquefied natural gas (LNG) exporter; however, maintaining complacency in Canberra's current export activities will ultimately lead to a long-term security crisis. Australia lacks institutional insight into Russian energy interests in Canberra's prime energy market—the Asia-Pacific. This book seeks to fill this knowledge gap by providing policymakers, academics and tertiary-level students with up-to-date insight and analysis of Russia's foreign energy strategy in the region. By comparing and contrasting this to Australia's energy security over-reliance throughout the Asia-Pacific region (APR), this book highlights serious energy security concerns on the not too distant horizon.

The concept of energy security is an age-old challenge for national strategy and, for Daniel Yergin, it consistently elicits 'new answers'.[1] A constantly evolving issue, energy security is shaped by both internal state forces and external international ones. With an array of definitions and priorities, most experts at least agree on the fact that global energy demand is continuing to increase in step with dwindling *known* supplies of existing energy resources. Put simply, 'easy access' to 'known' or 'proven' energy reserves (namely hydrocarbons—oil and natural gas) is getting harder. Existing wells are dry and explored energy frontiers are in technically challenging and financially prohibitive spaces, such as the

1    Daniel Yergin, 'Ensuring Energy Security', *Foreign Affairs*, March/April 2006, doi.org/10.2307/20031912.

offshore Arctic Ocean. Some of the 'new answers' to this challenge include renewable energy sources and the development of non-traditional energy ventures. While there are various definitions of energy security, common components include:

- secure, uninterrupted supply of energy resources
- secure, forecasted demand of energy resources
- safe, environmentally sound energy sources
- diversity of energy supply and demand
- efficiency of energy supplies.

In a constructivist sense, a state's energy security is what the state in question makes of it. Resource-export intensive states like Australia, in theory, ought to be diversifying and securing their energy export market and working to bolster sea lines of communication to secure their oil import needs. Therefore, an added element to an Australian energy security strategy would incorporate an understanding of changing consumption patterns in the targeted export market. Energy security is akin to a coin—it has two equally important and weighted sides. While Australian energy exports are breaking new records and, on face value, look promising, exports are predicated on secure customer or market demand. Australia may be rich in LNG reserves and export potential, but if the customer base and market are supplied elsewhere, or our exports are unable to reach market destinations, the entire energy security paradigm is impacted. Conflict in the South China Sea would indeed threaten Australia's sea lines of communication and may delay LNG exports from reaching Asian clients, thus eroding Australia's ability to ensure supply security to customers, who then necessarily look to other supply avenues and diversify away from Australian gas and coal.

Australia has continued to 'dodge' accountability in terms of energy security concerns. Void of a national energy security strategy, it may be the case that Canberra is set to learn the necessity of having an energy security policy the hard way—via regional shocks and their domestic economic knock-on effects.

This book critically examines Russian energy strategy in the Asia-Pacific with a view to determining the security implications for Australia. Of course, Russia is important for global energy security chains because of its vast resource wealth and its geographical position—a pivotal position to supply both the European and Asian markets. Geographically constrained as an island continent, Australia has no such luxury. Canberra relies on the nearby Asia-Pacific import market to demand our energy and to facilitate the delivery of our national oil supplies.

Russia ranks among the world's leading countries in terms of reserves in all three primary energy spheres: natural gas, coal and oil. Traditionally, European and former Soviet Union markets have absorbed the bulk of Russian energy exports. However, the rise of China and India, along with the advent of LNG, have seen the Asia-Pacific market emerge as the centre of gravity for future energy demand. In a few short years, the US managed to flip their energy reliance around to be a net exporter of LNG. Washington too has increasingly targeted the Asia-Pacific gas market. These geopolitical shifts in energy markets will have long-term implications for Australia's LNG export 'dream'.

This book comprises four sections with chapters contributed by some of the world's leading Russian energy scholars. An overview of the Asia-Pacific energy outlook, including energy security trends in the region, is first provided. Drivers for Russian strategy in the region are also explored. Next, Russian foreign energy strategy and the role that Moscow's quest for great power plays in energy policy under Putin are discussed. It then tackles the implications of Russian aggression in 2014 on the Crimean Peninsula in terms of how the events have shaped Russian foreign energy strategy.

Part 1 examines the broader Asia-Pacific energy outlook. There is a strong market for natural gas in the Asia-Pacific. Both the production and consumption levels of LNG have increased dramatically in recent years and are expected to continue to grow. China, Japan and South Korea, in particular, are leading consumers of energy and rely heavily on foreign energy imports. Russia has shown intense LNG ambitions through its export strategy to increase its export capacity of LNG by 400 per cent by the mid-2030s. Of course, success is contingent on the realisation of Russia's Arctic region gas projects and the continued cooperation of key Asian partners like China. The US is also placed to increase LNG exports in the region following the domestic shale gas revolution.

However, global political factors are increasing the uncertainty of energy security in the APR. For example, in the face of a protracted US–China economic 'war', China may wish to increase energy imports from Russia, rather than from the US. Here, Russia has identified the opportunities for LNG exports to Asia and has shifted its focus away from Europe and into the Asian region. While Russia's energy exports to Europe have been used before as political leverage (e.g. various instances of supply cuts to Ukraine), it is expected that gas trade between Russia and Asia will remain largely unpoliticised.

Shoichi Itoh opens Part 1 with a study of the Asia-Pacific energy outlook, focusing on the reality that global energy demand has increasingly shifted towards the Asia-Pacific. Market dynamics in the region are investigated and the threats and opportunities associated with the concentration of economic growth in the Asia-Pacific is examined. The chapter ends with an assessment of the APR as host to the new great energy game— the role of LNG in the emerging Asian market. Itoh highlights the fact that Australian, US and Russian LNG export interests compete in the Asia-Pacific theatre and this market competition is only set to increase into the future.

Morena Skalamera presents a study of Russia's foray into the Asia-Pacific energy market. The emergence of US shale upended global energy markets and created a dual challenge for Russia; in oil, it suppressed long-term prices with potentially devastating consequences for the country's budget. For natural gas, the shale gas revolution created a new rival in the increasingly competitive LNG market. While Russia anticipated European demand decline, Moscow began to turn to the East—towards the Asia-Pacific market. Skalamera argues that 2014 was a turning point in the pace of this pivot to Asia, wherein, following Russian action on the Crimean Peninsula, Western sanctions upended Russia's energy strategy in various ways. China became a crucial part of Moscow's ability to lessen the impact of Western sanctions, as it presented an alternative market and source of capital.

In the past few years, Russia has diversified this pivot within the Asia-Pacific to avoid an increasing over-reliance on China. Moscow's push to be a major LNG exporter is on track. However, Skalamera notes that Moscow might not be able to replicate the unusually strong hold it enjoys over European gas markets. For Australia, this means Russian energy exports will no doubt shape the Asia-Pacific market and this reality presents a potential hinderance to Canberra's long-term energy export strategy.

Part 2 delves into Russian foreign energy strategy and the question of what role energy plays in Russia's grand strategy. There are continuing debates as to whether Russia has a grand strategy in relation to its use of energy security. Some argue that Russia's policies since the mid-2000s have shown elements of a grand strategy. What is clear is that Putin is an exceptional opportunist and has sought to maintain Russia's survival and ensure its political, economic and military power. As such, energy is used by Russia as a key tool to achieve the realisation of its grand strategy. The Asian energy market provides Russia with a wide range of strategic relationships, an ability to limit Western influence and also significant economic stimulation. However, these opportunities for Russia in Asia are met with numerous challenges.

Bilateral energy cooperation has been central to the development of the broader Sino-Russian relationship under Putin. Of course, this partnership is merely one of strategic convenience, rather than an example of authoritarian cooperation. Russia has increased its focus on the Asian energy market to improve Moscow's political leverage to offset some of Beijing's political dominance. Increasingly, Russia is also seeking Chinese capital for its Russian Arctic energy projects. Yet, China also needs Russian energy sources to fuel its own projects, such as the Belt and Road Initiative. China wants to increase Russia's dependence on it as a buyer as a tool to control prices. Further, Beijing seeks access to the 'Polar Silk Road' that runs within the Russian Arctic Exclusive Economic Zone.

Overall, Russian energy firms have a clear Asia-Pacific strategy and, by extension, given the state-controlled nature of these entities (Gazprom and Rosneft in particular), Moscow has clear ambitions for the region. Rosneft, Russia's oil giant, has had success in China with pipeline infrastructure, namely the Power of Siberia, which facilitated Moscow in becoming the largest exporter of crude oil to China. Russia's LNG sector has been slow to improve its energy infrastructure projects; however, projects within the Russian Arctic have proliferated. These new Russian energy projects are key to Russia lifting its LNG revenue from Asian markets. Of course, China is expected to be the price setter moving ahead, given its huge consumption of LNG from a wide variety of sources.

Jakob Godzimirski outlines the ways in which energy is both central to the Russian economy and Moscow's grand strategy in providing the country with an important external leverage. In 2018, the energy sector represented 20 per cent of the country's GDP, and generated 45 per cent of budget revenue and 60 per cent of Russia's export revenue. This narrative is not new. Energy played an important role in Russia's strategy both before the collapse of the Soviet Union and in the post-Soviet period. Beyond the capital flows, energy has been used as a tool to help Russia establish long-term strategic relations with countries to which energy resources have been exported.

Although there is no agreement among Russian nor Western experts on whether the current Putin regime has a consistent long-term grand strategy or conducts mostly a reactive, opportunistic policy, it is widely accepted that Russian energy resources play an important part in Russian strategic designs today. Godzimirski's chapter illustrates how revenue generated by production and trade in energy resources have allowed critical investments and increases in defence spending to be made, which in turn has helped Russia re-establish its position as an important regional and global player. Energy (i.e. holding the world's largest hydrocarbon resource deposits) has also assisted Moscow to act as an agenda setter, which is one of the hallmarks of Russia's grand strategy under Putin.

It is useful to view Russian energy resources from a strategic perspective. As Godzimirski notes, energy is largely facilitating the achievement of other strategic goals for Russia, for instance, the re-establishment of Russia's position as a great power. Energy is employed as an instrument to help Russia project its economic and political power to areas that depend on energy supplies coming from Russia. Increasingly, energy resources play an important role, securing the stability and survival of the current Putin regime as a result of the financial windfalls that oil and gas garner.

The popular Russian 'pivot to Asia' became even more apparent following the 2014 crisis in Ukraine that resulted in Western sanctions, Russian countersanctions and the worsening of ties between Russia and the West. Moscow's pivot to Asia has included a focus on strengthening energy relations between Russia and its key Asian partners such as China, India, South Korea and Japan. However, for the time being, Russia's position on the Asian energy market is relatively weak: in 2018, Russia exported 34 per cent of its crude oil to Asia, but this represented only 8 per cent of oil imports to Asia; 16 per cent of Russian export of petroleum products went to Asia, but they represented only 6 per cent of the overall import to Asia; 69 per cent of Russian LNG export (17.2 bcm) went to the Asian market, but this represented only 5 per cent of LNG imports to this area and only 2.1 per cent of the gas consumption in the APR. The situation in the natural gas sector shifted in 2019 when the Power of Siberia pipeline started supplying piped gas to China, strengthening Russia's position in the Chinese and Asian market.

An important strategic change is also the increase in investment in Russian strategic energy projects made by Asian states. In particular, China and India support these projects through providing funding and some technological solutions. Godzimirski argues that this trend will likely continue for years to come, helping Russia diversify not only markets but also partnerships and thus interdependencies. Russia's energy interdependencies present challenges to Moscow's overall grand energy power strategy. There are questions over whether Russia remains an 'energy superpower' post events on the Crimean Peninsula in 2014. Russia's over-reliance on energy revenue has hurt Putin's reputation domestically and internationally. Russia's energy rents have resulted in increased military spending and also the consolidation of oligarchical power. This makes long-term security outlooks problematic. Climate change also poses challenges to Russia as the country has no direct policies in place to promote renewables beyond nuclear power and hydropower.

Peter Rutland presents an analysis of the post-Crimea 2014 implications on Russia's energy 'superpower' quest. In the 2000s, analysts started talking about Russia as an 'energy superpower'. A top three global producer of oil and gas, Russia seemed willing to use energy sales as a lever to exert influence over neighbouring countries. However, after 2008 the situation changed, and worries about Russia as an energy superpower have receded. Since 2008, Russia has been willing to use hard power to advance its interests—through military intervention in Georgia (2008), Ukraine (2014) and Syria (2015). These actions achieved Moscow's immediate goals. Russia's success in part was due to the fact that Putin has tripled military spending in real terms since 2000. Putin has also rattled the nuclear sabre, investing in new weapons and more aggressive deployment of existing weapons. These hard power actions posed a more immediate threat to the security of other countries than vulnerability to disruptions in Russian energy supplies, which could easily be insured against through investment in diversification of supplies.

Rutland delves into the domestic climate, in which Putin increased the concentration of political and economic power in the hands of his inner circle. This group of 'oligarchs' benefited from much of the energy rents. As such, Rutland argues that, over time, Russia has exhibited more of the characteristics of a 'petrostate': corruption, authoritarianism and decreasing economic competitiveness. And, further, that it is these features of the domestic political system that dominate Russia's image in the West.

At the same time, important shifts in global energy markets have weakened Russia's position in global energy markets. The rise of China as the world's largest energy importer has led Russia to start shifting its oil and gas exports to the Chinese market. However, the costs of developing fields and transport networks to feed the Chinese market are high, and Russia's bargaining position vis-à-vis China is weaker than with Europe. Likewise, the US fracking revolution has put a cap on global oil prices and has led to a halving of the global LNG price, cutting Gazprom's revenue stream. Overall, Rutland argues that Russia's capacity to wield the energy 'weapon' to advance its interests looks more questionable today than it did in 2008. The main geopolitical importance of energy when it comes to understanding Russia is its role in shaping the behaviour of the Russian power elite. There are some important feedback loops—both positive and negative—between the domestic political regime of the 'petrostate' and the aspirational international role as an 'energy superpower'.

Part 2 of the book closes with Keun-Wook Paik's study of Russian energy firms in the Asian market. Overall, the result of Russian firms entering into the Asia-Pacific market since 2000 is mixed—very positive results from the oil sector, and mixed results from the gas sector. Paik argues that the oil sector's performance was excellent based on the Eastern Siberia – Pacific Ocean (ESPO) pipeline completion in 2009. The ESPO pipeline played a key role in making Russia the biggest crude oil exporter to China in 2018, with a volume of 71.5 mt/y, more than Saudi Arabia's volume of 15 mt/y. The driving force behind this tangible result was Russia's state-owned company Rosneft. However, Russian firms in the gas sector's performance is mixed. Even though Gazprom started supplying Power of Siberia gas to northern China in 2019, it will take five years to increase the volume of supply to reach the target volume of 38 bcm/y. The two-thirds of Power of Siberia gas covering Heilongjiang, Jilin, Liaoning and Hebei province will not be affected by the competition from LNG supply, but the one-third of Power of Siberia gas will be quite vulnerable given competitive LNG pricing. A further challenge for Gazprom is whether and when the long-negotiated Altai gas line or a second Power of Siberia line can be introduced to China's Xinjiang Province during the first half of the 2020s.

Part 3 moves to examine Australian energy strategy and energy interests in the Asia-Pacific. An insight by a internal policy practitioner is provided by Vice Air Marshall (retired) John Blackburn. Reflecting on a career at the centre of fuel contingency planning, Blackburn presents a dire reality in his chapter on Australian energy insecurity. Australia does not have an energy security strategy and Canberra's fuel import dependency has grown to over 90 per cent since 2010. Australia's strategic fuel reserves are so low that a serious disruption in oil supply would lead to domestic market failure. For instance, tensions in the South China Sea could affect shipping routes and lead to disruptions in oil supply that would have national security implications for Australia. Blackburn argues that the topic of energy security in Australia is highly politicised when it should instead be addressed with nonpartisan political support.

Australia is the only International Energy Agency (IEA) member country that fails to meet its membership oil/fuel stockholding obligations. The IEA has also reported that Australia's stocks are at an all-time low, with the country having no strategic oil stocks (in country) and not placing any stockholding obligation on industry. Canberra's last National Energy Security Assessment (NESA) was published in 2011. The scenarios it used to assess Australian fuel security were inadequate for the risks faced in the APR, particularly with respect to the growing tensions in the South China Sea. As Blackburn notes, an updated NESA was due in 2015 but has not yet been produced, despite separate Senate and Parliamentary Joint Committee recommendations.

Despite the dire domestic energy security situation, Australia's energy exports to the Asia-Pacific are impressive. In 2019, Australia overtook Qatar to become the world's largest LNG producer. Akin to the Australian 'mining boom' of the 2000s, Australia's LNG revolution is threatened by Russian Arctic LNG and US LNG targeting the same Asian market. Another energy export sector in which Australia finds itself in competition with Russia is the coal sector. In his chapter, Stephen Fortescue presents an assessment of Russian coal export strategy in Asia. In 2017, Russia was the world's sixth largest producer behind Australia, which placed fourth, and the world's third largest exporter behind Australia, which placed first. Moscow has set ambitious targets out to 2030 to topple Australia's lead in the coal export industry. Fortescue argues that, while Russia's coal exports may increasingly be competitive with Australia, Russia's production costs are increasing and its labour productivity is still low. While it appears that Canberra will hold the competitive edge in the coal export market, the coal market itself may wind down under global climate change movements and emissions targets. Indications of this precedent gaining momentum are evident in China's (the world's largest coal importer) plans to move away from its coal-intensive economy, thereby 'greening' its footprint.

Part 4 of the book considers the future of Russia's energy strategy in the APR. Maria Shagina presents an analysis of Moscow's adaptation strategy to the 2014 Western sanctions, predominantly applied to the energy industry. Shagina notes that, by design, Western sanctions do not limit the current supply of energy exported from Russia, but instead aim to raise costs for Russia to develop its long-term and technologically challenging projects. Most of these projects are located in the Russian Arctic region. For Shagina, the short-term effect of sanctions is modest at best, given Russia's oil and gas production is currently at record high levels. The ban on Western equipment and limited access to Western capital has negatively impacted Russia's capital-intensive offshore and shale gas projects that require advanced technology. However, in the long run, the impact may be more discernible.

Shagina argues that the combination of financial and technological sanctions will affect Russia's ability to maintain production volumes in the future. With the brownfields in Western Siberia gradually depleting, access to enhanced oil recovery technology will be crucial, yet it is currently denied by the sanctions. In Eastern Siberia, both financial restrictions and a ban on technology transfer will be critical for the development of new fields. As the majority of Eastern Siberian fields are underdeveloped, larger investments and advanced technology will be necessary for the exploration and development of resource deposits. Accelerated by Western sanctions, Russia's import substitution aimed to safeguard the country's economic and technological sovereignty. It was originally designed as a way to stimulate economic growth and competitiveness, but it has descended into selective protectionism with political undertones, favouring state-controlled firms in the capital-intensive sectors.

For Moscow, the pivot to Asia has proven to be an alternative energy market and source of advanced technology and financial support. However, Russian energy companies are becoming increasingly over-dependent on the Chinese market and Chinese equipment and services. In the long run, this over-reliance on China will be detrimental to Russia's local manufacturing, as Beijing's financial support often comes with binding contracts. Japan and South Korea have been instrumental in supporting technologically and financially vital, yet not sanctioned, areas of the energy sector such as shipbuilding, LNG and nuclear power.

Tatiana Romanova's chapter unpacks the most recent Russian Energy Security Doctrine (ESD). While the 2019 ESD is a conceptual document with an opaque legal status, it nevertheless illustrates the Kremlin's priority energy plans. The ESD indicates that the Russian foreign energy policy sector will continue to be driven by geopolitical realities rather than purely market concerns. The doctrine also highlights the sceptical way in which Moscow continues to view clean energy. The ESD acknowledges that decreased energy demand as a result of Europe's clean energy and diversification strategy poses an economic challenge. At the same time, the broader climate change agenda is creating external political challenges. Debates within Russia following the ESD's release in 2019 focused primarily on this juncture—clean energy scepticism and fears of substantial energy rent revenue loses. On the role of the Asia-Pacific market in Russian energy export strategy, the ESD falls short of identifying Western sanctions and reduced European energy demands as the driving forces behind the pivot to the East. Instead, Moscow appears to be communicating that geographical diversification has been a hallmark of Russian foreign energy strategy for quite some time.

This volume fills a knowledge gap by boosting understanding of Russian foreign energy strategy in the region. Given the growing energy requirements in Australia's emerging Asia-Pacific arena that Russia may exploit, this knowledge is crucial. Further, given that Australia's own energy export strategy (primarily in terms of coal, LNG and uranium) relies heavily on the Asia-Pacific market, it represents a security challenge for Canberra. Traditionally, Russian foreign energy strategy has prioritised the European market. However, post-Ukraine 2014, Russia started to eye the Asian market and, in particular, China's energy requirements.

This book seeks to rectify the historical gender imbalance in security studies, particularly in the fields of energy security and Russian studies. It not only supports the research of young women emerging in the field but also incorporates early career researchers to reinvigorate the field of security studies. To the best of my knowledge, and in so far as there are no other books on the market that delve into Russian energy strategy in terms of the specific implications for Australia's foreign energy interests, this book is unique.

# Part 1:
# An Asia-Pacific
# Energy Outlook

# 1

# Energy Outlook in the Asia-Pacific

Shoichi Itoh

The gravity of the global energy demand has increasingly shifted towards the Asia-Pacific. The International Energy Agency (IEA) forecasts that primary energy demand in the Asia-Pacific will increase by 1.4 times in 2017–40.[1] Compared to the total energy consumption of the EU, that of the Asia-Pacific was 3.6 times more in 2017 and is estimated to be 5.2 times more in 2030. Following China as the world's largest energy consumer, India and South-East Asia will also increase energy demand dramatically to 2040. In particular, the role of natural gas has come under the spotlight to meet the growing energy demand as well as environmental needs to reduce greenhouse emissions in the world today. The Asia-Pacific is increasingly no exception to this global trend.

The Asia-Pacific also has gigantic exporters of natural gas, including liquefied natural gas (LNG)—namely Australia, Russia and the US. As a result of the US shale gas revolution, the role of LNG as a means of inter-regional long-distance transportation of natural gas is increasing. The US is projected to become the world's largest LNG exporter by the mid-2020s, by which time China is forecast to top the list of LNG importers by overtaking Japan. Russia, the biggest piped gas exporter in the world, is also striving to become a major LNG exporter in the 2020s.

---

1    International Energy Agency, *World Energy Outlook 2018* (Paris: OECD Publishing, 2018), 40 (hereafter *WEO 2018*).

Energy is securitised from different standpoints by policymakers, businessmen and mass media. The energy landscape is not necessarily transformed simply by the balance of energy supply and demand. Some focus on the security of energy markets. Security of supply is crucial for energy consumers, whereas security of demand is a major concern for energy producers. Others highlight the linkage between energy and security, which goes beyond a mere question of commercial deals. Energy is sometimes used as a means of political leverage to exert impacts on interstate relations.

The first part of this chapter provides an overview of the energy outlook in the Asia-Pacific with a special emphasis on natural gas. In the second part, Russia's growing presence in the Asia-Pacific's LNG market with dynamically changing trade flows is examined from both economic and geopolitical standpoints. We examine China's surging gas demand, the US shale gas revolution and Japan's positioning against its diminishing gas demand as market conditions that await Russia's LNG supplies. Then, the escalation of US–China relations, Tokyo's non-economic approach to Russian energy and the US–Japan joint initiative to create new demand for US LNG exports are discussed.

# Asia-Pacific Energy Outlook

## Primary Energy Demand

According to the Institute of Energy Economics, Japan's (IEEJ) *Outlook 2019*, the global primary energy demand is projected to increase by 1.4 times from 2016 to 2050, of which China, India and the ASEAN (Association of South-East Asian Nations) countries combined will account for 63 per cent of the increment. Asia's primary energy demand is projected to increase by 1.6 times against the background of robust economic growth in 2016–50.[2]

---

2    Institute of Energy Economics, Japan, *IEEJ Outlook 2019* (Tokyo: IEEJ, October 2018), 45 (hereafter *IEEJ 2019*). The reference scenario is drawn from *IEEJ 2019* in this chapter. The IEEJ defines a reference scenario as a scenario that reflects past trends with current energy and environment policies without taking any aggressive policies for low-carbon measures into account. Asia, defined in the *IEEJ 2019*, includes China (including Hong Kong), India, Japan, South Korea, Taiwan, the ASEAN countries (including Brunei, Indonesia, Malaysia, Myanmar, Philippines, Singapore, Thailand and Vietnam), Bangladesh, North Korea, Mongolia, Nepal, Pakistan, Sri Lanka and other countries included in the category 'other Asia' in IEA statistics.

The IEA's *World Energy Outlook 2018* (*WEO 2018*) forecasts that total primary energy demand in the Asia-Pacific will increase from 5,789 mtoe to 8,201 mtoe from 2017 to 2040. During the same period, it is estimated that China's demand will increase at an average annual rate of 1 per cent, whereas that of India and South-East Asia will expand by 3.3 per cent and 2.3 per cent, respectively.[3] As late as 2040, the Asia-Pacific is projected to account for 46 per cent of the global primary energy demand. It is forecast that China's share in this region will decrease from 53 per cent to 47 per cent in 2017–40, whereas that of India and South-East Asia will increase from 16 per cent to 23 per cent, and from 11 per cent to 14 per cent, respectively.[4] In the same time frame, Japan's primary energy demand is forecast to decrease at an average annual rate of 0.5 per cent, while its share in the Asia-Pacific will reduce from 7 per cent to 5 per cent.

Energy consumption in India and the ASEAN combined is projected to reach almost the same level of China and to account for 20 per cent of the global primary energy demand in 2050.[5] India and the ASEAN countries will gradually increase dependency on hydrocarbon fuels in the course of rapid economic growth.[6] It is forecast that China's energy consumption will peak in the mid-2040s with its ageing and decreasing population, but that energy demand in India and the ASEAN countries will continue to increase against the backdrop of their relatively younger demographic composition and high economic growth rates. It is estimated that India and the ASEAN will account for 43 per cent and 25 per cent, respectively, of the incremental growth of primary energy demand in Asia in 2016–50, with Indonesia the fastest-growing energy consumer, followed by Vietnam, in the region.[7] In 2016–50 the energy self-sufficiency ratio is projected to decrease from 72 per cent to 63 per cent in Asia, and from 117 per cent to 66 per cent in the ASEAN as a whole.[8]

---

3    IEA, *WEO 2018*, 40.
4    IEA, *WEO 2018*, 40. The new policies scenario (NPS) is drawn from *WEO 2018*. The IEA defines an NPS as a scenario that 'aims to provide a sense of where today's policy ambitions seem likely to take the energy sector. It incorporates not just the policies and measures that governments around the world have already put in place, but also the likely effects of announced policies, including the Nationally Determined Contributions made for the Paris Agreement'.
5    IEEJ, *IEEJ 2019*, 36.
6    IEEJ, *IEEJ 2019*, 37.
7    IEEJ, *IEEJ 2019*, 45. Indonesia and Vietnam are projected to account for 43 per cent and 25 per cent, respectively, of the increment of the ASEAN's energy consumption during the same period.
8    IEEJ, *IEEJ 2019*, 49.

## Natural Gas

According to IEA's *Gas 2019*, natural gas consumption is forecast to increase at an average annual rate of 1.6 per cent to 2024.[9] Natural gas consumption in the Asia-Pacific is projected to increase by an average annual rate of 4 per cent in 2018–24, contributing to 57 per cent of the global growth of gas demand.[10] China's natural gas demand grew by 14.5 per cent in 2017 and by 18.1 per cent in 2018, but the IEA predicts it will slow to an average annual rate of 8 per cent to 2024.[11] China, however, is expected to account for 42 per cent and 74 per cent of natural gas consumption in the world and the Asia-Pacific, respectively.[12]

The global natural gas demand in 2016–50 is forecast to increase by 1.7 times from 3,505 bcm to 5,986 bcm, of which non-OECD (Organisation for Economic Cooperation and Development) countries will account for 87 per cent of the increment. During the same period, it is estimated that natural gas will have the highest growth rate among all the fuels and account for approximately 40 per cent of the increase in the global primary energy demand: the share of natural gas in the global energy demand will increase from 22 per cent to 27 per cent.[13] Natural gas consumption is forecast to grow by 2.7 times in Asia from 2016 to 2050: its share in the world will increase from 19 per cent to 29 per cent.[14] Natural gas consumption will increase at an average annual rate of 1.6 per cent and overtake coal as the second energy fuel after oil in the latter half of the 2030s in the global market; however, coal will still remain the biggest component of Asia's energy mix as late as 2050.[15]

China's demand for natural gas is projected to expand by 2.8 times in 2016–40, when China alone will account for approximately 20 per cent of the global gas consumption.[16] During the same period, gas demand in

---

9    IEA, *Gas 2019*, 9 (Paris: OECD Publishing, 2019), www.iea.org/reports/gas-2019 (hereafter *Gas 2019*).

10   IEA, *Gas 2019*, 14.

11   IEA, *Gas 2019*, 9.

12   IEA, *Gas 2019*, 19.

13   IEEJ, *IEEJ 2019*, 41.

14   IEEJ, *IEEJ 2019*, 47.

15   IEEJ, *IEEJ 2019*, 172–73. According to *WEO 2018*, the shares of coal and natural gas in primary energy demand will change from 27 per cent to 22 per cent, and 22 per cent to 25 per cent, respectively, from 2017 to 2040 in the world. In contrast, the share of coal will remain the predominant part of the energy mix at 38 per cent in 2040, even if it decreases from 48 per cent in 2017, and that of natural gas will increase from 11 per cent to 15 per cent.

16   IEEJ, *IEEJ 2019*, 172.

ASEAN countries is forecast to increase by 2.1 times. Indonesia, which has hitherto been one of the main gas exporters in the region, is projected to become a net importer of natural gas in the mid-2030s and to increase its natural gas consumption by 2.8 times in 2040, compared to 2016.[17] Malaysia, Thailand and Vietnam are forecast to increase demand for natural gas by 1.6 times, 1.5 times and 3.6 times, respectively, in the same time frame.[18] The natural gas demands of Japan, one of the biggest LNG importers, is projected to decrease due to the restart of its nuclear reactors, the improvement of energy efficiency and the utilisation of non-fossil fuel energy sources, etc.[19]

It is projected that Asia's power generation will almost double in 2040, compared to 2016: that of China, India and ASEAN countries will increase by 1.7 times, 3.1 times and 2.7 times, respectively.[20] By 2040, natural gas consumption for power generation is forecast to increase by 1.4 times in China, by 6.5 times in India and by 2.1 times in ASEAN countries. The ratio of coal in power generation is projected to decrease from 69 per cent to 52 per cent in China, and from 75 per cent to 63 per cent in India, but is to increase from 37 per cent to 46 per cent in ASEAN countries from 2016 to 2040.

## Coal

Coal consumption is forecast to increase by 14 per cent from 2016 to 2050, whereas its share in the global primary energy demand will reduce from 27 per cent to 22 per cent.[21] During the same period, it is estimated that OECD countries will decrease coal consumption by 42 per cent; however, its demand will increase by 34 per cent in non-OECD countries, of which Asia will consume 91 per cent of the increment, especially India and ASEAN countries.[22]

Notwithstanding the overall reduction of coal's share in Asia's power mix, coal will still have the largest share in the region through 2050.[23]

---

17    IEA, *South-East Asia Energy Outlook 2017* (Paris: OECD Publishing, 2017), 83.

18    IEEJ, *IEEJ 2019*, 180–85.

19    IEEJ, *IEEJ 2019*, 47.

20    IEEJ, *IEEJ 2019*, 174–75, 179. Global power generation is forecast to increase at an average annual rate of 1.9 per cent from 2016 to 2050, while non-OECD countries will account for approximately 90 per cent of the incremental growth.

21    IEEJ, *IEEJ 2019*, 42–43.

22    IEEJ, *IEEJ 2019*, 43.

23    IEEJ, *IEEJ 2019*, 73.

# Oil

The share of non-OECD countries in the global oil consumption will increase from 48 per cent in 2016 to 64 per cent in 2050, when approximately 40 per cent of the demand will be concentrated in Asia, which will have about two-thirds of the global increase in oil consumption during the same period.[24] It is projected that about 80 per cent of the international oil trade will be destined for Asia as late as 2050.[25]

China is forecast to top the list of oil consumers by overtaking the US by around 2030: its oil demand will peak in the mid-2040s, due largely to a decrease in demand for fuel for automobiles because of improvements in energy efficiency and depopulation.[26]

Oil consumption in India and ASEAN countries is projected to increase by 2.9 times and 2.1 times, respectively, in 2016–50.[27] India will replace the US as the second-biggest oil consumer in the latter half of the 2040s.[28]

In 2016–50, the self-sufficiency ratio of oil will decrease from 37 per cent to 23 per cent in China, from 19 per cent to 4 per cent in India and from 55 per cent to 21 per cent in ASEAN countries.[29]

# Non-Hydrocarbon Energy Sources

It is estimated that demand for non-fossil energy will almost double in Asia, accounting for 19 per cent in 2050, a 3 per cent increase from 2016. Renewables, excluding biomass and nuclear power, will account for 57 per cent and 34 per cent, respectively, of the incremental non-fossil energy consumption.[30]

---

24 IEEJ, *IEEJ 2019*, 47.
25 IEEJ, *IEEJ 2019*, 47.
26 IEEJ, *IEEJ 2019*, 3, 39.
27 IEEJ, *IEEJ 2019*, 39.
28 IEEJ, *IEEJ 2019*, 3.
29 IEEJ, *IEEJ 2019*, 39.
30 IEEJ, *IEEJ 2019*, 48.

# Natural Gas Supply Outlook

According to estimates of *WEO 2018*, the global natural gas production will increase at an average annual rate of 1.6 per cent from 3,769 bcm in 2017 to 5,399 bcm in 2040.[31] It is forecast that five countries will have more than 80 per cent of the production growth in 2017–25 with the US accounting for 40 per cent of the increment. Thereafter, the supply sources will increase and the top 10 producers will account for about two-thirds of the increases in natural gas production to 2040.[32]

Russia is projected to remain the second-largest gas producer through 2040 with increasing gas supplies mainly from the Arctic region, Eastern Siberia and the Far East. China is expected to become the newly expanding gigantic market for Russia's gas exports, especially after the commissioning of the 4,000 km pipeline (Power of Siberia-1) between the two countries, planned for completion by the end of 2019. In 2017–40, Russia is forecast to account for 12 per cent of the gas production growth in the world, to be followed by Australia, sharing 10 per cent of the increment.[33]

Natural gas production in the Asia-Pacific is projected to increase at an average annual rate of 2.5 per cent (approximately 100 bcm per annum) in 2018–24, of which Australia and China will account for about 55 per cent of the regional incremental production.[34] Australia is expected to increase natural gas production at an average annual rate of 2.3 per cent from 132 bcm in 2018 to 152 bcm in 2024.[35] As a result of intensive investments and the gradual increase in unconventional gas production, China is forecast to increase its natural gas production at an average annual growth rate of 7.1 per cent from 160 bcm in 2018 to 242 bcm in 2024. However, the gap between domestic production and consumption will keep widening.[36] Natural gas production in emerging Asian economies, including Indonesia, Malaysia, India, Pakistan, Bangladesh, etc., is projected to plateau at 330 bcm per annum in 2018–24, while the gap between the regional soaring demand and supply continues to widen.[37]

------

31　IEA, *WEO 2018*, 179.
32　IEA, *WEO 2018*, 180.
33　IEA, *WEO 2018*, 180.
34　IEA, *Gas 2019*, 79.
35　IEA, *Gas 2019*, 86, 175.
36　IEA, *Gas 2019*, 81, 175.
37　IEA, *Gas 2019*, 86.

# Natural Gas Trade

According to IEA's *Gas 2019*, the total volume of global natural gas trade is forecast to increase at an average annual rate of almost 4 per cent to 2024, reaching 32 per cent of the world's gas consumption. Global LNG trade is projected to increase to 546 bcm or about 60 per cent of inter-regional gas trade by 2024.[38] In this time frame, Australia, Russia and the US are expected, altogether, to supply about 90 per cent of the global LNG export growth, of which the US alone will account for two-thirds of total growth.[39] The US is expected to increase its exports at 113 bcm and to top the list of LNG exporters at 113 bcm by surpassing Qatar and Australia by 2024.[40]

China is projected to account for one-third of the total growth in the global LNG trade in 2018–24 and to overtake Japan as the largest LNG importer at 109 bcm (or about 80 mt) by 2024.[41] China is also expected to become the largest pipeline importer during this period. It is estimated that the total volume of piped gas from Russia and Central Asia will amount to 100 bcm per annum, accounting for 48 per cent of China's total natural gas imports by 2024.[42]

With the Power of Siberia-1 pipeline, Russia is expected to become the largest contributor of incremental gas supplies to China by the middle of the 2020s.[43] Russia is also forecast to increase LNG exports by approximately 50 per cent to 38 bcm (or about 28 mt) per annum by 2024.[44]

---

38   IEA, *Gas 2019*, 115.
39   IEA, *Gas 2019*, 135.
40   IEA, *Gas 2019*, 113.
41   IEA, *Gas 2019*, 113.
42   IEA, *Gas 2019*, 113.
43   IEA, *Gas 2019*, 120.
44   IEA, *Gas 2019*, 136.

# Political Economy of LNG and the Russian Factor

## Russia's LNG Ambition

Amid the intensifying competition among natural gas producers, Russia has been stepping up its efforts to become one of the major LNG suppliers in the world.[45] The Yamal LNG project, the second LNG export facility after the Sakahalin-2 project, rapidly expanded LNG export capacity following the first shipment from its first train with the maximum capacity of 5.5 mt/y in December 2017. Its second and third trains, each having the same nameplate liquefaction capacity as the first, were commissioned in 2018, ahead of the original schedules. With the completion of the Yamal Project's fourth train, which has a smaller capacity, Russia's total liquefaction capacity, including the Sakhalin-2 Project, reached 26 bcm by the end of 2019.[46]

In June 2018, Russian Deputy Energy Minister Pavel Sorokin said that Russia might increase its LNG production up to 100 or 120 mt/y by 2035.[47] As late as April 2019, President Putin also emphasised Russia's plan to increase its LNG capacity to 100 mt by 2035.[48] To this end, Russia aims to expand the number of LNG export facilities in the High North. However, this entails an enormous amount of capital and associated investment risks.

China is a key stakeholder of Novatek's Yamal LNG project.[49] China National Petroleum Corporation (CNPC) and Novatek inked an agreement in October 2013 for the supply of 3 mt/y for 20 years, and its first LNG cargo arrived in China in March 2018.

---

45   Russia started to export LNG from the Sakhalin-2 Project in 2009.
46   IEA, *FIDs for new LNG liquefaction capacity, 2014–2019,* 10 June 2020, www.iea.org/data-and-statistics/charts/fids-for-new-lng-liquefaction-capacity-2014-2019.
47   Oksana Kobzeva and Olesya Astakhova, 'Russia to Boost Presence on Global LNG Market, Helped by Lower Costs', *Reuters*, 1 June 2018, www.reuters.com/article/us-russia-lng/russia-to-boost-presence-on-global-lng-market-helped-by-lower-costs-idUSKCN1IX4FI. According to IEA's *World Energy Outlook 2017*, it was estimated that the United States would increase its liquefication capacity to 104 mt (140 bcm) in 2025 and over 126 mt (170 bcm) in 2040.
48   Atle Staalesen, 'Putin's Biggest Oil Company Promises 100 Million Tons on Arctic Route', *Barent's Observer*, 3 April 2019, thebarentsobserver.com/en/industry-and-energy/2019/04/putins-biggest-oil-company-promises-100-million-tons-arctic-route.
49   CNPC and China's Silk Road Fund have 20 per cent and 9.9 per cent stakes, respectively, in this project.

In addition to the sheer size of China's growing natural gas market, which could easily absorb Russia's LNG exports, Moscow has been desperately seeking Chinese financial commitments against the backdrop of escalating Western economic sanctions following Russia's illegal annexation of Crimea in March 2014.

As late as April 2019, Novatek signed binding agreements with CNPC and the China National Offshore Oil Corporation to have 10 per cent stakes in the Arctic LNG 2 project with a nameplate capacity of 19.8 mt/y.[50]

# Market Dynamics

## China's Gas Demand

As noted above, China's share in the global as well as the Asia-Pacific's gas consumption is rapidly expanding. In July 2018, China's National Development and Reform Commission announced a plan to increase the share of natural gas in primary energy consumption up to around 15 per cent in 2030.[51] As of 2017, this target is still behind the world's average; however, given the sheer size of total energy consumption, its absolute volume is enormous.[52] Further, given the urgency to improve air quality, the Chinese Government is aggressively revisiting the role of natural gas to reduce coal consumption, thereby alleviating mounting frustration among the population. Compared to 2018, China is expected to consume 58 per cent more natural gas by 2024.[53]

China's total gas imports increased by 7.4 times from 16.4 bcm in 2010 to 121.4 bcm in 2018.[54] According to the IEA's forecast, the total volume of China's gas imports will overtake that of the EU by 2040. Turkmenistan accounted for 27 per cent of China's portfolio of gas imports in 2018 and is projected to remain the largest gas exporter to China to 2024.[55] With the gradual increase in gas supplies by the Power of

---

50 Its first train is planned for commissioning in 2023.
51 As late as 2018, natural gas accounted for only 8 per cent of China's primary energy mix.
52 IEA, *Gas 2019*, 20.
53 IEA, *Gas 2019*, 21.
54 BP, *BP Statistical Review of World Energy 2019* (London: British Petroleum, 2019), www.bp.com/content/dam/bp/business-sites/en/global/corporate/pdfs/energy-economics/statistical-review/bp-stats-review-2019-full-report.pdf.
55 IEA, *Gas 2019*, 120.

Siberia-1, Russia is projected to overtake Turkmenistan soon afterwards. However, China has so far developed reasonably diversified natural gas supply routes—pipelines and LNG—in advance of the start of piped gas supplies from Russia.

# US Shale Gas Revolution

During the shale gas revolution, future prospects of natural gas production in the US and its LNG exports have undergone upward revisions. According to estimates by the US Energy Information Administration (EIA) as late as 2019, the projected volumes of natural gas production, including shale gas, in 2030 and 2040 increased by 1.3 times and 1.2 times, respectively, compared to the data published in 2013. Correspondingly, forecast LNG exports increased by 3.1 times and 3.2 times, respectively, in the same time span.[56] As noted above, the US is projected to become the world's largest LNG exporter by the mid-2020s.

The US shale gas revolution has triggered seismic effects in the global natural gas market in four ways. First, it has prompted a rising share of LNG in international long-distance gas flows. The International Association for Natural Gas (CEDIGAZ) estimates that long-distance trade by pipeline and LNG will increase at average annual rates of 1 per cent and 4.9 per cent in 2017–40. LNG accounted for 37 per cent of the total inter-regional gas flows in 2017, whereas its share is projected to increase to 58 per cent in 2040.[57] Second, gas pricing mechanisms, still largely indexed to oil especially in Asia, are gradually diversified with the increasing number of gas-indexed contracts.[58] Third, relaxation or abolishment of destination clauses, which restrict buyers from reselling or swapping LNG cargos, is increasing in number. Fourth, the hitherto globally compartmentalised regional gas markets in North America, Europe and Asia are being converged. This would likely foster further correlation of gas prices across regions.

---

56   EIA, *Annual Energy Outlook 2013* (Washington, DC: EIA, 2013), www.eia.gov/outlooks/archive/aeo13/; EIA, *Annual Energy Outlook 2019* (Washington, DC: EIA, 2019), www.eia.gov/outlooks/archive/aeo19/.
57   *CEDIGAZ World LNG Outlook 2019* (Rueil Malmaison: CEDIGAZ, August 2019), 12.
58   Japan has traditionally purchased LNG indexed to crude oil prices, known as JCC (Japan Crude Cocktail). The IEA predicts that most natural gas consumption will still be indexed to oil or regulated prices outside North America and Europe in the foreseeable future. Only 34 per cent of LNG is priced by gas-to-gas competition in the world today. IEA, *Gas 2019*, 152.

# Japan's New Positioning

Japan imported 8–10 per cent of its total LNG imports from Russia in 2010–18. After the Fukushima Daiichi Plant's nuclear accident in March 2011, Japan suffered from the sudden jump of LNG imports due to the full-scale operation of gas-fired thermal plants to make up for the nuclear shutdowns. This entailed tremendous financial costs for Japan since LNG prices soared against the backdrop of the subsequent tightening of the global LNG market with relatively high oil prices. Japan in 2011 recorded an annual trade deficit for the first time since 1981, and the deficit hit historical highs for the next three years. The total costs of Japan's LNG imports mounted by approximately 2.3 times that of 2010.[59]

However, concern over procuring enough LNG at internationally competitive prices has now significantly reduced. Indeed, Japan's gas demand has already peaked and begun to decrease since 2015. According to *WEO 2018*, Japan's natural gas demand is forecast to decrease by 0.7 per cent per annum from 2017 to 2040.[60] Unlike the case for crude oil, which is heavily dependent on imports from the Middle East, Japan's portfolio of LNG imports is fairly diversified.[61]

Japanese buyers, including gas companies, electrical utilities and trading houses, already signed a grand total of approximately 15 mt/y of LNG to be supplied from the US by the early 2020s. This volume is equivalent to about 18 per cent of Japan's LNG imports as late as 2018, whereas not all of those LNG cargos will be delivered to the Japanese market, since Japanese buyers are becoming portfolio players in the global LNG market.[62]

---

59  Shoichi Itoh, 'Japan's Energy Security in the Age of Low Oil Prices', National Bureau of Asian Research, Pacific Energy Summit, Policy Brief, 26 May 2016, www.nbr.org/publication/japans-energy-security-in-the-age-of-low-oil-prices/.
60  IEA, *WEO 2018*, 586.
61  Australia, Malaysia and Qatar accounted for 34 per cent, 14 per cent, 12 per cent, respectively, of Japan's LNG imports in 2018. Ministry of Finance (Japan), Trade Statistics of Japan. See, *2020 EDMC Handbook of Japan's & World Energy & Economic Statistics 2019 Edition* (Tokyo: IEEJ, 2019).
62  The total LNG volume includes both purchasing and sales agreements and tolling agreements.

# Political Factors

## US–China Conflict

China is set to become the world's largest LNG importer in 2024 when the US is forecast to top the list of LNG exporters globally.[63] However, Beijing has found fresh incentive to further consolidate a strategic energy partnership with Russia by the escalation of relations with the US under the Trump administration. The ongoing Sino-US trade war has inflated uncertainties with regard to the future of bilateral LNG trade. In 2018, when China's LNG imports expanded by 38 per cent to 54 mt, US LNG exports to China dropped by 10.5 per cent. China imposed 10 per cent tariffs on LNG imports from the US in retaliation for its imposition of tariffs on Chinese goods in September 2018. China raised the tariffs of US LNG to 25 per cent in retaliation for increased US tariffs in June 2019. There was no US LNG export cargo delivered to China in the second quarter of 2019.[64]

Rising concerns have emerged that the current Sino-US standoff entails Chinese state-backed buyers losing confidence in US LNG projects as long-term stable supply sources, and that US sellers may lose big market opportunities that were previously factored in for the planned expansion of LNG exports. China would be encouraged to tilt towards non-US LNG exporters, including Russia. The aggravation of Sino-US relations could also augment the significance of securing increased access to natural gas supplies by land from Russia, provided against a conceivable US naval blockade on oil tankers to China in military contingencies.

# Japan's Politicisation of Energy Vis-à-Vis Russia

Prime Minister Shinzo Abe has identified radical improvement of Japan–Russia relations as one of Japan's diplomatic priorities. Tokyo has singled out energy as a priority area for bilateral cooperation, since this

---

63    IEA, *Gas 2019*, 113.

64    'Europe and South America Jump in as China sees no US LNG in Q2', *Hellenic Shipping News*, 4 July 2019, www.hellenicshippingnews.com/europe-and-south-america-jump-in-as-china-sees-no-us-lng-in-q2/.

strategic sector would likely capture Moscow's attention more than any other sector.[65] The Abe administration initially anticipated Moscow's concession on the Northern Territories issue in return for a massive economic cooperation package. Tokyo also sought to make reinforcement of Japan–Russia relations a hedge against the rise of China and a means to circumvent further consolidation of the Sino-Russian partnership. Yet, these naively optimistic targets have been dashed to date.

Notwithstanding that Russia increased its presence in Japan's portfolio of oil and LNG imports in the past decade, an economically feasible mega energy project could no longer be easily identified. As a matter of fact, the Japanese Government's extra effort to politically encourage its domestic private companies to develop more business opportunities in Russia's energy sector has resulted in only limited success. Although the Abe administration has virtually minimised Japan's commitment to move in step with the US and the EU to impose economic sanctions against Russia, the Japanese private sector has increased concerns about the possibility of getting involved in the consequences of Russia's escalating relations with the West. Apart from the question of political risks, Japanese buyers can easily procure LNG at internationally competitive prices elsewhere.

Nonetheless, Japan has increased its commitment to economically dubious LNG projects in the Arctic. Following a memorandum of understanding between Novatek and JOGMEC (Japan Oil, Gas and Metals National Corporation) to develop additional LNG projects and new marketing opportunities for Russia in September 2018,[66] JOGMEC signed a share purchase agreement with Novatek and Mitsui & Co. in relation to the sale of a 10 per cent participation interest in the Arctic LNG 2 project in June 2019.[67]

---

65   For the details, see Shoichi Itoh, 'Japan's Opaque Energy Policy toward Russia: Is Abe Being Trumped by Putin?', in *The Emerging Russia-Asia Energy Nexus*, ed. Erica Downs, James Henderson, Mikkal E. Herberg, Shoichi Itoh, Meghan L. O'Sullivan, Morena Skalamera and Can Soylu, *NBR Special Report* 74 (December 2018): 33–42; Shoichi Itoh, 'Japan's Russia Policy at a Crossroads: New Phase for Geopolitics of Energy', in *Change and Continuity in Japan-Russia Relations: Implications for the United States*, ed. Paul J. Saunders and John S. Van Oudenaren, 17–26 (Washington, DC: Center for the National Interest, 2019).

66   'JOGMEC and NOVATEK Signed a Memorandum of Understanding', JOGMEC, last modified 12 September 2018, www.jogmec.go.jp/english/news/release/news_03_000002.html.

67   'JOGMEC Provides Equity Financing and Loan Guarantee for Mitsui's Participation in the Arctic LNG 2 Project and Signed Share Purchase Agreement', JOGMEC, last modified 29 June 2019, www.jogmec.go.jp/english/news/release/news_03_000009.html.

# The US–Japan Agreement

Tokyo and Washington agree on the importance of creating new LNG demand, especially in the Asia-Pacific, to absorb the growing scale of LNG exports from the US. Despite the decrease of Japan's LNG demand and its reasonably diversified import portfolio, Tokyo has good reasons to maximise LNG supplies from the US, Japan's ally, from both geopolitical and economic standpoints. The increase of LNG transportation across the Pacific Ocean would relax Japan's dependence on the other seaborne routes cutting across the Strait of Hormuz and the South China Sea, where seeds for geopolitical conflicts are simmering almost endlessly. Besides, the expansion of LNG exports from politically reliable partners, including the US, would further increase the liquidity of LNG trade flows in which Japanese stakeholders are becoming portfolio players in the world.

The Japan–US Strategic Partnership was established in November 2017 with the aim of developing new LNG markets globally. A memorandum of cooperation to boost bilateral cooperation on the creation of energy infrastructure in third countries was inked by Japan's Ministry of Economy, Industry and Trade and the US Trade and Development Agency.[68] Additionally, the US Overseas Private Investment Corporation signed a memorandum of understanding with the Japan Bank for International Cooperation and Nippon Export and Investment Insurance separately in view of developing joint-financing opportunities in the field of LNG-related infrastructure in third countries in Asia, Africa, the Indo-Pacific and Middle East.[69]

Given the US–Japan agreement of joint enterprise to expand new market opportunities for US LNG exports, it is no wonder that Tokyo may find it difficult to keep politically covering up the lack of economic rationality to help Russia's ambition to increase its LNG supplies into international markets. It would be especially so in the case of further escalation of negative US–Russia relations.

---

68  'Japan and the United States Affirm Advancement of Cooperation in the Fields of Energy and Infrastructure', Ministry of Economy, Trade and Industry, accessed 3 September 2020, www.meti.go.jp/english/press/2017/1107_001.html.
69  'JBIC Signs MOU with OPIC of the US', Japan Bank for International Cooperation, accessed 3 September 2020, www.jbic.go.jp/en/information/press/press-2017/1108-58390.html; 'United States of America/Memorandum of Understanding on Cooperation between NEXI and Overseas Private Investment Corporation (OPIC)', Nexi, last modified 8 November 2017, www.nexi.go.jp/en/topics/newsrelease/2017110701.html.

The surging demand for natural gas in the Asia-Pacific has created a new arena for competition for LNG suppliers. Russia is accelerating efforts to drastically expand its LNG export capacity; however, amid the West's economic sanctions, its future will depend on the scale of greenfield Arctic projects, which are in need of tremendous investment. The US, which is projected to become the largest LNG exporter globally by the mid-2020s, has an increasingly optimistic future scenario in regard to shale gas production; however, it still needs to find new markets to make the best of its export potential. China is forecast to overtake Japan as the world's largest LNG importer by 2024, while the former is also to become the largest pipeline importer with gradual increases of gas supplies by land from Russia by around the same time.

A market-based projection of the regional energy landscape is subject to a range of political uncertainties and challenges. The aggravation of US–China relations may slow final investment decisions of US LNG projects, which have hitherto taken the huge Chinese gas market for granted. China, instead, could be encouraged to increase its commitment to Russia's gas sector, which is under mounting financial pressure due to the West's economic sanctions. Tokyo's strategy of politicising energy to capture Moscow's attention, thereby improving bilateral relations, if somewhat ignorant of economic rationality, may negatively affect marketing opportunities for US LNG suppliers.

# 2

# Russia's Foray into Asia's Energy Market

Morena Skalamera

'Sanctions are counterproductive and senseless, especially against such country as Russia.'[1] President Putin used these words immediately after the Trump–Putin Helsinki summit in August 2018. By then Russia had already launched its pioneering Yamal liquefied natural gas (LNG) project, representing Putin's defiant stance against Western sanctions. Yamal signalled that Russian LNG activities aimed at the Asian market had not been constrained by Western sanctions since 2014.

Russia's move into the Asian energy market was no easy feat and many of Russia's initial forays had failed. By mid-2014, the effect of geopolitical pressure on Russia was magnified by a collapse in global oil prices. This dual condition inflicted hardship on the Russian economy, with some fearing Moscow could be headed for a recession. While sanctions were consequential, the Russian economy struggled more from the swift decline in global oil prices. The devastating effect of the collapse in oil prices, and the low oil prices since, have overall dwarfed the shock of the sanctions for the Russian economy.

---

1    Clark Mindock, 'Putin Says New US Sanctions on Russia are "Senseless"', *Independent*, 22 August 2018, www.independent.co.uk/news/world/americas/us-politics/us-russia-sancions-latest-putin-trump-washington-moscow-a8503371.html.

# America's Challenge

The fall in the price of oil was largely a consequence of oversupply—a result of new technology and capital investments in the US; weakening demand, particularly from China;[2] and the increasingly self-sufficient US energy market.[3] By injecting new oil and gas supplies into a well-fed market, America's 'unconventional' boom was shaking up the energy world and posing an existential threat to traditional oil and gas producers. The challenge in oil affected the so-called OPEC (Organization of the Petroleum Exporting Countries) grouping, too, and was not confined to Russia. But the challenge in gas was more targeted; it had the potential of weakening Russia's dominance over its holy of holies—the European gas market.

European gas markets had never been as lucrative as the budget-sustaining revenue that Russia made with the black stuff, but gas trade with Europe has always been about much more than profits. Since Soviet times, these pipelines—whose life cycle spans over 25 years or more—enabled Russia to project political influence and, occasionally, helped Moscow to drive wedges between 'old' and 'new' EU member states. This ability to play pipeline politics in Europe and transit countries in-between had great repercussions in the policy world as it helped Putin's efforts to demand geopolitical deference and transmit the impression that Russia stood tall in world affairs.

Between 1999 and 2008, oil rents were a bonanza for Putin's exuberant economic growth. The Russian Government used the budget surplus to close the state debt, increase social spending and finance an ever-expanding military apparatus. Today, just as then, energy revenue is critical for the country's federal budget, with oil revenue accounting for about 40 per cent of the Russian budget, and gas revenue for far less, about 10 per cent, while still playing a large role in Russia's efforts at restoring its 'rightful' place on the world stage.[4]

---

2    China had seen GDP growth drop from 10.3 per cent in 2010 to 6.9 per cent in 2015.

3    Several analysts anticipated the subsequent decline by evaluating investment patterns in oilfields over the past decade. See, Leonardo Maugeri, 'Oil: The Next Revolution', Discussion Paper, 2012, Belfer Center for Science and International Affairs, Harvard Kennedy School.

4    'The Ministry of Finance Disclosed the Size of Future Windfall Oil Profits', *Vedomosti*, 9 July 2018, www.vedomosti.ru/economics/news/2018/07/09/774948-minfin-raskril-razmer-buduschih-sverhdohodov-ot-nefti. The total oil and gas revenues of the federal treasury in 2018 will amount to ₽7.23 trillion (42.4 per cent of total income); in 2019, ₽8.32 trillion (41.9 per cent); in 2020, ₽7.9 trillion (39.5 per cent); in 2021, ₽7.77 trillion (37.8 per cent). See, Ministerstvo finansov Rossijskoj Federacii, 'Osnovnye Napravlenija Bjudzhetnoj, Nalogovoj I Tamozhenno-Tarifnoj Politiki na 2019 God I na Planovyj Period 2020 i 2021 Godov', [Main directions of the budgetary, tax, customs and tariff policies for 2019, and for the planned period of 2020 and 2021], 2018, accessed 1 September 2020, www.komitet-bn.km.duma.gov.ru/upload/site7/ONBNiTTP(2).pdf.

Given this strong dependence on energy revenue, when the US shale boom hit global markets, some authors argued that this transformative change posed a major geopolitical quandary for conventional oil and gas producers, primarily OPEC and Russia.[5] Some energy analysts, along with the International Energy Agency, were quick to emphasise that Russia was likely to emerge as the industry's top loser.[6] Opposite this, some argued that, for all the challenge, Russia would maintain its dominant role in supplying gas to Europe. They also contended that, to the extent that Russia was forced to modify its modus operandi in Europe, it was more due to the EU's regulatory efforts than to any impending competition by US LNG.[7]

While nearly everyone agreed that the unconventional revolution was a negative development for Russia, analysts debated the extent to which this was likely to be consequential. For many it seemed likely to make Russia less economically robust, more vulnerable to external actor influence and with fewer tools to shape the international arena.[8] Given the large role that energy revenue played in determining Russia's political trajectory, some predicted greater impetus for political reform, others more foreign policy adventurism to compensate for imminent domestic instability and yet others speculated about the need to find new markets for hydrocarbon export-oriented growth. One thing, however, was clear: the emergence of US shale upended global energy markets and created a dual challenge for Russia. In oil, it suppressed long-term prices with

5    For example, see Andrei V. Belyi and Andreas Goldthau, 'Between a Rock and a Hard Place: International Market Dynamics, Domestic Politics and Gazprom's Strategy', EUI Working Paper RSCAS 2015/22; James Henderson and Arild Moe, 'Gazprom's LNG Offensive: A Demonstration of Monopoly Strength or Impetus for Russian Gas Sector Reform?', *Post-Communist Economies* 28, no. 3 (2016): 281–99, doi.org/10.1080/14631377.2016.1203206.
6    Andrew Critchlow, 'Russia Will Be Biggest Loser from Oil Price Fall, Warns IEA', *Telegraph*, 10 February 2015. See also Clifford Krauss, 'Boom in American Liquefied Natural Gas Is Shaking Up the Energy World', *New York Times*, 16 October 2017, www.nytimes.com/2017/10/16/business/energy-environment/liquified-natural-gas-world-markets.html.
7    Tim Boersma, Tatiana Mitrova, Geert Greving and Anna Galkina, *Business As Usual. European Gas Market Functioning in Times of Turmoil and Increasing Import Dependence* (Washington, DC: Brookings, Policy Brief, 2014); Tatiana Mitrova and Tim Boersma, 'The Impact of US LNG on Russian Natural Gas Export Policy', Columbia's Center on Global Energy Policy, December 2018, energypolicy.columbia.edu/sites/default/files/pictures/Gazprom%20vs%20US%20LNG_CGEP_Report_121418_2.pdf; Morena Skalamera and Andreas Goldthau, 'Russia: Playing Hardball or Bidding Farewell to Europe?', Discussion Paper, Belfer Center for Science and International Affairs, Harvard Kennedy School, June 2016, www.belfercenter.org/sites/default/files/files/publication/Russia%20Hardball%20-%20Web%20Final.pdf.
8    Meghan O'Sullivan, *Windfall: How the New Energy Abundance Upends Global Politics and Strengthens America's Power* (New York: Simon & Schuster, 2017).

potentially devastating consequences for the country's budget. In natural gas, it created a new rival in the increasingly globalising markets for LNG, both in Europe and in Asia. Russia needed to react to maintain key social provisions, or worse, contain potential instability at home.

# Europe's Long Game

In Europe, as the market for LNG was becoming, well, more liquid,[9] this development was married with the EU's regulatory efforts to deliver a competitive and transparent gas market, and to force longstanding external suppliers, like Gazprom, to compete. In 2015, a newly self-contained American gas market had weakened Russia's hold on the European market (even before the US had yet exported a single molecule of gas), by creating a gas bubble in a well-supplied market. The effects of the US natural gas boom were propelled by a parallel rapid expansion of other LNG, such as plentiful Qatari alternatives, which were now hitting the lower-priced European LNG hubs, forcing competition with its dominant pipeline gas supplier, Gazprom. With the spectre of true competition looming over Gazprom, an emboldened EU pushed for effective liberalisation of the gas market through the so-called 'Third Energy Package', and made supply systems more resilient via new interconnectors between countries dependent on Russian gas imports.

Gazprom did eventually adapt—with some notable concessions such as a partial erosion of oil-indexed pricing and more flexible pricing—as it sought to preserve market share in its most prized market.[10] And Gazprom certainly is able to compete; the company's main advantage is price. Its upstream production costs are one of the industry's lowest at around US$20 per 1,000 cubic metres.[11] Rouble devaluation supports the attractiveness of Russian gas (as the majority of the cost is indexed in roubles) and piped gas is generally a cheaper transportation method than

---

9   Given that new LNG deliveries were increasingly freed from the so-called destination clauses—an old regime of rigid contracts with fixed destinations.

10   By shifting parts of its contract to 'spot' pricing, which itself is formed through the daily interactions of thousands of buyers and dozens of sellers.

11   'UPDATE 1–Gazprom Sees No Need for Europe Price War, No US LNG Threat', *Reuters*, 31 May 2016, www.reuters.com/article/russia-gazprom/update-1-gazprom-sees-no-need-for-europe-price-war-no-u-s-lng-threat-idUSL8N18S230.

LNG. Hence, while demand for Russian gas in Europe has risen in recent years, prices—and thus Gazprom's revenue per cubic metre—have fallen amid pressure from competitors.

In 2018, Gazprom doubled net profit to a record high as it exported more gas than ever to Europe and Turkey for a third year in a row, pushing its market share to 37 per cent.[12] In 2020, Russia had planned to start gas flows via two geopolitically critical export pipelines. The first, TurkStream, connecting Russian gas to Turkey and onto South-East Europe, came online in early 2020. However, the second pipeline, a second line of Nord Stream (Nord Stream II) linking Russian gas to Germany and Northern Europe, remains incomplete. Again, Gazprom's advantages are low production and transportation costs. Russia's gas deliveries to Europe have been consistently competitive in the last couple of years (and by US$1–1.5 per mmbtu cheaper than those of its LNG competitors) and so, the gas behemoth is likely to continue servicing about one-third of EU needs in the next decade or so.[13]

Longer term, however, Europe presents very few growth opportunities. A key factor here is Europe's gas demand. Given sluggish economic growth, most analysts bet on flat demand in the near term, but imports will grow due to falling domestic production in countries such as the United Kingdom or the Netherlands.[14] In such a situation, Russian gas remains the most competitive source.[15] However, crucial parts of Western Europe are now committed to an ambitious zero-carbon emissions target by 2050. This new age of renewables means that there is limited room for natural gas in Europe's future energy mix, with obvious challenges for traditional gas players in the region and especially for Europe's gas

12 'Russia's State-Owned Gazprom Doubles Profit on Higher Gas Sales', *Financial Times*, 29 April 2019.

13 For a detailed analysis see Tatiana Mitrova, 'Russian Natural Gas Supplies to Europe Competition with the US LNG', Presentation, Hague Centre for Strategic Studies, 8 September 2016, 7. See also James Henderson, 'Russian Gas in Europe: How Competitive and How Secure', Oxford Institute for Energy Studies, June 2016, slideplayer.com/slide/10879936/.

14 For a more detailed discussion, see for instance, IEA, *Gas 2019* (Paris: IEA, 2019), www.iea.org/reports/gas-2019; BP, *BP Energy Outlook 2035*, January 2014, www.bp.com/content/dam/bp/business-sites/en/global/corporate/pdfs/energy-economics/energy-outlook/bp-energy-outlook-2014.pdf.

15 European gas demand is expected to reach 564 bcm in 2020 and 618 bcm in 2030, according to the Oxford Institute for Energy Studies. From the production cost perspective, Russian gas is the EU's cheapest option. This, in turn, means that despite the EU's strong move towards renewables, Russian gas deliveries to the continent will likely stay stable at about one-third of EU's gas imports. See, Anouk Honoré, *The Outlook of Natural Gas Demand in Europe* (Oxford: Oxford Institute for Energy Studies, NG 87, 2014), doi.org/10.26889/9781784670030.

overlord—Gazprom. For all of the EU Competition Commission's mettle in taking on Gazprom, and America's relentless efforts 'to wean Europe of Moscow's energy grip over the continent', ironically, it may well be Europe's ambitious 'greening' agenda that presents the strongest challenge to Russia maintaining strength in its preferred gas market.[16]

Anticipating a steady decline in Europe's demand, Russia has long advocated the need to turn to Asia, the world's epicentre of economic growth. Yet, easy money in Europe had, over the years, made Gazprom fat and slow to change course. The EU had been a lucrative market and more attractive culturally speaking. China represented a bet on uncharted territory, and Beijing refused to pay the high European prices for piped gas. As long as Russia could sell to Europe all the gas required to keep the Russian economy growing, it did not have to budge over price or share its energy wealth with Chinese investors.[17] Ongoing plans included two gas pipelines from Siberia to China that were discussed over the 2000s but never finalised as the two sides bickered over prices.

In 2014, all this had changed. Western sanctions mixed with the tangible results of the US unconventional revolution (by 2014, the US already had three operational LNG production trains[18] and the first US LNG cargo set sail two years later, in 2016[19]) upended this picture in fundamental ways. Given the extent of the challenge, it was decided at the time that Gazprom would keep its monopoly of piped gas to Europe and concentrate on maintaining European market share; that Rosneft would become the national champion in oil; and that Novatek, a more agile company, would take on the task of directing a swift commercial and diplomatic focus to the growing Asian LNG markets. China was a crucial part of this plan to lessen the impact of Western sanctions by finding alternative markets and sources of capital, but the strategy, allegedly, was to 'pivot' Russia's economy towards Asia, and not just to China.

---

16  'Energy Diversity and Security Remarks By Secretary Rick Perry', US Department of Energy, 14 November 2018, www.energy.gov/articles/energy-diversity-and-security-remarks-secretary-rick-perry.
17    China was hoping to gain equity stakes in Russia's unrivalled gas fields as a quid pro quo in return for the pipeline deal. Due to resource nationalism and low trust, Russia was not excited to share the domestic pie. This had, at times, involved retrospective legislation concerning major projects and, in turn, threatened the country's reputation as a reliable investment partner.
18    With a total capacity of 13.5 mt/y (18.6 bcm/y). For more information, see International Gas Union, *IGU 2018 World LNG Report*, www.igu.org/resources/2018-world-lng-report-27th-world-gas-conference-edition/.
19    Daniel J. Graeber, 'First US LNG Cargo Sets Sail', *UPI*, 26 February 2016, www.upi.com/Energy-News/2016/02/25/First-US-LNG-cargo-sets-sail/9231456403122/.

# Russia's Reaction to America's Shale Boom

Some believed that the effects of America's reshaping of the world markets for natural gas would force the Russian Government to spur reform in its gas sector. The government did not rise to the occasion; instead, these developments were accompanied by protectionism, the bolstering of massive state-owned energy enterprises and an ever-assertive Russian posture on the international stage. The failure to reform, in turn, meant that new markets for Russia's prime export commodities—oil and gas—would become crucial to economic and political stability. The government's line continued to be that Gazprom's hold on its export monopoly raised the competitiveness of Russian gas in export markets. Domestically, through price controls, the government kept control over the regions, provided a safety net for the poor and kept potentially explosive areas (such as Chechnya and Dagestan) in check. Rather than competing with each other in the face of economic challenges, Russian companies were encouraged to find a way to split the market pie at home. One expert, close to the Russian Government, said at the time, 'there is a hybrid situation—an oligopoly with regional monopolies—Rosneft, Gazprom, and Novatek divide the market among themselves and try not to interfere in each other's business'.[20]

Such division of labour also applied to export markets; the recognition of Gazprom's role as the sole exporter of piped gas meant that, in return, everyone concerned would accept Novatek's role as the prime exporter of Russian LNG while Rosneft would receive the government's backing for a further expansion in the oil sector. The billionaire chief executives of all three companies—Aleksei Miller (Gazprom), Gennady Timchenko (Novatek) and Igor Sechin (Rosneft)—are long-term associates of Russia's commander in chief, and, given President Putin's role as distributor of patronage, arbiter of opportunities and disputes, and protector of a balance in the various groups' influence, it is no surprise that Novatek, a so-called 'independent' producer, succeeded in sidelining Gazprom in the rush to

---

20   Aleksei Grivach, interview by Morena Skalamera, Moscow, Russia, 2 June 2015.

Asian LNG.[21] The rise of Novatek, however, does not suggest that the Kremlin 'set out to create competition' in gas. It is the result of liberalising LNG exports and betting on a very capable company (Novatek) that has been attentive to delivering its projects on time and on budget, as well as being considered capable enough to take on the challenge of delivering Russia's response to America's unconventional revolution.[22]

# Russia's Foray to Asia Picks up Steam

The initial pivot to gas markets in the Asia-Pacific had a rough start, amid cooling relations with Japan over the disputed Kuril Islands and Tokyo's endorsement of sanctions against Russia. With South Korea, it was the US—not Russia—that was managing to score most market share in the country's burgeoning LNG market. Meanwhile, Russia was edging closer to entering into a potentially smothering embrace with China.

In LNG, there is Sakhalin-2, Gazprom's LNG terminal that, before the opening of Yamal LNG, was Russia's only LNG terminal. Two other proposed projects that meant to target Asia, Vladivostok LNG (Gazprom) and Sakhalin-1 (Rosneft and Exxon Mobil), have both stalled. As for piped exports, we will only see concrete numbers once the Power of Siberia is launched. Then, in December 2017, with much fanfare, President Putin personally sent off Yamal LNG's first tanker to China, having been able to secure the project's financing from the French company Total (20 per cent), China's state-owned energy company China National Petroleum Corporation (20 per cent) and Beijing's state-owned Silk Road investment fund (9.9 per cent), a special financial mechanism to support China's ambitious aims with the Belt and Road Initiative (BRI).[23] China's state-owned companies, which already retain nearly a third of Novatek's first liquefaction plant, have in 2019 signed agreements to buy

---

21 In a recent study, Lamberova and Sonin estimate the relationship between Putin's inner circle's wealth and the closeness of their relationship to the chief executive, and find that the strength of the correlation is enormous in high oil and gas price years. See, N. Lamberova K. and Sonin, 'Economic Transition and the Rise of Alternative Institutions: Political Connections in Putin's Russia', *Economics of Transition* 26, no. 4 (2018): 615–48, doi.org/10.1111/ecot.12167.
22 The answer has been developing the Arctic's resources for exports to Asia.
23 The Silk Road Fund that took a stake in Yamal is a US$40 billion special purpose vehicle to back Chinese President Xi Jinping's BRI—a US$1 trillion plan to build infrastructure across Eurasia.

a combined 20 per cent stake in Novatek's new Yamal LNG 2, which will produce a projected 19.8 mt of Arctic LNG per year and is expected to go online by 2023.

Novatek boasts that further expansion will transform Russia into one of the biggest LNG exporters within a decade. The gas producer has aggressive plans to command a tenth of the global market by 2030, its CFO Mark Gyetvay says, and position Russia as one of the world's largest exporters alongside the US, Qatar and Australia.[24] Novatek admits its plans are ambitious but insists they are realistic, well-calculated and concrete.

In 2018, according to Russia's Federal Customs Service, Gazprom's Sakhalin Energy and Novatek's Yamal LNG revenue spiked by 49.8 per cent, reaching US$1.95 billion.[25] According to reports, Yamal LNG alone contributed a 40 per cent increase in net profits.[26] In the first six months of its operation, Yamal LNG produced around 2 mmt of LNG.[27] Such extraordinary spikes in production, rising gas sales and recent acquisitions by prominent investors increased Novatek's net profit nearly six-fold between January and June 2019.[28]

In 2017, at the launch of Yamal LNG, Putin stated 'the development of Arctic reserves is the engine of Russia's economic development in the 21st century'.[29] Such words testify the degree of political and financial support that the goal of 'carving out the niche that Russia deserves in this field' enjoys.[30] Yamal LNG 1 and 2 aim to help Russia double the country's share of the global LNG market by 2020 from about 4 per cent in 2018 (in comparison, the US global market share for the same year was higher, at about 4.5 per cent, and Australia's was about six times higher).[31]

---

24    'Russia Eyes Greater Energy Dominance with Arctic LNG Push', *Moscow Times*, 8 April 2019, www.themoscowtimes.com/2019/04/08/russia-eyes-greater-energy-dominance-with-arctic-lng-push-a65140.

25    'Russia Increased Profits from Oil and LNG Exports', *News*, 13 May 2019, news.ru/en/economics/russia-increased-profits-from-oil-and-lng-exports/.

26    Nastassia Astrasheuskaya, 'Russia's Novatek to Sell Stake in Arctic Gas Project to Chinese Partners', *Financial Times*, 25 April 2019.

27    Oksana Kobzeva and Olesya Astakhova, 'Russia to Boost Presence on Global LNG Market, Helped by Lower Costs', *Reuters*, 1 June 2018, www.reuters.com/article/us-russia-lng/russia-to-boost-presence-on-global-lng-market-helped-by-lower-costs-idUSKCN1IX4FI.

28    'Profits at Russia's Novatek Soar on LNG Sale', *Financial Times*, 24 July 2019.

29    'Ceremony of First Tanker Loading Under the Yamal LNG Project', President of Russia, 8 December 2017, en.kremlin.ru/events/president/news/56338.

30    'Putin Says Russia to Boost LNG Output for Greater Market Role', *Reuters*, 24 April 2019, af.reuters.com/article/energyoilnews/idafr4n22004k.

31    International Gas Union, *IGU 2018 World LNG Report*, 9.

Both Russia's and the US's deliveries are growing fast and present a real challenge for Australia in the traditionally attractive Asian LNG markets.[32] By 2019, and in defiance of US-led sanctions, Novatek had already successfully attracted other, non-Chinese suitors for its Yamal LNG 2 plant, such as France's Total (with a 10 per cent stake) and Japan's Mitsui & Co. and JOGMEC (10 per cent),[33] with Saudi Aramco, the kingdom's state oil producer, keen to follow suit. These deep-pocketed investors bring Novatek closer to its goal of ramping up Russian LNG production to as much as 120 mmt by 2035 and taking market share from Australia and the US.[34] China's involvement with Russian LNG extends far beyond the role of financier and is linked to the potential of the so-called Northern Sea Route (NSR), or, as China sees it, the Polar Silk Road.

## China's Silk Route on Ice

In 2018, China published an Arctic policy paper that explicitly linked the NSR to its ambitious BRI strategy, dubbing it the 'Polar Silk Road'—a useful alternative to the Strait of Malacca—a maritime chokepoint whose vulnerability to blockade by the US military has for years haunted Chinese leaders.[35] For Novatek, the route is attractive because it provides much more direct access to the world's largest LNG consumers in Asia. It is these large-volume customers that Russia covets; the Asia-Pacific region (APR) would receive about 70 per cent of production, with shipments planned via the NSR.[36] For other shipping companies—most

---

32    Asia and Europe are the two distinct LNG-importing regions, and, typically, though not without exceptions, robust demand from China, South Korea and Japan have kept the Japan–Korea Marker, the Asian benchmark, higher than the European equivalent.

33    'Japan Teams Up with Russia in Big Arctic LNG', *Moscow Times*, 2 July 2019, www.themoscow times.com/2019/07/02/japan-teams-up-with-russia-in-big-arctic-lng-a66248.

34    Kobzeva and Astakhova, 'Russia to Boost Presence on Global LNG Market'.

35    The State Council, The People's Republic of China, 'China's Arctic Policy', last modified 26 January 2018, english.gov.cn/archive/white_paper/2018/01/26/content_281476026660336.htm. The paper mainly focuses on climate research and environmental protection, as well as identifying China as a 'near-Arctic state'. The paper is notably silent on China's interest in accessing the colossal oil and gas resources locked under the region's permafrost.

36    The potential of the Northern Sea Route was brought up in the Kremlin's 2008 Arctic Concept. See, 'Osnovy gosudarstvennoj politiki Rossijskoi Federatsii v Arktike na period do 2020 goda i dal'nejshuiu perspektivu' [The foundations of the Russian Federation's policy for the arctic zone to 2020 and beyond], Russian Government, 18 September 2008. The same is reiterated in 'Foreign Policy Concept of the Russian Federation', The Ministry of Foreign Affairs of the Russian Federation, 1 December 2016, www.mid.ru/en/foreign_policy/official_documents/-/asset_publisher/CptICkB6BZ29/content/id/2542248.

notably the China Ocean Shipping Company (COSCO) but also the Danish company Maersk—the route has the potential to cut the costs and time between European and Asian markets.

Despite misgivings by some in Moscow that the Chinese BRI already encroaches on Russian interests in Central Asia, and that the rhetoric of benign environmental protection along the 'Polar Silk Road' belies an interest in Russia's vast Arctic hydrocarbon resources, there are big advantages for both sides. China has been eager to invest in shipping through this route and has set aside money for the development of the Arctic. Russia, for all the talk about not selling on the cheap, needs China if it wants to tap the Arctic's full commercial potential and set itself as the dominant Arctic shipping state. It is in this context that we should interpret Putin's statement at the 2019 BRI forum in Beijing: 'Russia has emphasized on numerous occasions that PRC [People's Republic of China] President's Belt and Road initiative rimes with Russia's idea to establish a Greater Eurasian Partnership.'[37]

For all Russia's excitement about cutting the journey time between Asia and Europe by one to two weeks, the NSR still requires nuclear icebreakers to accompany vessels, is more costly than other routes and is only usable for six months a year at most. It is well-suited, however, as a shipping route for transporting oil and gas produced in the Arctic, which is where Russia's competitive advantage lies.[38] In an attempt to make the route commercial, Russia plans to hand control of shipping to Rosatom, the state-run nuclear group, to pilot freighters along the route and allow year-round navigation.[39] Russia hopes that a fleet of nuclear icebreakers will encourage investment across the NSR, increase commercial shipping through this emerging trade artery, and give more opportunities to Russian companies to supply LNG to East Asia (especially to China—already the world's second-largest market), and by doing so it hopes to undercut rivals including the US and Australia. In July 2019, Novatek shipped its first ever LNG cargo through the NSR and, while traffic is light today, it is reasonable to expect that it will grow as the polar ice recedes.

37   'Belt and Road Forum for International Cooperation', President of Russia, 26 April 2019, en.kremlin.ru/events/president/transcripts/statements/60378.

38   Richard Milne and Henry Foy, 'Maersk Launches Container Ship on Arctic Route', *Financial Times*, 21 August 2018, www.ft.com/content/fb38b6ac-a484-11e8-8ecf-a7ae1beff35b.

39   Natassia Astrasheuskaya, 'Russia Gives Nuclear Group Control of Arctic Sea Route', *Financial Times*, 13 December 2018, www.ft.com/content/b5dc9c38-fd56-11e8-aebf-99e208d3e521.

For China, investing in the 'Polar Silk Road' is a golden opportunity to potentially gain greater access at favourable prices to Russia's natural resources that would otherwise remain stranded, to secure access to big infrastructure contracts that might have gone to Western competitors and to provide financing for projects that will benefit Chinese firms. This underlines that, for as long as Western sanctions persist, Russia is going to need China more than the other way around, and China's bilateral cooperation with Russia—in the Arctic and elsewhere—is seen as part of President Xi Jinping's extensive Belt and Road diplomacy to realise China's broader aspirations in Eurasia.

## China–Russia Edging Closer and Closer …

There is substance beyond the pomp of the China–Russia relationship. Bilateral trade rose 27.1 per cent in 2018, to a record high of US$107 billion, trade increased to US$110 billion in 2019.[40] At the same time, the EU's share (of trade with Russia) fell from 49.6 per cent to 43.8 per cent. Europe is still Russia's biggest trading partner but EU–Russia trade has continuously decreased since 2012, dropping by 44 per cent between 2012 and 2016.[41]

Beyond (energy) economics, Russia and China increasingly share a view of how the world ought to be reordered. They resent America's 'hegemony' and share a desire for a more multipolar world order. Putin and Xi also have a personal bond forged by their common fear of 'colour revolutions' (popular uprisings), which they see as having been America's doing. The fact remains, however, that their economic power is impressively dissimilar (Russia's economy is about one-tenth the size of China's) and while their strategic partnership is growing—for instance, in 2019 Russia's biggest military drills since the Cold War included units from China—ultimately, the common question of whether a true Sino-Russian strategic alliance has materialised is nonsensical. What is clear from years of research into the Sino-Russian partnership is that to concentrate persistently on this

---

40  'Russia's Trade with China Surges to More than $107 Billion', *RT*, 14 January 2019, www.rt.com/business/448783-russia-china-trade-turnover; 'Russia–China Bilateral Trade Hit US$110 Billion in 2019—What Is China Buying?, *Russia Briefing*, 14 January 2020, www.russia-briefing.com/news/russia-china-bilateral-trade-hit-us-110-billion-2019-china-buying.html/.

41  From €339 billion in 2012 to €191 billion in 2016. See, 'Countries and Regions: Russia', European Commission, last modified 20 May 2020, ec.europa.eu/trade/policy/countries-and-regions/countries/russia/.

question is to do irreparable damage to the nuances of the Sino-Russian partnership. In a world of uncertainty, these two powers rely on the depth of their relationship, on trust, habits of thought, on the alleged personal chemistry between Xi and Putin, and on innovative practices to reshape the institutional contexts within which they manage. At the same time, their hands are free to adapt to the unpredictability of world politics, make adjustments as they go and tackle their still many divergent interests. As seen from Beijing, its objectively much needier neighbour can help develop pathways for Sino-centric trade and influence across Eurasia while at the same time delegitimising America's liberal agenda and supporting China's push for a multilateral trading system that better serves its interests.

In energy, big milestones on this journey have been the signing in May 2014 of a 30-year deal worth US$400 billion to deliver Siberian gas to China through the 4,000 km long Power of Siberia, which is set to start pumping in December 2019, joining an already-operating oil supply pipeline link. In 2015, Chinese oil group Sinopec bought 10 per cent of SIBUR for US$1.3 billion, in 2016 Gazprom borrowed €2 billion from the Bank of China in its largest ever bilateral loan and in July 2017 an US$11 billion financing agreement by China's Development Bank underlined the extent to which the Kremlin had turned its economic focus to China.[42]

These mega-deals are critical for both sides. In 2016, Russia surpassed Saudi Arabia as China's largest crude supplier and, over the years, has strengthened its position.[43] The colossal Power of Siberia pipeline, which is devoid of in-between transit countries, will arguably service China with cheaper and reliable piped gas for decades to come. Crucially, from Moscow's perspective, the benefits of such an expanded Chinese presence are not just financial. The burgeoning partnership also sends a message to those who thought such mega-deals would be impossible under the sanctions regime. China's tens of billions of dollars worth of cash have

---

42    'Gazprom Secures €2bn Loan from Bank of China', *Financial Times*, 3 March 2016.
43    'Russia Leads as Top Crude Supplier to China Overtakes Saudi', *Reuters*, 25 June 2019, www. reuters.com/article/us-china-economy-trade-crude/russia-leads-as-top-crude-supplier-to-china-overtakes-saudi-idUSKCN1TQ1MS.

helped offset the effect of ever-tougher rounds of Western sanctions by 'insulating' Russian companies, and have supported Moscow in defying the image of an industry that struggles or feels abandoned.[44]

When asked recently whether Russia was putting too many eggs in the Chinese basket, Putin replied: 'We have sufficient eggs but there are not too many baskets to put those eggs in'.[45] The Kremlin has been acutely aware of the need not to be overly dependent on the Xi–Putin alignment, especially in pursuit of Russia's goals in Asia. Moscow needed to move fast to grab larger parts of the Asia-Pacific LNG market. Taken together, the Novatek deals are a notable breakthrough in this endeavour.

# The Asia-Pacific 'Basket'

In the aftermath of the Ukraine crisis, the energy partnership with China served to show the world that Moscow always had a plan B. Yet, Moscow's 'China-first' policy in Asia also had a constraining effect on its engagement with other Asian players, especially with countries that have difficult relations with Beijing, as is the case with India and Japan.[46] This has now changed. Increasingly, there is action in addition to diversity talk in Russia's pivot to Asia, thereby somewhat moderating the notion of Russia's difficulty in pursuing a fully independent foreign policy in Asia given its near-total reliance on China. In a matter of only a few years, Russia has been able to forge deeper military and energy links with countries such as India and Japan, both of which are rivals of China. Despite the still deep mistrust and the unresolved Kuril Island issue, Moscow has also been able to capitalise on stronger energy ties with a key country that is concerned about China's growing regional hegemony—Japan.

---

44    For instance, on 26 June 2015, the EU foreign ministers decided to extend sanctions against Russia until January 2016, following breaches of the Minsk ceasefire plan and a general impasse in negotiations on resolving the conflict in eastern Ukraine. See, 'EU–Russia: Moment of Truth Extended by Another 6 Months', *RBTH*, 26 June 2015.

45    Quoted in Lionel Barber and Henry Foy, 'Vladimir Putin: Liberalism Has "Outlived Its Purpose"', *Financial Times*, 17 September 2019, www.ft.com/content/2880c762-98c2-11e9-8cfb-30c211dcd229.

46    Bobo Lo, 'New Order for Old Triangles? The Russia-China-India Matrix', *Russie.Nei.Visions*, no. 100 (April 2017): 18; Shoichi Itoh and Andrew Kuchins, 'The Energy Factor in Russia's "Asia Pivot"', in *Energy Security in Asia and Eurasia*, ed. Mike M. Mochizuki and Deepa M. Ollapally (New York: Routledge, 2017), Ch. 7.

Prior to the launching of Yamal LNG, Japan imported approximately 10 per cent of LNG from Russia,[47] and Moscow was fourth in the list of Japan's LNG suppliers, behind Qatar, Malaysia and Australia.[48] Since 2016, however, the US has jumped into the LNG market in a big way. In 2017, US LNG exports quadrupled, with most of the fuel going to Asia, as the result of the continuing expansion of US LNG export capacity.[49] In 2018, American producers shipped around 15 bcm of LNG to Japan, China and other Asian countries,[50] closing in on Russia's exports of 18.6 bcm to the APR, according to the Russian news agency TASS.[51] The US Energy Information Administration (EIA) projects that US LNG export capacity will reach 8.9 bcf/d by the end of 2019, making it the third largest in the world behind Australia and Qatar.[52] This extraordinary expansion in the US energy sector upped Russia's sense of urgency to capture a larger market share in Asia.

Despite Gazprom's early moves with an LNG terminal on the Sakhalin island, Gazprom has been slow to secure a stronger position in the Asian LNG market due to its longstanding focus on pipeline deliveries to Europe.[53] Now Novatek—not Gazprom—is eager to take up Russia's 'deserved niche'. Closer cooperation with Japan, the world's largest LNG buyer, is crucial to this goal. Most recently, on the sidelines of the G20 summit, two Japanese energy companies acquired a 10 per cent share

---

47    'Japan, Russia Need to Enhance Trust before Gas Pipeline Plans: Minister', *Reuters*, 7 August 2017, www.reuters.com/article/us-japan-russia-gas-idUSKBN1AN0OO.
48    'Japan: Liquefied Natural Gas (LNG)', International Trade Administration, last modified 13 October 2019, www.trade.gov/knowledge-product/japan-liquefied-natural-gas-lng.
49    'US Liquified Natural Gas Exports Quadrupled in 2017', US Energy Information Administration (EIA), 27 March 2018, www.eia.gov/todayinenergy/detail.php?id=35512. See also International Gas Union, *IGU 2018 World LNG Report*, 21.
50    According to the EIA, total exports amounted to about 30 bcm, with about 47 per cent being delivered to the Asia-Pacific region. See, 'US Natural Gas Exports and Re-exports by Country', EIA, 31 July 2020, www.eia.gov/dnav/ng/ng_move_expc_s1_a.htm. See also 'US LNG to Asia in Question as Prices Fall, Shipping Costs Rise, *Hellenic Shipping News*, 29 October 2018, www.hellenic shippingnews.com/us-lng-to-asia-in-question-as-prices-fall-shipping-costs-rise/.
51    'Russia Increases LNG Exports to Asia-Pacific Countries by 29.2%', *Tass*, 2 December 2018, tass.ru/ekonomika/5861682.
52    'US Liquified Natural Gas Export Capacity to More than Double by the End of 2019, EIA, 10 December 2018, www.eia.gov/todayinenergy/detail.php?id=37732.
53    Until recently, the country had just one liquefaction project in operation, the Gazprom-led Sakhalin 2 project in its far-east region near Japan, with an annual capacity of about 10 mt.

in Novatek's Arctic LNG 2. The deal also stipulates that Novatek will supply Japan with around 2 mt of LNG annually—about one-tenth of the facility's capacity.[54]

Budding relations with Vietnam[55] have reinforced a sense of depth to Russia's foray into Asia, while occasional deals with India hold out the prospect of a more systematic relationship with Asia as a whole. While such relationships are not based solely on energy matters, Russian supplies do figure prominently in each. For instance, in October 2016, Indian state companies signed energy deals worth billions of dollars with Rosneft to buy into the Vankor oilfield, some of Russia's most promising assets in Siberia. In 2017, Rosneft bought a 49 per cent share of India's Essar Oil Ltd, while in March 2018, Novatek started supplying India with Arctic LNG.[56]

In the case of South Korea, new momentum has been seized following the election in 2017 of President Moon Jae. Prior to the power transition in Seoul, Russia–South Korea commodity turnover had been US$15 billion,[57] but Moon's administration wants to double that by 2020.[58] However, it is the US that has been able to seize a substantial share of South Korea's LNG market, exporting 392.6 bcf between February 2016 and December 2018, or about 20 per cent of US total LNG exports.[59]

Yet, unlike the US or Australia, Russia also hopes to reach two of its major Asia-Pacific LNG buyers, Japan and South Korea, via pipeline. There are two pipeline projects, with both Koreas and Japan, which

---

54  'Russia Looks for Asia LNG Buyers to Blunt Western Sanctions' Bite', *Nikkei Asian Review*, 14 July 2019, asia.nikkei.com/Business/Energy/Russia-looks-for-Asia-LNG-buyers-to-blunt-Western-sanctions-bite2.

55  For instance, in the first seven months of 2017, trade turnover between Vietnam and Russia reached nearly US$2 billion, up 27 per cent year-on-year. See, 'Vietnam, Russia Determined to Raise Trade to $10 Bln by 2020', VietnamNet, 27 October 2017, english.vietnamnet.vn/fms/business/189085/vietnam--russia-determined-to-raise-trade-to--10-bln-by-2020.html.

56  'Russia's Rosneft Closes Deal to Buy 49 Pct Stake in India's Essar Oil', *CNBC*, 21 August 2017, www.cnbc.com/2017/08/21/russian-oil-major-rosneft-seals-biggest-foreign-purchase-ever-in-india-with-49-percent-stake-in-essar-oil.html.

57  'Here Is Why South Korea May Be Turning to Russia', *National Interest*, 6 February 2018, nationalinterest.org/blog/the-buzz/here-why-south-korea-may-be-turning-russia-24370.

58  Ria Novosti, 'Yuzhnaya Koreya khochet v 2020 godu uvelichit' tovarooborot s Rossiyey do $30 Mlrd' [South Korea wants to increase trade with Russia to $ 30 billion in 2020], accessed 28 August 2020, ria.ru/20171130/1509937590.html; Timothy Stanley, 'The Growing Russia–South Korea Partnership', *Diplomat*, 24 May 2018.

59  US Department of Energy, Office of Oil and Natural Gas, 'LNG Monthly', 2018, www.energy.gov/sites/prod/files/2019/03/f61/LNG%20Annual%20Report%20-%202018_1.pdf.

continue to be discussed periodically, but both, for different reasons, are unlikely to be built. One is the long-desired Trans-Korean natural gas pipeline—a 1,200 km (740 mile) long pipeline to bring Russian gas through North Korea to the South's industrial hubs. Beyond obvious political risks, the biggest obstacles are sanctions, which block joint ventures with North Korean firms, prohibit financial transactions with North Korea, and forbid sales and purchases of commodities. Hence, the pipeline's chances might be reconsidered only if international sanctions are lifted.[60]

The second one is a 1,500 km gas pipeline that is proposed to run from Russia's Sakhalin to the vicinity of Tokyo at an estimated cost of US$6 billion. In theory, this pipeline would provide Japan with a source of cheap and reliable gas while also lessening the country's over-reliance on LNG. Meanwhile, Russia would further its goal of rebalancing energy exports and becoming an influential energy player in Asia. However, in the current environment of booming global LNG supplies, Japan might simply not need to be tied to Moscow via pipes, as the glut means that prices can only fall further. Japan is well aware that restoration of five of its nuclear power reactors in 2018, compounded to additional volumes of LNG from the US, Australia or, for that matter, Russia, will fuel yet more competition.[61]

Beyond the geo-economics of the Trans-Korean pipeline, Russia has long looked for a way to insert itself into negotiations over Pyongyang's nuclear program, seeking to cultivate ties that date to the Soviet era. Most recently, Moscow hoped to use the highly choreographed and largely symbolic April 2019 visit of Kim Jong Un to Vladivostok to cast itself as a regional powerbroker and geopolitical heavyweight.[62] Both China and Russia have voiced support for Kim's gradual approach to disarmament and sanctions relief and the Vladivostok summit seemed intended to highlight that the Kremlin's support for a step by step de-escalation provides Kim with another tangible partner, beyond Beijing.[63] China

60    Jane Chung, 'Trans-Korea Gas Pipeline Project Reappears, but Challenges Remain', *Reuters*, 29 June 2018, www.reuters.com/article/us-northkorea-southkorea-gas-russia-expl/trans-korea-gas-pipeline-project-reappears-but-challenges-remain-idUSKBN1JP0UN.
61    'Japan Has Restarted Five Nuclear Power Reactors in 2018', EIA, 28 November 2018, www.eia.gov/todayinenergy/detail.php?id=37633.
62    'Kim Kong-un Meets Putin in Russia with US Talks Faltering', *New York Times*, 24 April 2019.
63    'News conference following Russian–North Korean talks, President of Russia, 25 April 2019, en.kremlin.ru/events/president/news/60370. Both countries, moreover welcome a revival of multilateral talks on North Korea, known as the six-party negotiations, which the Trump administration opposes.

is the North's biggest business partner by far, accounting for more than 90 per cent of Pyongyang's trade according to estimates. Still, in 2018, the North imported US$21.6 million worth of mineral fuels and oil from Russia, out of US$32.1 million of total fuel imports.[64]

# Game On: The Price Issue

Having only recently ramped up LNG production, the Kremlin is perfectly aware that Russia is a long way from fending off established rivals in the Asia-Pacific LNG battleground. Be that as it may, in its rapid and determined push, the Russian energy sector's main competitive advantage is low production and transportation costs. The gas in the Yamal Peninsula is low cost; according to the Moscow-based Skolkovo think tank, average production and transportation costs at Yamal LNG for exports to Shanghai are seen at just above US$8 per million British thermal units by 2025. That is roughly the same as the cost for LNG projects in Western Australia and less than the approximately US$9 for LNG exports from the south-eastern US.[65] The same figure for Sakhalin-2, a brownfield, stands at below US$4, the lowest among current global projects. Recently, Novatek CFO Mark Gyetvay noted that 'not only does Novatek manage in the harsh environment but it sees the Arctic's location as a competitive advantage, because the lower temperatures actually make production costs cheaper, given that less energy is needed to chill the gas'.[66]

That might well be true, but, as the above Skolkovo report notes, the harsh geography of Arctic projects inevitably affects transportation and construction costs.[67] Moreover, as the same report notes, a great part of the first Yamal LNG's profits are reinjected into foreign markets due to payments for equipment that Russia imports from South Korea. The lack

---

64    Kim Jong Un Woos Vladimir Putin as North Korean Laborers Toil in Russia, *Japan Times*, 17 July 2019.
65    Tatiana Mitrova, Alexander Sobko and Zlata Sergeeva, 'Global LNG Market Transformation: To Miss the Windows of Opportunities for Russia', Energy Centre, Moscow School of Management SKOLKOVO, June 2018, 22, energy.skolkovo.ru/downloads/documents/SEneC/News/Russia-on-global-spg-market-Eng.pdf.
66    He further added that: 'The cost of producing Yamal gas is only around $0.1 per million British thermal units, whereas US producers typically buy their gas on a market such as the Henry Hub, where prices are currently about $2.60'. 'Russia Eyes Greater Energy Dominance with Arctic LNG Push', *Moscow Times*, 8 April 2019, www.themoscowtimes.com/2019/04/08/russia-eyes-greater-energy-dominance-with-arctic-lng-push-a65140.
67    'Russia Eyes Greater Energy Dominance with Arctic LNG Push'.

2. RUSSIA'S FORAY INTO ASIA'S ENERGY MARKET

of homegrown technologies for large-scale liquefaction and transportation will continue to erode parts of the profits—and Moscow's ability to compete—unless Russia develops its own LNG technology soon.[68]

These setbacks notwithstanding, since the US and EU sanctions against Russia (implemented after Moscow's invasion and annexation of Crimea in 2014) restricted foreign capital and technology, high-profile partners have continued to pour finance into Russia's energy sector, from China's loans to large equity stakes (such as Indian companies' 49 per cent in the Vankor oilfields) to share purchases (such as Japanese firms' 10 per cent stake in Novatek's Arctic LNG 2 or French Total's 10 per cent in both Yamal LNG 1 and 2). These are just some examples of the many joint venture agreements across Russia's energy sector since March 2014, which have notably also included new-found friendships and energy deals with countries in the Middle East. Russia's go-to partners and financiers for major energy projects emphasise that business relationships built over decades are not easily curtailed. Five European companies are partnering with Gazprom in constructing the Nord Stream 2 pipeline: Germany's Uniper and Wintershall, Engie of France, Anglo-Dutch Shell and Austria's OMV. These five EU energy companies have done business with Gazprom for decades and most recently have agreed to finance half of the North Stream II €9.5 billion cost.

The companies behind Russia's Arctic Yamal projects are similarly undeterred; abundant gas will be coming to Europe or Asia whatever the political impediments thrown up by Brussels or Washington.[69] The UK is one of the most hawkish towards Moscow, but British energy group BP is one of Russia's biggest foreign investors through its 19.75 per cent stake in Rosneft. Bob Dudley, BP's chief executive, has recently summarised this attitude by saying: 'It is very difficult to remain in business for a long time by taking sides … we try to build bridges.'[70] The message is simple and clear: Russia's underdeveloped energy fields are too large and lucrative to be ignored or to let politics get in the way. Western and Eastern companies alike have found ways around the restrictions considering how profitable Russia's unrivalled energy resources still are. Acquisitions and international expansion projects have followed.

---

68    Mitrova, Sobko and Sergeeva, 'Global LNG Market Transformation', 23.
69    Natassia Astrasheuskaya, 'Russia Defies Pipeline Threats over Gas for Europe', *Financial Times*, 18 June 2019, www.ft.com/content/1f6ac3d6-861f-11e9-97ea-05ac2431f453.
70    Henry Foy, 'Russian Sanctions: Why "Isolation Is Impossible"', *Financial Times*, 12 November 2018, www.ft.com/content/c51ecf88-e125-11e8-a6e5-792428919cee.

In light of the above, it is important that scholarship on hydrocarbon markets recognises the pervasive influence of creative action by the executives who run the world's energy firms.[71] It is no surprise that Western sanctions had been largely ineffective in persuading non-US companies to stop doing business in Russia. As Rawi Abdelal notes, firms have relationships with one another—relationships of great political consequence and considerable variability and even as they seek profits, uncertainty pervades these firms' decision-making. In such circumstances, their strategies build on their pasts—on business partnerships that have lasted for decades—and, by doing so, they actually make and remake energy geopolitics. This is evinced by Dudley's statement that: 'More and more there is a great importance that business plays in bringing the world closer. There are a lot of forces trying to push us apart'.[72] Occasionally, in energy trade and in politics, governmental priorities override the interests of firms, but on a day-to-day basis, the commercial logic of firms prevails. Meanwhile, all the recent activity of European companies makes it clear that even targeted asymmetric sanctions come at a cost to the countries imposing them, which is why parts of Europe, for all the anti-Kremlin rhetoric, have been reluctant to sever energy trade and investment with Russia. That said, future energy sector growth comes at a cost as sanctions will curb Russia's companies' ability to deploy advanced international technologies, and therefore restrain its drive to grow in new Arctic locations.[73] They might, however, also spur the development of in-house technological advances.

# Russia's Interests in Global Energy Markets

Since the early 2000s, the Kremlin has talked about the need to diversify its energy and economies to the East. While these efforts had been initially slow, after 2014 Moscow has made sharp strides in its economic focus there. Overall, at home, Moscow's interests lie in attracting more non-

---

71   Rawi Abdelal, 'Firms in Firmament: Hydrocarbons and the Circulation of Power', in *Protean Power: Exploring the Uncertain and Unexpected in World Politics*, ed. Peter J. Katzenstein and Lucia A. Seybert (Cambridge: Cambridge University Press, 2018), 147–65, doi.org/10.1017/9781108597456.008.
72   Quoted in Foy, 'Russian Sanctions'.
73   These measures limit Russia's access to new technology needed to keep its traditional oil and gas fields productive. Russia's energy companies still lag behind the technological might of their Western rivals. Many knowledge-sharing agreements and joint ventures terminated by the sanctions.

Western investments to the Arctic and in Russia's Far East, thus helping to regenerate the economy of this region. Internationally, however, it aims to keep world affairs at a low, not steaming, boil.

In oil, geopolitical turmoil in the Middle East and in other crude-producing regions only serves Russia's economic interests. Of course, geopolitical turmoil and the price of oil is closely correlated. Unsurprisingly, Russia backs Venezuela's President Nicolás Maduro; disruptions of crude supplies—such as oil from Iran and Venezuela—keep the market tight and raise prices, even as the transformative effects of the US's unconventional revolution stabilise the market (crude prices now sit between US$60 and US$70).[74]

In LNG, where the US's unconventional boom, too, has reshaped markets for decades to come, Russia has similar interests. An unsettled US–China trade war will alleviate US competition in Asia. The trade spat has already given exporters such as Qatar, Australia and Russia an edge in securing deals with the world's second-largest economy even as US companies seek to build new export terminals. Bloomberg New Energy Finance estimates that Australia, China's largest LNG supplier, stands to gain most from the escalation of US–China trade tensions.[75] Any imminent resolution of the trade spat would likely see more oil and LNG flow from the US to Asia, in turn triggering even more rivalry in the Pacific.

Bloomberg NEF expects that global LNG markets will face about 16 mmt/y of excess supply in 2019, exerting downward pressure on global LNG prices even in Asia, where prices tend to be higher due to huge demand and fewer alternative suppliers.[76] A BP report concurs, noting that global LNG supplies continued their rapid expansion in 2018, increasing by almost 10 per cent (37 bcm) as a number of new liquefaction plants in Australia, the US and Russia either were started or

---

74   By broadening supplies, they push oil prices down.
75   China applied a 25 per cent tariff on US goods, including LNG, from 1 June 2019. According to Bloomberg NEF, China has already substantially diversified its LNG supply, and Australia's and Malaysia's LNG share to China totalled 72 per cent in May 2019. Australian LNG comprised 52 per cent of Chinese imports in May, up from 43 per cent last year. Malaysian LNG is also benefiting from the absence of US LNG in China's supply mix, rising to 20 per cent in May from an average of 10 per cent in 2018. Abhishek Rohatgi, 'Trade War: The Impact on LNG', Bloomberg, spotlight. bloomberg.com/story/trade-war-the-impact-on-lng?src=LNGPortal&utm_medium=mktg_site&utm_ campaign=CoreProdAdmin&utm_source=Website&utm_content=LNGPortal&mpam=18961&bbgs um=DG-WS-PROF-LNGPORTAL.
76   Maggie Kuang, 'Global LNG: The Big Swing', Bloomberg, spotlight.bloomberg.com/story/ global-lng-the-big-swing.

ramped up.[77] Japan remains the world's largest LNG importer, but it is China, India and other emerging Asian markets that will see their share of trade increase substantially, reaching 45 per cent of trade volumes by 2023—more than double the share of 2013.[78]

As the US and other global LNG exporters rewrite the world's markets for natural gas, Russia has an interest in closer cooperation with Japan, China and South Korea, the world's fastest-absorbing LNG buyers. It also quietly welcomes an escalating US–China trade war.

# Russia as Australia's LNG Export Competitor

According to BP's 2019 annual report, for all of 2018 LNG imports from Australia were king in Japan, China and South Korea, the three core Asian markets in which Russia aims to secure a stronger grip.[79] But Asian demand is expected to slow down, a development further intensified by Japan's relaunch of four nuclear facilities and new LNG 'optionality' (from Russian LNG, among others). Conversely, Australia is traditionally a high-cost location.

The prospect of the further rapid increases of low-cost LNG in Russia means that the country represents an increasingly serious competitor in what, for now, is Australia's stronghold.[80] In the medium term, booming global LNG production will create a glut both in Europe and Asia.[81] In the long run, however, the APR is poised to become the catalyst of

77   *BP Statistical Review of World Energy 2019*, 6, www.bp.com/content/dam/bp/business-sites/en/global/corporate/pdfs/energy-economics/statistical-review/bp-stats-review-2019-full-report.pdf.
78   'Gas 2018: Analysis and Forecasts to 2023', IEA, www.iea.org/gas2018/.
79   *BP Statistical Review of World Energy 2019*, 39.
80   Beyond Russia, the Asia-Pacific battleground is expected to be flooded by plentiful supplies from the US (expected to double export capacity to more than 40 mmt in 2019), Malaysia, Indonesia and Qatar, among others.
81   Anna Shiryaevskaya, 'LNG Ships Are Turning Away from Europe's Gloomy Gas Market', Bloomberg, 5 July 2019, www.bloombergquint.com/business/lng-vessels-turn-away-from-europe-s-gloomy-natural-gas-market; Sabina Zawadzki, 'European Gas Prices Exceed Asian Spot LNG, Shuts Arbitrage', *Reuters*, 15 July 2019, www.reuters.com/article/us-global-lng-europe/european-gas-prices-exceed-asian-spot-lng-shuts-arbitrage-idUSKCN1UA1L6.

global LNG growth. Currently, the region accounts for approximately three-quarters of global LNG trade,[82] with that amount projected to increase to as much as 86 per cent in the next decade.[83]

The way Australia positions itself to preserve market share will determine its status in the region over the next decade. The *Financial Times* has recently reported that, in addition to overseas competition, chaotic policymaking is threatening to cut short Australia's tenure as the world's biggest exporter of LNG. Australia now faces intense competition from the likes of the US and Russia—producers that prioritise stable energy policies and clarity over the outlook for costs. Meanwhile, apparent lack of policy coordination and bickering at federal and state levels has become a risk for Australian LNG producers and has already delayed investment decisions in Canberra. Such hurdles are especially difficult when one has to compete with countries such as Russia, where handpicked mega-projects in the energy industry, once declared geopolitically critical, become patriotic national undertakings.

Homegrown Arctic LNG is an absolute priority of the Putin administration. This is somewhat reminiscent of the zeal with which Soviet mega-projects were implemented; there was scope for disagreement on how the economy should be organised until a decision had been reached, at which point the decision had to be implemented in a strictly disciplined manner at all affected levels of society. In Russia, rigid hierarchical subordination still dictates the execution of the most ambitious, costly and geopolitically critical energy projects—such as the two Yamal LNG plants. While deliberating on important issues such as a coherent national emissions policy and the need to balance between LNG exports and energy security at home, Canberra should do so with the awareness that some of its overseas competitors have a clear, top-down notion of what energy market competition means.

Already the world's top exporter of pipeline gas and second-biggest shipper of crude oil, Moscow's push to be a major LNG exporter is real. In the APR, however, Russia will not be able to replicate the unusually strong hold it enjoys over European gas markets or make use of heavy-handed pipeline politics essential to the Kremlin's claim of greatness. This

---

82 'Perspectives on the Development of the LNG Market Hubs in the Asia-Pacific Region', EIA, 2 March 2017, www.eia.gov/analysis/studies/lng/asia/.

83 'Asia to Dominate Long-term LNG Demand Growth', BloombergNEF, 12 September 2018, about.bnef.com/blog/asia-dominate-long-term-lng-demand-growth/.

has to do with the inherent characteristics of LNG transportation and trade along with well-established competition. In Asia, Russian LNG will be purely business; traded like Russian oil and very much deprived of its strategic foreign policy status.

That said, the many investment partners that Russia has been able to secure in its post-Ukraine phase have succeeded in lessening the country's dependence on Western financing, blunting the concerted efforts by the US to economically isolate Russia. Stakes, joint ventures, foreign direct investment and other types of corporate agreements with energy firms from Europe, Japan, India and the Middle East have supported Russia's foray to Asia and, to some extent, belie the narrative of a Russian Pivot to Asia that stops at China.

New competition by Russia will shape the Asia-Pacific market and may be a hindrance to Australia's business. However, on the question of whether Australia will be able to maintain its crown as the world's largest LNG exporter, Russia is not likely to be a singularly determinative factor.

# Part 2:
# Russian Foreign
# Energy Strategy

# 3

# Russian Grand Strategy and Energy Resources: The Asian Dimension[1]

Jakub M. Godzimirski

This chapter addresses a set of strategically important questions about the relationship between Russian strategy and the country's energy resources. It is divided into three sections. The first presents a brief discussion of the concept of a 'grand strategy' and its application in the Russian context. The second examines the role of energy resources in a grand strategy in general, and in the current Russian context in particular. The final section considers the importance of Asia in the realisation of Russian energy and grand strategy.

The chapter seeks to answer the following questions:

- What is a grand strategy?
- Does Russia have a grand strategy?
- What is the connection between grand strategy and energy?
- What is the role of energy resources in Russia's grand strategy?
- What is the role of Asia in Russia's grand and energy strategy designs?

1    Research for this chapter was made possible through a grant from the Research Council of Norway for the project 'Evaluating Power Political Repertoires' (EPOS) (project no. 250419).

The term 'grand strategy' was officially introduced by Basil Henry Liddel Hart in his 1929 text on indirect strategy (published in a revised version in 1967);[2] however, it appeared in public debates somewhat earlier. A search for the term in the web archive of one of the most respected journals on foreign affairs and national security, *Foreign Affairs,* conducted in August 2019 returned 809 hits, with the oldest one stemming from 1924, and no less than 108 hits before 1967. Debate on the meaning and content of the term gained momentum after 1967 and especially after the end of the Cold War, with 156 hits returned in the period between 1967 and 1991, and 529 hits between 1992 and the end of 2018.[3]

This study uses three widely accepted operational definitions of 'grand strategy'. Peter Feaver defines grand strategy as: 'The collection of plans and policies that comprise the state's deliberate effort to harness political, military, diplomatic, and economic tools together to advance that state's national interests.'[4] J. L. Gaddis describes grand strategy as: 'The calculated relationship of means to large ends. It's about how one uses whatever one has to get to wherever it is one wants to go.'[5] Conversely, Biddle argues that:

> Grand strategy identifies and articulates a given political actor's security objectives at a particular point in time and describes how they will be achieved using a combination of instruments of power—including military, diplomatic, and economic instruments.[6]

---

2    Basil Henry Liddell Hart, *Strategy: The Indirect Approach*, rev. ed. (London: Faber and Faber, 1967).

3    Search for the term 'grand strategy' was conducted by the author on 10 August 2019 at www. foreignaffairs.com. For an overview of this debate see John Lewis Gaddis, *On Grand Strategy* (New York: Penguin Books, 2019); Nina Silove, 'Beyond the Buzzword: The Three Meanings of 'Grand Strategy', *Security Studies* 27, no. 1 (2018): 27–57, doi.org/10.1080/09636412.2017.1360073; Tami Davis Biddle, *Strategy and Grand Strategy: What Students and Practitioners Need to Know* (Carlisle: US Army War College, The Strategic Studies Institute, 2015); Harry R. Yarger, *Strategic Theory for the 21st Century: The Little Book on Big Strategy* (Carlisle: Strategic Studies Institute, US Army War College, 2006); Paul M. Kennedy, *Grand Strategies in War and Peace* (New Haven: Yale University Press, 1992).

4    Peter Feaver, 'What Is Grand Strategy and Why Do We Need It?', *Foreign Policy*, 8 April 2009, shadow.foreignpolicy.com/posts/2009/04/08/what_is_grand_strategy_and_why_do_we_need_it.

5    John Lewis Gaddis, 'What Is Grand Strategy?', Karl Von Der Heyden Distinguished Lecture, Duke University, Durham, 26 February 2009, tiss-nc.org/wp-content/uploads/2015/01/KEYNOTE. Gaddis50thAniv2009.pdf.

6    Biddle, *Strategy and Grand Strategy*, 5.

Therefore, the three key elements of any grand strategy can be said to be: 1) the ends/objectives it seeks to achieve, 2) the means/resources it has at its disposal while trying to achieve its goals, and 3) the ways/instruments/tools it can use to make these happen.

# Does Russia Have a Grand Strategy?

There is an abundance of literature on Russian foreign, security and defence policy and the topic became even more relevant in the wake of the 2014 conflict in Ukraine. Scholars working in this area seek to understand the role of various institutions and individuals, including Putin, in the formulation and implementation of policy; the extent to which Russian policymaking and implementation is centralised and well-coordinated; the short-, mid- and long-term objectives of Russian policy; and the instruments it uses to achieve these objectives.

Christopher Marsh describes the question of whether Putin has an overarching strategy or is merely reacting to international events as they unfold as 'one of the most significant questions surrounding Russian foreign policy'.[7] Posing this type of question is well justified, as today's Russia can be suspected of having inherited some of the approaches characteristic of its Soviet past, when policy planning and teleological—goal-oriented—approaches to policymaking were an important part of the Soviet tradition.

As usual, there are many different opinions. For instance, Anne Applebaum argues that Putin's policy lacks a grand strategic cut; she describes it as a strange strategy of regime survival.[8] Others, like Sarah Topol, argue that, while there are elements of grand strategic thinking and design in Russian policy, the country mostly responds to opportunities in order to be an autonomous player—that is, to uphold its identity as a great power that is strategically independent from other centres of global power.[9] Then there

---

7    Christopher Marsh, 'Russia Sees Its Future in China and Eurasia', *National Interest*, 22 April 2019, nationalinterest.org/feature/russia-sees-its-future-china-and-eurasia-53702.
8    Anne Applebaum, 'Putin's Grand Strategy', *South Central Review* 35, no. 1 (2018): 22–34, doi. org/10.1353/scr.2018.0001.
9    Sarah Topol, 'What Does Putin Really Want?', *New York Times Magazine*, 30 June 2019.

are those like Marsh, Kofman, Person and others[10] who argue that the country's current policies 'combine into a coherent global foreign policy agenda that seeks to reposition Russia as a great power in the emerging world order',[11] and that Russia has indeed a grand strategy—one that seeks to achieve some long-term goals and has, at its disposal, tools to facilitate its realisation. These include the country's abundant energy resources[12] that force, for instance, 'Eastern Europe as well as Western Europe to "play nice" with Russia as a major energy source and political and military power'.[13]

# Russia's Strategic Objectives

Before examining the role of energy in Russia's strategic designs, it is necessary to better understand the objectives of this apparent Russian grand strategy and the extent to which they can be viewed as representing a 'strategic continuity'. There is a large body of literature on the persistence of Russian objectives and how they have been translated into short-, mid- and long-term goals.[14]

---

10  Marsh, 'Russia Sees Its Future in China and Eurasia'; Michael Kofman, 'Drivers of Russian Grand Strategy', Stockholm Free World Forum, 23 April 2019, frivarld.se/wp-content/uploads/2019/04/Drivers-of-Russian-Grand-Strategy.pdf; Robert Person, *Russian Grand Strategy in the 21st Century* (West Point: US Military Academy, 2019), doi.org/10.1016/j.orbis.2019.02.002; Joseph Roger Clark, 'Russia's Indirect Grand Strategy', *Orbis* 63, no. 2 (2019): 225–39, doi.org/10.1016/j.orbis.2019.02.002; Andrei P. Tsygankov, 'Preserving Influence in a Changing World. Russia's Grand Strategy', *Problems of Post-Communism* 58, no. 2 (2011): 28–44, doi.org/10.2753/PPC1075-8216580203; Andrew Monaghan, 'Defibrillating the *Vertikal*?: Putin and the Russian Grand Strategy', Chatham House, 7 October 2014, nllp.jallc.nato.int/IKS/Sharing%20Public/Defibrillating%20the%20Vertikal%20Putin%20and%20Russian%20Grand%20Strategy.pdf.
11  Marsh, 'Russia Sees Its Future in China and Eurasia'.
12  Tsygankov, 'Preserving Influence in a Changing World'; Person, *Russian Grand Strategy*; Marsh, 'Russia Sees Its Future in China and Eurasia'.
13  Marsh, 'Russia Sees Its Future in China and Eurasia'.
14  Cyril C. Black, 'The Pattern of Russian Objectives', in *Russian Foreign Policy. Essays in Historical Perspective*, ed. Ivo Lederer (New Haven: Yale University Press, 1962), 3–38. Edward N. Luttwak, *The Grand Strategy of the Soviet Union* (New York: St Martin's Press, 1983); Alfred J. Rieber, 'Persistent Factors in Russian Foreign Policy', in *Imperial Russian Foreign Policy*, ed. Hugh Ragsdale (Cambridge: Cambridge University Press, 1993), 315–59; Alfred J. Rieber, 'How Persistent Are Persistent Factors?', in *Russian Foreign Policy in 21st Century. The Shadow of the Past*, ed. Robert Legvold (New York: Columbia University Press, 2007), 205–71, doi.org/10.7312/legv14122-005; Margot Light, 'Russian Foreign Policy Themes in Official Documents and Speeches: Tracing Continuity and Change', in *Russia's Foreign Policy Ideas, Domestic Politics and External Relations*, ed. David Cadier and Margot Light (London: Palgrave Macmillan, 2015), 13–29, doi.org/10.1057/9781137468888_2; A. Radin and C. B. Reach, *Russian Views of the International Order* (Santa Monica: RAND Corporation, 2017).

Having studied the pattern of Russia's long-term objectives, Cyril Black lists stabilisation of frontiers, assurance of favourable conditions for economic growth, unification of Russian territories, and participation in alliance systems and international institutions as the main leitmotifs in Russian foreign and security policy.[15] Margot Light, in her study of the patterns of Russian objectives in the post-Soviet period, argues that Russia's policymaking community was mostly preoccupied with establishing the Commonwealth of Independent States as a buffer zone, opposition against the North Atlantic Treaty Organization's (NATO) eastward expansion, defence of Russia's sovereignty and territorial integrity, countering Western plans to deploy a ballistic missile defence system, efforts to create a multipolar international system and recognition of Russia as a great power.[16] A RAND study published in 2017 concluded that Putin's regime was most interested in defence of the nation and the regime, increasing the level of influence in the near abroad, creating conditions that would limit other states' ability to interfere in Russia's domestic affairs, strengthening the perception of Russia as a great power, and political and economic cooperation as a partner equal to other great powers.[17]

A recent reading of Russian strategic intentions by NSI Inc., a US-based analytics company, concluded that Russia's core objectives are to reclaim and secure the country's influence over former Soviet nations; regain worldwide recognition as a 'great power'; and portray Russia as a reliable actor, key regional powerbroker and successful mediator in order to gain economic, military and political influence over other nations and to refine the liberalist rules and norms that currently govern the world order.[18] One of the contributors to the NSI study summed up his findings on Russian grand strategy by saying that:

> The main 'end' of Russian grand strategy in the 21st century is establishing a 'Yalta 2.0', in which Russia enjoys an uncontested sphere of influence in the post-Soviet region, broadcasts Russian voice and influence globally, and establishes reliable constraints on American globe-trotting and regime-change activities.[19]

---

15   Black, 'The Pattern of Russian Objectives'.
16   Light, 'Russian Foreign Policy'.
17   Radin and Reach, *Russian Views of the International Order*.
18   J. Arquilla et al., 'SMA TRADOC White Paper—Russian Strategic Intentions', NSI, May 2019, nsiteam.com/sma-white-paper-russian-strategic-intentions/.
19   Person, *Russian Grand Strategy*.

# Grand Strategy and Energy

According to Meghan O'Sullivan, energy that is the basis of economic growth can be found at the heart of virtually every country's strategic evaluations.[20] She argues that to understand how energy policy forms part of national grand strategy, how energy and security are intertwined and how energy factors into a whole host of interactions between countries, actors and global institutions, one should examine energy policies in the context of national grand strategy. In her view, grand strategy is a 'concept guiding a country in its efforts to combine its instruments of national power in order to shape the international environment and advance specific national security goals'.[21] Energy-related issues can thus have various roles in this grand strategic context. For some actors, getting access to energy is one of the main goals of a grand strategy; some may view energy as a means to achieve other grand strategy–related goals; while others use their endowment with energy resources as a tool and instrument in realisation of their grand strategy. How do these energy-related questions figure in Russia's grand strategic designs? Is energy an objective to be achieved, an instrument or a means—or all of them combined?

# Russian Grand Strategy and Energy

There are various possible ways of examining this issue. I will approach the question of the relationship between Russian energy resources and the country's grand strategy from several angles. First, I will examine the place of energy in Russia's foreign, defence and security policy. Second, I will consider how studies of Russian energy strategies published over the past 20 or so years have addressed this issue. Third, I will explore how the main priorities in Russian energy policy are defined in the current situation and the role of Russia's foreign energy policy in Russian strategic designs. Finally, I will present some conclusions on how to understand the role of energy in Russian grand strategy and the role assigned to Asia in Russian strategic energy designs.

---

20    Meghan L. O'Sullivan, 'The Entanglement of Energy, Grand Strategy, and International Security', in *The Handbook of Global Energy Policy*, ed. Andreas Goldthau (London: Wiley-Blackwell, 2013), 30–47, doi.org/10.1002/9781118326275.ch2.
21    O'Sullivan, 'The Entanglement of Energy'.

**Table 3.1: What makes Russia important in energy terms and what makes energy important in the Russian strategic context?**

| Category | Amount |
|---|---|
| Energy consumption, mtoe[i] | 720.7 |
| Energy production, mtoe[ii] | 1373.7 |
| Net energy exports, mtoe[iii] | 624.4 |
| Energy export value, US$ billion[iii] | 307 |
| Share of fuels in export in %[iv] | 65.7 |
| Share of global fuel exports in %[iv] | 12 |
| Oil reserves, billion tons/share of global/RPR ratio[i] | 14.7/6.1/25.4 |
| Oil production, mtoe/share in %/rank[i] | 566.3/12.6/3 |
| Oil crude exports, mtoe/share in %/rank[i] | 275.9/12.8/2 |
| Natural gas reserves, tcm/share/RPR ratio[i] | 38.9/19.8/58.2 |
| Gas production, bcm/share in %/rank[i] | 669.5/17.3/2 |
| Gas export piped, bcm/share in %/rank[i] | 223/23.6/1 |
| Gas export LNG, bcm/share in %[i] | 24.9/5.8 |
| Share of petroleum sector in state revenue in % 2014/2018[v] | 51/46 |
| Share of oil, oil products and natural gas in export 2000–18 (highest/2018)[vi] | 66.9/57.9 |
| Value of oil, oil products and natural gas export 2000–18/share in total exports[vi] | 3, 807, 106/62.1 |

[i] BP, *Statistical Review of World Energy 2019* (London: British Petroleum, 2019), www.bp.com/content/dam/bp/business-sites/en/global/corporate/pdfs/energy-economics/statistical-review/bp-stats-review-2019-full-report.pdf.

[ii] IEA, *World Energy Outlook 2018* (Paris: OECD Publishing, 2018).

[iii] World Trade Organization, *World Trade Report 2010. Trade in Natural Resources* (Geneva: World Trade Organization 2010), see data for 2008.

[iv] World Trade Organization, *World Trade Report 2010*.

[v] 'Annual Information on the Execution of the Federal Budget (Data from January 1, 2006)', Ministry of Finance of Russia, accessed 3 September 2020, minfin.gov.ru/ru/statistics/fedbud/execute/?id_65=80041-yezhegodnaya_informatsiya_ob_ispolnenii_federalnogo_byudzhetadannye_s_1_yanvarya_2006_g.

[vi] calculated by the author based on data provided by the Central Bank of Russia, see 'External Trade in Goods (Balance of Payments Methodology)', Bank of Russia, accessed 3 September 2020, cbr.ru/eng/statistics/macro_itm/svs/.

The strategic importance of energy resources is well understood in Russia. When the Russian Federation's *Energy Strategy through 2020* was published in 2003, the first paragraph stated:

> Russia has abundant energy resources and a powerful fuel and energy sector that forms the basis of economic development and is an instrument in [the] realisation of domestic and foreign policy. The role of the country at the global energy market in many respects defines geopolitical influence.[22]

Finnish expert Kari Liuhto identified the strategic importance of various sectors in the Russian economy in 2007: Russia's oil and gas industries were defined as highly strategic to the national economy and national security.[23]

In his 2011 article on Russian grand strategy, A. Tsygankov described Russia's energy clout as an important tool helping Russia to regain its great power status and emerge as a power 'capable of defending its international prestige using economic, military, and diplomatic means' after a period when the country looked like a 'weak and inward-looking nation'.[24] According to Tsygankov, energy is one of five strategic tools that Russia can use to fashion a comprehensive policy, the other four being diplomacy, military power, cultural and historical capital, and technological expertise.[25]

When summing up the economic results of 2018, a group of Russian experts stated that, although the country had managed to become less dependent on energy resources in its pursuit of strategic goals, the oil and gas sector still represented 20 per cent of the country's GDP, and generated 45 per cent of the state budget revenue as well as 60 per cent of the country's export revenue.[26] Energy resources are not only important as a tool in Russian foreign and security policy, but also in the domestic context. Further, having access to, or direct or indirect control over, energy resources gives various actors important political leverage on the Russian political scene. Figure 3.1 shows the position of four key players in the Russian energy sector—Igor Sechin, head of Rosneft; Alexei Miller, head of Gazprom; Vagit Alekperov, owner of Lukoil; and Gennadii

---

22 Government of the Russian Federation, *Energeticheskaya Strategiya Rossii Na Period Do 2020 Goda* [Energy strategy of Russia through 2020] (Moscow: Government of the Russian Federation, 2003).
23 Kari Liuhto, 'A Future Role of Foreign Firms in Russia's Strategic Industries', *Electronic Publications of Pan-European Institute* 4 (2007).
24 Tsygankov, 'Preserving Influence in a Changing World', 28.
25 Tsygankov, 'Preserving Influence in a Changing World', 35.
26 Elizaveta Gorodishchiva, 'Let's Go on the Mend', Lenta.Ru, accessed 19 August 2020, lenta.ru/articles/2019/04/24/independence.

Timchenko, co-owner of Novatek—on an informal map of political power, as presented in the *Nezavisimaya Gazeta* (NeGa) annual rankings of the top 100 most influential figures in Russia.

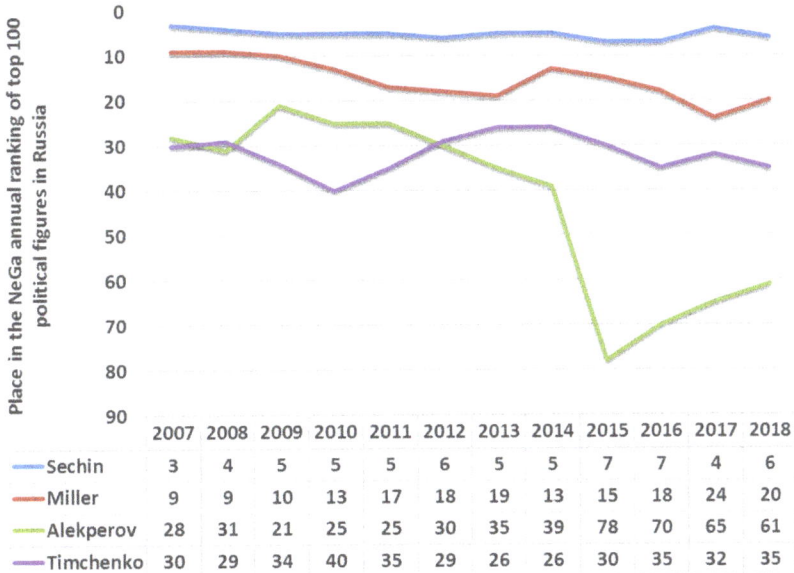

| | 2007 | 2008 | 2009 | 2010 | 2011 | 2012 | 2013 | 2014 | 2015 | 2016 | 2017 | 2018 |
|---|---|---|---|---|---|---|---|---|---|---|---|---|
| Sechin | 3 | 4 | 5 | 5 | 5 | 6 | 5 | 5 | 7 | 7 | 4 | 6 |
| Miller | 9 | 9 | 10 | 13 | 17 | 18 | 19 | 13 | 15 | 18 | 24 | 20 |
| Alekperov | 28 | 31 | 21 | 25 | 25 | 30 | 35 | 39 | 78 | 70 | 65 | 61 |
| Timchenko | 30 | 29 | 34 | 40 | 35 | 29 | 26 | 26 | 30 | 35 | 32 | 35 |

**Figure 3.1: Russian energy actors on a map of reputational power. Annual rankings of top 100 political figures presented by *Nezavisimaya Gazeta* (NeGa) between 2007 and 2018.**

Source: These rankings are published annually. See, Dmitrii Orlov, '100 vedushchikh politikov Rossii v 2007 godu' [Top 100 leading politicians in Russia in 2007], *Nezavisimaya Gazeta*, 17 January 2008; Dmitrii Orlov, '100 vedushchikh politikov Rossii v 2018 godu' [Top 100 leading politicians in Russia in 2018], *Nezavisimaya Gazeta*, 9 January 2019.

# Energy in Russian Doctrines

To test whether this academic and journalistic assessment of the strategic importance of Russian energy resources is reflected in official thinking, it is crucial to examine how energy-related questions figure in Russian strategic documents on foreign, defence and security policy.

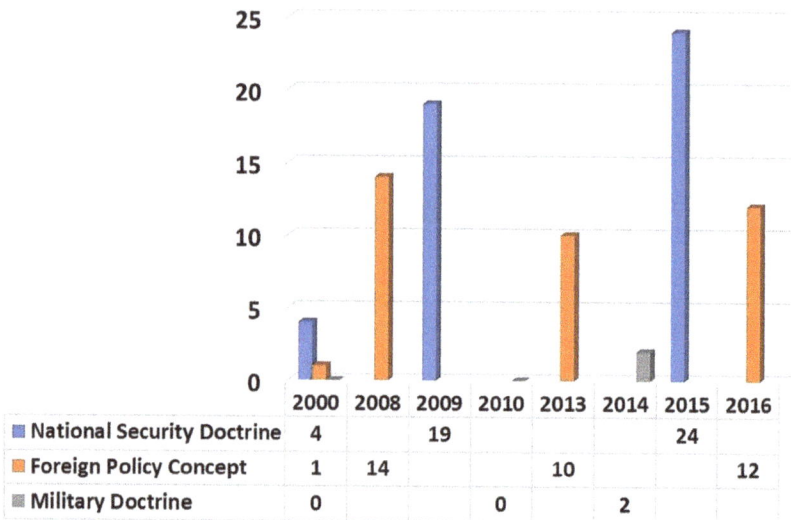

| | 2000 | 2008 | 2009 | 2010 | 2013 | 2014 | 2015 | 2016 |
|---|---|---|---|---|---|---|---|---|
| ■ National Security Doctrine | 4 | | 19 | | | | 24 | |
| ■ Foreign Policy Concept | 1 | 14 | | | 10 | | | 12 |
| ▥ Military Doctrine | 0 | | | 0 | | 2 | | |

**Figure 3.2: Frequency of term 'energy' in Russian doctrines, 2000–18.**[27]

In the period after the collapse of the Soviet Union, several national security, defence and foreign policy doctrines have been published in Russia. Doctrines published after 2000 show a growing interest in energy in the strategic context—especially in the field of national security and foreign policy, and, to a lesser extent, in the military context. One of the factors that explains this phenomenon is the coming to power of Vladimir Putin, who earlier in his career had shown great interest in the management of the country's natural resources.[28]

When analysing the strategic context today, it is crucial to understand how energy-related questions figure in the current set of strategic doctrines. The 2014 *Military Doctrine* mentions energy twice: once in the context of the threat posed by nuclear energy facilities, which was to be dealt

---

27 The list of examined documents includes the following official Russian doctrines published after Vladimir Putin's ascent to power: *2000 National Security Concept; 2000 Foreign Policy Concept; 2000 Military Doctrine; 2008 Foreign Policy Concept; 2009 National Security Strategy until 2020; 2010 Military Doctrine; 2013 Foreign Policy Concept; 2014 Military Doctrine; 2015 National Security Strategy; 2016 Foreign Policy Concept.*

28 Vladimir Putin, 'Mineral'no-Syr'evye Resursy V Strategii Razvitiya Rossijskoj Ekonomiki' [Mineral resources in the development strategy of the Russian Federation], in *Rossiya V Okruzhayuschem Mire: 2000 (Analiticheskij Ezhegodnik)* [Russia in the surrounding world: 2000 (analytical yearbook)], ed. N. N. Moiseev and S. A. Stepanov (Moscow: MNEPU, 2000); Harley Balzer, 'Vladimir Putin's Academic Writings and Russian Natural Resource Policy', *Problems of Post-Communism* 55, no. 1 (2006): 48–54; Harley Balzer, 'The Putin Thesis and Russian Energy Policy', *Post-Soviet Affairs* 21, no. 3 (2005): 210–25, doi.org/10.2747/1060-586X.21.3.210.

with by the Russian military, and once in relation to the formation of territorial troops, which was described as means of dealing with threats to critical infrastructure, including energy infrastructure. The *2015 National Security Strategy* mentions energy 24 times, paying special attention to energy security; volatility in the energy market; ensuring state and public security in fuel and energy industries; and state protection of Russian producers active in the sphere of military, food, information and energy security. In addition, it devotes two entire paragraphs (60 and 61) to discussing various aspects of energy security, and describes energy security as: 'One of the main avenues of ensuring national security in the sphere of the economy for the long term'.[29]

Finally, the 2016 *Foreign Policy Concept* mentions energy 12 times. Placing energy-related questions in the broader context of the evolution of the international system, it pays special attention to qualitative changes in the sphere of energy caused by the introduction of new technologies to extract hard-to-recover hydrocarbon reserves, and the expanded use of renewable sources of energy. This strategic document also addresses the question of 'groundless restrictions and other discriminatory measures' in the field of energy in a situation in which 'states need to diversify their presence on global markets to ensure their energy security'.[30] It states that Russia's interests and approaches should be taken into account when dealing with issues related to energy security and multilateral cooperation in the peaceful use of nuclear energy, and that 'Russia enhances cooperation with the leading energy producers, promotes equal dialogue with consumer and transit countries assuming that stable demand and reliable transit are needed to guarantee energy supplies'.[31] In addition, the document describes the EU as 'an important trade and economic and foreign policy partner, including in the energy segment'.

29 President of the Russian Federation, *Strategiya natsional'noj bezopasnosti Rossiyskoy Federatsii* [National security strategy of the Russian Federation] (Moscow: President of the Russian Federation, 2015).
30 Ministry of Foreign Affairs of the Russian Federation, *Foreign Policy Concept of the Russian Federation* (Moscow: MFA).
31 Ministry of Foreign Affairs of the Russian Federation, *Foreign Policy Concept of the Russian Federation*.

# Energy Strategies

Strategic energy issues are not only discussed in Russian doctrines on national security, defence and foreign policy, but also, and more comprehensively, in the set of documents that could be labelled Russian energy strategies. In the period after the fall of the Soviet Union, at least seven Russian official documents of this type were published by the Russian policymaking community (for an overview see Figure 3.3). These documents outline short-, mid- and long-term goals to be achieved by the country's energy sector; ways of achieving them; and challenges that the sector needs to deal with in order to succeed. As mentioned earlier, these documents also present some thoughts on the strategic importance of the sector in the broader strategic national security and foreign policy context.

The 2019 *Energy Security Doctrine of the Russian Federation* reflects the official view on how to ensure Russia's energy security. The document expands and develops the provisions of the *National Security Strategy of the Russian Federation* and other strategic planning documents in the field of national security.[32] It starts by defining key concepts, such as energy security, threats, challenges and risks to energy security, and identifies some of the challenges, threats and risks the country's energy sector must deal with if it wants to remain relevant in the global context and be able to supply energy to domestic consumers. These crucial issues include sanctions restricting Russian energy companies' access to modern technology; long-term funding and joint projects and measures undertaken by other actors, which are viewed as discriminating against Russian energy actors; and international climate policies and accelerating green energy transitions that may lower global demand for energy resources, which is especially challenging in a situation in which global hydrocarbon reserves are growing and the energy momentum is shifting to the Asia-Pacific region (APR) where Russia lacks adequate infrastructure to become an important supplier. Also, the emergence of the global liquefied natural gas (LNG) market and new gas suppliers is viewed as posing a threat to Russian energy security. Further, the Russian energy sector faces several legal and regulatory challenges, especially in relations with the EU, while, domestically, the sector must deal with issues related to lower-quality resources, corruption and uncertainty over future demand, at the same time as overcoming obstacles caused by what is regarded as excessive environmental regulations.

---

32    President of the Russian Federation, *Energy Security Doctrine of the Russian Federation* (Moscow: President Administration, 2019).

| ENERGY POLICY CONCEPT OF RUSSIA IN THE NEW ECONOMIC CONDITION | MAJOR DIRECTIONS OF ENERGY STRATEGY OF RUSSIA FOR THE PERIOD UP TO 2010 | ENERGY STRATEGY OF RUSSIA FOR THE PERIOD UP TO 2020 | ENERGY STRATEGY OF RUSSIA FOR THE PERIOD UP TO 2030 | ENERGY SECURITY DOCTRINE OF THE RUSSIAN FEDERATION | ENERGY STRATEGY of RUSSIA FOR THE PERIOD UP TO 2035 | ENERGY SECURITY DOCTRINE OF THE RUSSIAN FEDERATION |
|---|---|---|---|---|---|---|
| 1992 | 1995 | 2003 | 2009 | 2012 | 2015 | 2019 |

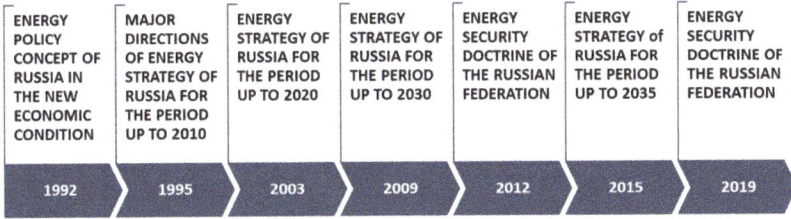

Figure 3.3: Russian energy-related doctrines published between 1993 and 2019.

# Russian Energy Resources as a Means of Grand Strategy

Russian energy resources play an important role in creating the economic framework and conditions that have allowed the current regime to increase its stability on the domestic front and have helped Russia to punch above its economic weight in the international arena. The ability of the current Russian regime to achieve its strategic objectives both domestically and internationally depends on revenues generated by the country's energy sector. According to Russian official data (e.g. Ministry of Finance and CBR), the share of petroleum revenues in the budget reached more than 50 per cent some years ago, declined to below 40 per cent in 2016 and 2017, and reached 46 per cent in 2018 (see Figure 3.4).

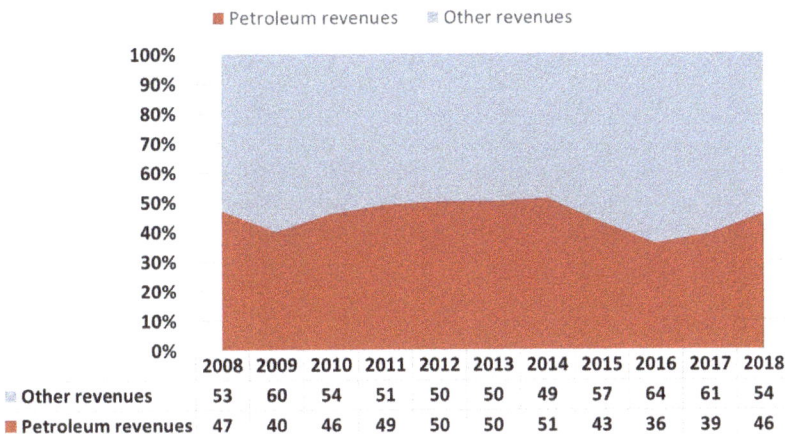

| | 2008 | 2009 | 2010 | 2011 | 2012 | 2013 | 2014 | 2015 | 2016 | 2017 | 2018 |
|---|---|---|---|---|---|---|---|---|---|---|---|
| Other revenues | 53 | 60 | 54 | 51 | 50 | 50 | 49 | 57 | 64 | 61 | 54 |
| Petroleum revenues | 47 | 40 | 46 | 49 | 50 | 50 | 51 | 43 | 36 | 39 | 46 |

Figure 3.4: Share of petroleum revenue in the Russian state budget.

Source: Data from the Russian Ministry of Finance and Central Bank of Russia.

Petroleum-related revenue has allowed the regime to pursue a double-track strategy. The first track of this strategy involved heavy investment in defence- and security-related matters—as promised by Putin during his 2012 presidential campaign.[33] This helped Russia increase its military capabilities as well as its ability to project military power beyond its borders, thereby improving its clout in international relations. The second track involved heavy investment in social programs that helped to secure the stability as well as the survival of the current regime, which is one of the key objectives of what some have labelled 'grand strategy' and others describe as 'strange strategy'.

To illustrate how important petroleum-related revenue was in allowing the regime to pursue this double-track strategy in the years after Putin's return to power in 2012, it is enough to mention that the share of petroleum revenue reached 50 per cent of the budget revenue in 2012, 50 per cent in 2013, 51 per cent in 2014 and dropped to 43 per cent in 2015. The share of defence- and security-related spending (combined) in the Russian state budget reached the level of 24.8 per cent in 2012, 31.3 per cent in 2013, 30.8 per cent in 2014 and 32.95 per cent in 2015, while the share of social spending reached slightly lower levels: 29.9 per cent in 2012, 28.7 per cent in 2013, 23.3 per cent in 2014 and 27.31 per cent in 2015. Therefore, one can ask a highly relevant, and not only rhetorical, question: how would Russian policymakers be able to realise this type of double-track strategy without revenue generated by the country's petroleum sector? The fact that Russian policymakers announced a 20 per cent cut in spending on defence in 2016—in a year in which petroleum-generated revenue formed only 36 per cent of the budget revenue—is a very convincing example of how important energy resources are as a means of realising Russia's grand strategic designs.

The very same energy revenue—or what is referred to as Russian oil and gas rents—have also provided an important economic cushion that has helped Russia deal with external pressures, as illustrated by Clifford Gaddy and Barry Ickes.[34]

---

33    Vladimir Putin, 'Russia Muscles up—the Challenges We Must Rise to Face', Archive of the Official Site of the 2008–2012 Prime Minister of the Russian Federation, 6 January 2012, archive.premier.gov.ru/eng/events/news/17755/; Vladimir Putin, 'Being Strong: National Security Guarantees for Russia', Archive of the Official Site of the 2008–2012 Prime Minister of the Russian Federation, 20 February 2012, archive.premier.gov.ru/eng/events/news/18185/; Vladimir Putin, 'Russia and the Changing World', Archive of the Official Site of the 2008–2012 Prime Minister of the Russian Federation, 27 February 2012, archive.premier.gov.ru/eng/events/news/18252/.
34    Clifford Gaddy and Barry W. Ickes, 'Can Sanctions Stop Putin?', *Brookings*, 3 June 2014, www.brookings.edu/research/articles/2014/06/03-can-sanctions-stop-putin-gaddy-ickes.

# Russian Energy Resources as an Instrument of Grand Strategy

Russian energy resources can be viewed as a means of grand strategy *and* as an instrument in the realisation of grand strategic goals. This is clearly visible in the role these resources play in Russia's relationship with the outside world. In addition to generating revenue, Russian energy resources serve as instruments of political influence. By establishing energy links with buyers of Russian energy resources, a situation of mutual interdependence between Russia and these actors is created: Russia depends on revenue generated by its sale of energy and the buyers depend on energy supplied by Russia to make their economies and societies work.

Energy resources are the most important Russian export commodity. In the period between 2000 and 2018, exports of Russian oil, petroleum products and natural gas generated US$3.807 trillion in revenue, and represented 62.1 per cent of the total value of Russian exports in that period. Analysis conducted by NSI in 2019 concluded that energy has been a key source of Russian power and influence; globally, many countries have developed a strong energy relationship with Russia; Russia's energy priorities extend worldwide; and European nations in particular have become dependent on Russia for access to these resources.[35] In addition, Africa and the Arctic have also become significant as Russia looks to exploit opportunities for energy-related commerce.

According to S. Kardas, the EU was the main energy partner of Russia both before and after the 2014 crisis. The share of the EU in Russian oil export was 72 per cent in 2008 and 63.4 per cent in 2015, and in the gas export 57 per cent in 2008 and 72 per cent in 2016.[36] The situation did not change despite growing tensions between Russia and the West in the wake of the 2014 crisis in Ukraine, and the EU remains the main target area for the export of Russian energy commodities.[37] In 2019, Russia and the EU still depended on each other in terms of energy. While

---

35    Arquilla, 'SMA TRADOC White Paper—Russian Strategic Intentions'.

36    Szymon Kardaś, *The Twilight of the Oil Eldorado. How the Activity of Russian Oil Companies on the EU Market Has Evolved* (Warsaw: Ośrodek Studiów Wschodnich im. Marka Karpia, 2016). Szymon Kardaś, *At Crossroads. Current Problems of Russia's Gas Sector* (Warsaw: Ośrodek Studiów Wschodnich im. Marka Karpia, 2017).

37    Jakub M. Godzimirski, 'Russia–EU Energy Relations: From Complementarity to Distrust?', in *EU Leadership in Energy and Environmental Governance? Global and Local Challenges and Responses*, ed. Jakub M. Godzimirski (New York: Palgrave Macmillan, 2015), 89–112, doi.org/10.1057/9781137502766_5.

this situation provides Russia with certain opportunities, it also creates challenges, as identified in the 2019 official *Energy Security Doctrine of the Russian Federation.*

According to some studies, situations of interdependence create positive incentives for actors to avoid situations of conflict; however, other studies suggest the opposite. Irina Busygina and Mikhail Filippov examined the issue of what they labelled the 'energy curse' in the context of Russian–EU energy dependence, and concluded that, 'as the dependence of both sides on mutual trade increased, their political relations deteriorated'.[38] They argue that this was the result of a strategic choice made by Russian leadership that, at the time, sought to sustain a certain level of political conflict with the EU and many post-Soviet countries for domestic political reasons.[39]

According to C. Egmond, R. Jonkers and G. Kok, there are four major instruments that can be used when designing and implementing energy policy–related measures: judicial-legal, economic, communicative and infrastructural.[40] Judicial-legal instruments prescribe desired behaviour and set norms; they influence the behaviour of actors by making them understand what is desired and accepted and what is not. If actors comply, they can expect rewards; if they do not play by the rules, they can expect a kind of punishment or sanction. Many of these judicial-legal instruments have been used in the Russian context: for instance, the 2010 agreement whereby the Ukraine was given a special gas price in return for its willingness to meet Russia's strategic expectations. The use of various forms of legal instruments is clearly visible in Russia's dealings with various energy actors: those who are more willing to show understanding for Russian interests are given more beneficial legal conditions than those who are less inclined to meet Russian demands. The recent Stockholm arbitration court's decision on the whole body of issues in Russian–Ukrainian gas relations shows how legal instruments can be used in the energy context by both sides.

---

38  Irina Busygina and Mikhail Filippov, '"Resource Curse" and Foreign Policy: Explaining Russia's Approach Towards the EU', in *Russian Energy in a Changing World: What Is the Outlook for the Hydrocarbons Superpower*, ed. Jakub M. Godzimirski (Farnham: Ashgate, 2013), 91–109.
39  Busygina and Filippov, '"Resource Curse"', 105.
40  C. Egmond, R. Jonkers and G. Kok, 'One Size Fits All? Policy Instruments Should Fit the Segments of Target Groups', [English] *Energy Policy* 34, no. 18 (2006): 3464–74, doi.org/10.1016/j.enpol.2005.07.017. For an interesting overview, see Randall Newnham, 'Oil, Carrots, and Sticks: Russia's Energy Resources as a Foreign Policy Tool', *Journal of Eurasian Studies* 2, no. 2 (7/2011): 134–43, doi.org/10.1016/j.euras.2011.03.004. For a more general discussion of these issues in the current context, see Michael Rühle and Julijus Grubliauskas, 'Energy as a Tool of Hybrid Warfare', NATO Defence College, *Research Paper* 113 (April 2015), www.files.ethz.ch/isn/190791/rp_113.pdf.

Legal instruments are often combined with economic instruments that aim to influence the financial considerations of actors, providing economic incentives to those who accommodate Russian interests and de-incentivising those who could oppose Russia's plans. Gazprom's pricing policy, which has attracted the attention of the EU Commission, highlights the use of this type of instrument by Russian actors, and there are numerous other examples, such as Russia's preferential treatment of Belarus and other post-Soviet countries.

Communicative instruments that transfer knowledge for the purpose of informing, persuading, convincing or tempting are also often used in the pursuit of Russia's strategic and energy interests. These instruments can be combined with, and support, other types of instruments. They are often used to influence public opinion, to create social support or increase awareness. A 2011 study on how various communication strategies had been used to facilitate the realisation of the North Stream 1 project provides interesting insights on these questions.[41] This study was followed by one on Russian and Norwegian strategies of influencing EU energy policy, focusing on the use of various channels as a way of promoting national strategic energy interests.[42]

Physical, infrastructural instruments can be used to promote Russian interests. These can include the construction of various elements of physical energy infrastructure, or actions aimed at the existing infrastructure that work to change the physical and market parameters, thereby rendering them useful or useless to other actors. There are numerous examples of how these instruments have been used in the pursuit of energy and strategic goals by Russia: the construction of North Stream 1 and 2, the South Stream, the Turkish Stream and the Yamal LNG terminal; and, conversely, the stop in supplies of oil (explained officially as caused by technical problems to the Mazeikai refinery in Lithuania) and the redirection of oil flows from ports in the Baltic countries to new Russian facilities in Ust'-Luga.

---

41    Jakub M. Godzimirski, 'Nord Stream: Globalization in the Pipeline?', in *Russia's Encounter with Globalisation: Actors, Processes and Critical Moments*, ed. Julie Wilhelmsen and Elana Wilson Rowe (New York: Palgrave Macmillan, 2011), 159–84.
42    Jakub M. Godzimirski, 'Channels of Influence, or How Non-Members Can Influence EU Energy Policy', in *New Political Economy of Energy in Europe: Power to Project, Power to Adapt*, ed. Jakub M. Godzimirski (Cham: Palgrave Macmillan, 2019), 105–37, doi.org/10.1007/978-3-319-93360-3_5.

A detailed examination of the use of various instruments in Russia's energy relations with countries that have direct and indirect implications for Russia's ability to implement its strategic plans can be found in Larsson,[43] Larsson and Leijonhielm,[44] and Orttung and Øverland.[45] These studies—and many others—illustrate how Russian energy resources have been used instrumentally as a tool not only in Russian energy policy, but also in the context of Russian national strategy, grand or strange (see Table 3.2).

Table 3.2: Instruments and tools in Russian energy strategy[46]

| Tools and instruments | Legal | Economic | Communicative | Structural |
|---|---|---|---|---|
| Subsidies | | x | | |
| Gas pipelines shut offs | | x | x | x |
| Pipeline explosions | | x | x | x |
| Constructing alternative transit pipelines | x | x | | x |
| Heated rhetoric | | | x | |
| Import bans | | x | x | x |
| Cyber attacks | | x | x | x |
| Personal relationships | | | x | |
| Sophisticated PR campaigns | | | x | |
| Court cases | x | | | |
| Military sabre rattling | | | x | x |

In this context, it is important to mention that other instruments from Russia's strategic toolbox—which are not necessarily directly associated with energy strategy or policy—have also been used with some effect on Russian energy policy, which means that there is a sort of mutual grand strategic interdependence. On the one hand, energy is used as an instrument in Russia's pursuit of grand strategic goals; yet, on the other, military power, which is also a part of the grand strategic toolbox, can be used to change the parameters for Russian energy policy.

43    Robert Larsson, *Russia's Energy Policy: Security Dimensions and Russia's Reliability as an Energy Supplier* (Stockholm: Swedish Defence Research Agency, 2006).
44    Jan Leijonhielm and Robert L. Larsson, *Russia's Strategic Commodities: Energy and Metals as Security Levers* (Stockholm: Swedish Defence Research Agency, 2004).
45    Robert W. Orttung and Indra Overland, 'A Limited Toolbox: Explaining the Constraints on Russia's Foreign Energy Policy', *Journal of Eurasian Studies* 2, no. 1 (2011): 74–85, doi.org/10.1016/j.euras.2010.10.006.
46    Based on framework proposed by Egmond, Jonkers and Kok, 'One Size Fits All?', and empirical studies conducted by Orttung and Overland, 'A Limited Toolbox'.

Two recent examples illustrate this connection. The annexation of Crimea in 2014, in which the Russian military played an important part, provided Russia with new opportunities in energy policy, as some important energy deposits located in the region came under Russian control. Russia's military intervention in Syria in 2015 was predicted to have some impact on Russian energy producers, as it was expected that the increased level of conflict and Russia's direct military involvement would result in higher oil prices on the global market. However, the effect of Russian intervention in Syria on oil prices was short-lived: the price increased from US$38 per barrel on 24 August 2015 to US$49 on 9 October 2015, but then dropped to US$27 on 10 February 2016. Since then, and to the amazement of energy experts who had not expected the oil price to be decoupled from political events in the Middle East, it has swung independently of Russia's actions in Syria.

# Russian Energy Resources as a Goal of Grand Strategy

Due to the political and economic importance of Russian energy resources, they can be regarded not only as a means or a tool in pursuit of Russia's grand strategy, but also as a goal of this strategy. As indicated by our examination of Russian strategic documents, Russian policymakers understand the importance of the country's energy resources. Developing these resources and protecting them is viewed as an important goal of the country's national strategy for at least two intertwined reasons. Russian energy resources provide the general population and industry with access to affordable and reliable energy, securing the stability and survival of the regime as well as Russia's economic competitiveness in the global context.[47] Further, taking 'strategic care' of Russian energy resources enables the country to project its economic—and political power— beyond its borders, as shown in the previous section.[48]

---

47  For more detail on the Russian understanding of this, see President of the Russian Federation, *2015 National Security Strategy*, especially paragraphs 60 and 61.

48  On the role of economic power and instruments in Russian policy, see for instance, Maksim Braterskiy, *Ekonomicheskie Instrumenty Vneshnei Politiki I Politicheskie Riski* [Economic instruments in foreign policy and political risks] (Moscow: Higher School of Economics, 2010); Maksim Braterskiy, ed., *Nevoyennye Rychagi Vneshney Politiki Rossii: Regionalnyye I Globa' Nye Mekhanizmy* [Non-military leverages in Russian foreign policy: Regional and global mechanisms] (Moscow: Higher School of Economics, 2013).

To be able to provide energy to domestic consumers *and* foreign partners, Russia must identify and address the challenges faced by this sector. Hence, extending the lifespan of Russia's energy sector—one of the crown jewels in Russia's strategic toolbox—and making it better prepared to meet expected and unexpected current and future threats, challenges and risks is one of the key goals of Russian energy policy, and one of the key objectives of the country's grand strategy (if any such strategy exists).

A 2019 document prepared by the Russian Ministry of Energy outlines four main goals in Russian energy policy to be achieved in the coming years:[49]

1. Securing energy needs in the domestic market in line with the principles of energy saving and efficiency, as well as the fulfilment of foreign contracts.
2. Increasing the environmental efficiency of Russia's energy sector by reducing man-made negative footprints on the environment and increasing the level of innovation.
3. Changing the approach to questions related to the pricing of heat supply, leading to the creation of a heat supply market.
4. Introducing advanced and digital technologies in the Russian energy sector.

These goals are to be realised in cooperation with other actors who may play a crucial role as suppliers of necessary financing or technology, or as providers of access to markets, thereby generating revenue for both companies and the state. This explains why having a comprehensive external energy strategy is of crucial importance.

The authors of a project on Russian energy strategy to 2035 outlined four key strategies to be pursued in the coming years: first, establishing and maintaining stable relations with old and new consumers of Russian energy resources, and securing Russian shares on the global energy market; second, increasing the level of export diversification in terms of product portfolio and increasing the share of processed products; third, establishing Russia as an important player in the APR; and, fourth, increasing the

---

49    Ministry of Energy Russian Federation, *Ob Utverzhdenii Plana Deyatelnosti Ministerstva Energetiki Rossiyskoy Federatsii Na Period 2019–2024 Godov* [On the approval of the plan for activity of the Ministry of Energy of the Russian Federation for the period 2019–2024] (Moscow: Ministry of Energy Russian Federation, 2019).

level of cooperation between Russian energy companies and their foreign partners.[50] It remains to be seen how, or whether, these energy goals will be pursued in the coming years; having plans is one thing, but realising them is something completely different.[51] It is impossible to know how Russia's energy future will be shaped, what role its energy resources will play in the country's pursuit of grand strategic goals and what the short-, mid- and long-term effects of this energy/grand strategy interaction will be. Rather than examine this highly uncertain future, the next section focuses on the role of Asia in Russian energy and grand strategy.

# What Is the Role of Asia in Russian Energy and Grand Strategy?

The following brief examination of Asia's role in Russian energy and grand strategy, and the interconnection between Russian grand strategic objectives and the use of energy resources, is divided into two sections. The first describes Russia's energy relations with Asia in 2019.[52] The second discusses the role of Russian energy in Asia from three perspectives, treating energy as a means of Russian grand strategy, as an instrument and finally as a goal.

By 2019, Russia had managed to achieve some of the Asia-related energy objectives defined in official and unofficial statements. According to BP data, in 2018, 34 per cent of Russia's oil exports (94.8 mt) went to the APR, with China alone importing 71.6 mt, followed by other countries in the region (12.3 mt), Japan (7 mt), India (2.2 mt) and Singapore (1.7 mt). Although these figures look impressive, Russia's contribution represented only 8 per cent of the total oil exported to this region.

---

50   Vitaliy Bushuev, *Proyekt energeticheskoy strategii Rossii do 2035* [Project of the energy strategy of Russia until 2035] (Moscow: Institute of Energy Strategy, 2014), www.energystrategy.ru/ab_ins/source/Bushuev_ES-2035-17.02.14.pdf.
51   See L. S. Ruban, '"Vse, Chto Sbylos I Ne Sbylos". Prognozy Razvitiya Tek Rossii V Energeticheskikh Strategiyakh Rf Do 2020 G., Do 2030 G., Proekte Ec Do 2035 G. I Ekspertnykh Otsenkakh' ['All that's true and not true'. Prognosis of the Russian fuel and energy complex in the energy strategies of the Russian Federation up to 2020, to 2030, the draft ES up to 2035 and expert estimations], *Burene i neft* 11 (2017).
52   BP, *Statistical Review of World Energy 2019*, www.bp.com/content/dam/bp/business-sites/en/global/corporate/pdfs/energy-economics/statistical-review/bp-stats-review-2019-full-report.pdf.

In the same year, Russia exported approximately 28 mt of petroleum products to the Asia-Pacific. This represented 16.2 per cent of Russia's total export of petroleum products, but only 6 per cent of the total import of petroleum products to this region. In terms of importers, Singapore (10.5 mt) was the most important, with other Asia-Pacific countries importing 12.5 mt, and China (2.3 mt) and Japan (2.1 mt) playing a relatively small role in this regional context.

The role of Russian gas in the APR market deserves closer scrutiny. Russia has 19.8 per cent of global reserves of natural gas—more than two times the combined reserves in the whole APR (9.2 per cent). In 2018, Russia produced 669.5 bcm of gas (17.3 per cent of global production), which was slightly more than the total gas production in the Asia-Pacific (631.7 bcm, or 16.3 per cent of global production). Russia consumed 454.5 bcm of gas, while consumption in the Asia-Pacific was almost double (825.3 bcm). Russia exported 223 bcm of gas through its pipelines and 24.9 bcm as LNG, while Asian countries imported huge volumes of gas—most as LNG. China's imports totalled 121.3 bcm, of which 73.5 bcm was LNG and 47.9 bcm was piped gas from Turkmenistan, Uzbekistan, Kazakhstan and Myanmar. India imported 30.6 bcm of LNG; Asian members of the OECD (Organisation for Economic Cooperation and Development) imported 179.1 bcm, of which 173.2 bcm was LNG; and other Asian countries imported 45.6 bcm, all LNG.

According to BP data, there were no supplies of Russian piped gas to the APR market in 2018, but that situation changed at the end of 2019 when the first supplies of Russian gas via the Power of Siberia pipeline started and were expected to increase to 38 bcm/y some years later.[53] In 2018, 69.08 per cent of Russian LNG exports (17.2 bcm) went to this region; however, this represented only 5 per cent of LNG supplies reaching this area. Japan alone imported more than 50 per cent of Russian LNG reaching the Asia-Pacific market (9.4 bcm), followed by Taiwan (3.2 bcm), South Korea (2.6 bcm) and China (1.3 bcm). The 17.2 bcm of Russian LNG that reached the APR market in 2018 represented only 7.7 per cent of Russia's total gas export and 2.6 per cent of the country's gas production in 2018, while the share of Europe—mostly the EU—receiving exported Russian gas (piped and LNG combined) was above 80 per cent.

---

53  Ben Aris, 'Gazprom's Power of Siberia Gas Pipeline to China Is Finished', *Intellinews*, 14 March 2019, www.intellinews.com/gazprom-s-power-of-siberia-gas-pipeline-to-china-is-finished-157956/.

# Energy as a Means of Grand Strategy: What Role for Asia?

Although revenue from the energy trade with Asia is increasing, it has come at a relatively high cost due to the need to make investments in infrastructure, as illustrated by the huge investment in the Power of Siberia pipeline, the Sakhalin I and Sakhalin II projects, the planned Altai pipeline, and the development of oil and gas fields that are to be used to supply energy to an Asian market that has other options—such as LNG supplies from the Middle East, Australia or the US.

The economic value of Russian energy exported to the APR region in 2018 can be roughly calculated as follows: c. US$44 billion from oil, c. US$13 billion from petroleum products and c. US$3 billion from gas. This represents approximately 13.8 per cent of the revenue generated by the sale of oil, petroleum products and natural gas in 2018.[54] Therefore, in purely economic terms, it is clear that Asia's role as a generator of means that can be spent on other grand strategic objectives is still relatively marginal; however, Asia's role is expected to grow in line with new infrastructural developments, allowing higher levels of energy supplies to Asian markets.[55]

# Energy as an Instrument in Grand Strategy: What Role for Asia?

By building strategic partnerships with Asian countries that strengthen the multipolarity of the global system and reduce the influence of the West in global affairs, energy resources can play an instrumental role in Russian grand strategy. A number of energy deals and partnerships with Asian actors have already been signed and implemented. This realignment

54   Values calculated by author based on CBR data (value of exported Russian energy commodities in 2018) and BP data (share of APR market in total Russian exports of oil, petroleum products and natural gas in 2018).

55   See, for instance, V. V. Bessel, 'Perspektivy Aziatskogo Napravleniya Eksporta Uglevodorodov Iz Rossii' [Asian prospects directions of hydrocarbons export from Russia], *Burene i neft* 9 (2015); A. Mastepanov, 'Sotrudnichestvo Stran Briks V Energeticheskoj Sfere Kak Faktor Prognozirovaniya Mirovogo Energopotrebleniya' [The cooperation of Brics countries in the energy sector as a factor in forecasting global energy demand], *Burene i neft* 1 (2016).

towards Asia gained momentum in the wake of the 2014 Ukraine conflict and is a part of a conscious strategy of counterbalancing Western influence and market dependency.

When operating in the Asian landscape, Russia has to deal with groups of actors who have varying levels and types of strategic importance. During Y. Primakov's period as Russia's minister of foreign affairs, China and India were singled out as the most important partners in shaping a more multipolar global environment, and both countries figured as important arms customers of Russia. However, the dream of creating a Moscow–Delhi–Beijing axis that could challenge the Western hegemony has not come to fruition, as the strategic paths and choices of Beijing and Delhi differed.

China is undoubtedly Russia's most important strategic Asian partner—both in terms of limiting Western global influence and as the most promising energy market in the development of Russian energy resources.[56] Relations with India are also important, but they lack this grand strategic cut; there are also geographical and structural constraints that limit further development of this energy and political partnership. South Korea, already an important economic partner and supplier of technological solutions, serves an important role in strengthening Russia's grip on the Asian energy market. A fleet of ice-class LNG tankers that will serve Russia's Arctic LNG terminals is being built in South Korean shipyards, but relations with South Korea can be influenced by Russia's approach to North Korea, representing a security conundrum.

Japan figures high on Russia's map of energy interests in Asia and is already an important market for Russian gas and oil; however, there are sensitive issues that need to be resolved, such as the question of a peace treaty and the situation in the Kuril Islands. Placing further constraints on a future partnership, Japan is viewed as a staunch supporter of the US presence in Asia and as a strategic Western outpost in Asia.

Finally, there are several countries in Asia that play an important role in both Russian energy and strategic designs, such as Turkey. Russia is trying to build a kind of strategic partnership with Turkey in the Middle East at the same time as undermining the US position in the region. This has

---

56  Morena Skalamera, 'Understanding Russia's Energy Turn to China: Domestic Narratives and National Identity Priorities', *Post-Soviet Affairs* 34, no. 1 (2018): 55–77, doi.org/10.1080/106058 6X.2017.1418613.

caused tension between Turkey and other NATO members, as symbolised by the debate over Russia's sale of S-400 air defence systems to Ankara. Turkey also plays a pivotal role in Russia's energy strategy for Europe, having cooperated with Russia on the Turkish Stream pipeline and becoming an important transit area for Russian gas to Southern Europe.

Finally, Russia has invested in developing working relations with a number of Asian OPEC (Organization of the Petroleum Exporting Countries) members, such as Iran and Saudi Arabia, who, as energy producers and exporters, share strategic energy interests with Russia. This has resulted in the establishment of the OPEC+ format and the strengthening of cooperation within the Gas Exporting Countries Forum.

As well as using energy as an instrument to strengthen relations with Asian partners, Russia uses access to the Asian market and these bilateral energy relationships to reduce its dependence on access to the European market and to diversify its energy supplies away from Europe. This serves two strategic goals. In reducing Russia's dependence on European energy markets, it limits the country's exposure to EU and Western normative, regulatory, market and economic power. Further, by involving Asian actors, Russia may also become less dependent on the transfer of funding and technology from Western partners—who often tend to attach normative or political strings to their energy deals with Russia and are frequently seen as suffering from Russophobia.

# Extending the Lifespan of the Russian Energy Sector as a Goal in the Grand Strategy: What Role for Asia?

Asian partners can play a significant role in securing an extended lifespan for Russia's energy sector and in making it more competitive in the global context, which is, as I have demonstrated, one of the grand strategic goals of the current regime. This could involve co-financing various elements of critical infrastructure and/or providing access to vital technological solutions. In order to supply Asian markets, Russia has to develop new gas and oilfields that require financial resources; this presents another opportunity for Asian partners to play a role. Unlike the energy market in Europe, the Asian energy market is expected to grow. Moreover, unlike European policymakers, Asian policymakers are less likely to be influenced by climate concerns in designing and implementing their energy policies, all of which bodes well for Russia. The era of the so-called 'low hanging fruits' in Russia's energy sector seems to be over. The development of new fields will require significant investment and access to new technologies. Therefore, securing mid- and long-term access to growing Asian energy markets is of paramount importance for securing the future of the Russian energy sector, for making Russia less exposed to Western pressure and for securing Russia's further cooperation with, and influence in, the region emerging as the new global economic, political and normative powerhouse.

* * *

What, then, is Asia's role in Russia's grand strategic designs, and how should energy resources be viewed in this context? According to NSI, Russia wants:

> To portray itself as a reliable actor, a key regional powerbroker, and a successful mediator in order to gain economic, military, and political influence over nations worldwide and to refine the liberalist rules and norms that currently govern the world order.[57]

As stated above, the main goal is to establish a 'Yalta 2.0' system in which Russia enjoys an uncontested sphere of influence in the post-Soviet region, broadcasts Russian voices and influence globally, and establishes reliable constraints on American—or, more broadly, Western—globetrotting and regime-changing activities. According to Person, the key approach in Russia's grand strategy is 'asymmetric balancing' through grey zone challenges to prevent uncontested US influence from setting the global agenda.[58] In his opinion, Russia's means expanded with the oil boom, allowing critical investments and increases in defence spending to be made. At the same time, energy has been a key source of Russian power and influence, as many countries have developed a strong energy relationship with Russia.

Russia's turn to Asia seems to have clear strategic purposes. The country's cooperation with Asia—and especially with China—on energy is motivated by more than purely economic concerns and interest in market expansion and diversification. It will reduce Russia's strategic exposure

---

57 Arquilla, 'SMA TRADOC White Paper—Russian Strategic Intentions'.
58 Person, *Russian Grand Strategy*.

vis-à-vis the West by reducing the level of strategically constraining energy interdependence between Russia and the EU caused by the EU's dominant role in Russia's export of energy commodities. It will also reduce Russia's strategic exposure to possible consequences of the green energy revolution, promoted and implemented by the EU, which could, in the mid- and long-term perspective, undermine Russia's role as the leading producer and exporter of fossil fuels. The shift to Asia will also help Russia develop new energy provinces and infrastructure financed, at least partly, by Asian partners who can also provide some needed technological solutions and who seem to be interested in greater volumes of fossil energy imports from Russia as a way of addressing their own energy dilemmas. This in turn will contribute to extending the lifespan of the Russian energy sector, which will most probably remain the backbone of the Russian economy and the main source of state revenue in the foreseeable future. By developing stronger energy ties with a number of Asian countries, Russia will also be able to project not only its economic and energy power but also its political power, working with them on other issues of common interest, including construction of a new global order based on a new set of non-Western rules. This in turn could result in limiting the power of the West in the global context, which could be viewed as a beneficial development from the Russian strategic point of view, but at the same time poses a new strategic challenge to be dealt with by Russia—namely, how to avoid overexposure to the growing Chinese influence, locally and globally.

It is important to point out that the realisation of Russia's grand strategic energy plans towards Asia will depend not only on what Russia is going to undertake, but also on how the country's actual and potential strategic partners in Asia respond (i.e. how they factor Russia's strategic plans into their own strategic calculations). But this is a completely different history to be told by others …

# 4

# Energy and Russian Great Power Post-Crimea

Peter Rutland

Vladimir Putin has been in power for 20 years, longer than Leonid Brezhnev. (He was appointed prime minister on 9 August 1999 and president on 31 December 1999.) During that time there have been some important shifts in the balance between the different instruments in Russia's power projection toolkit.

In the 2000s, the biggest fear in the West was, it seems, the energy weapon. However, Russia's rebuilding of its military power and its demonstrated willingness to use armed force beyond its borders has shifted the balance towards hard power. This began with Russia's invasion of Georgia in 2008 and continued with the annexation of Crimea in March 2014 and the military intervention in Syria in September 2015.

At the same time, changes in global energy markets (the fracking revolution and the rise of China) have changed the equation of risks and rewards in Russian energy exports. Increasing global economic integration left Moscow vulnerable to fluctuations in world markets, and post-Crimea sanctions revealed its exposure to Western interruption of key technologies and financial services. Russia's capacity to wield the energy 'weapon' to advance its interests looks more questionable today than it did in 2008.

There is a curious imbalance between Russia's resurgence as a power on the world stage and its anaemic economic performance and dim growth prospects. This is largely explained by the decisive role that energy plays in structuring Russia's domestic political economy. Russia remains very much a 'petrostate', in which energy rent-seekers, in alliance with security forces, have the upper hand over profit-seekers. This is part of a broader pattern in emerging market economies in which 'the middle income trap is in the final analysis a political trap not an economic one'.[1] Therefore, the main geopolitical importance of energy when it comes to understanding Russia is its role in shaping the behaviour of the Russian power elite. There are some important feedback loops—both positive and negative—between the domestic political regime of the 'petrostate' and the aspirational international role as an 'energy superpower'.

# Russia as an Energy Superpower

Oil and gas were key to Russia's return to prominence on the international stage in the 2000s, when it became common to refer to Russia as an 'energy superpower'.[2] The *Economist* and many other Western publications were fond of cartoons showing the Russian bear sitting astride oil and gas pipelines, gleefully shutting the valves. There was growing concern that Russia was using energy dependency to pressure neighbouring states to accede to Russia's political or economic demands, and to project influence over customer states further afield. Robert Larsson identified 55 instances between 1992 and 2006 when Russia either cut off, or threatened to cut off, energy supplies.[3] For the Russian elite, too, the term 'energy superpower' was a useful rhetorical device justifying their rule, with the geopolitical utility of energy being expressed in the 2003 *Energy Strategy*.

There is no question that the raw data show Russia is an energy superpower. Russia is the second-largest producer of natural gas and third-largest producer of oil in the world. In 2016, Russia pumped 11 million barrels of crude oil a day, about 12 per cent of the global supply, placing third

1    Hartmut Elsenhaus and Salvatore Babones, *BRICS or Bust? Escaping the Middle Income Trap* (Stanford: Stanford University Press, 2017), 107, doi.org/10.1515/9781503604919.
2    The term was used a handful of times in the 1990s, but only came into more widespread usage in the wake of Russia's interruption of natural gas supplies to Ukraine in January 2006. See, Stefan Bouzarovski and Mark Bassin, 'Energy and Identity: Imagining Russia as a Hydrocarbon Superpower', *Annals of the Association of American Geographers* 101, no. 4(2011): 1–12, doi.org/10.1080/00045608. 2011.567942; Peter Rutland, 'Russia as an Energy Superpower', *New Political Economy* 13, no. 2 (June 2008): 203–10, doi.org/10.1080/13563460802018547.
3    Robert Larsson, *Russia's Energy Policy: Security Dimensions and Russia's Reliability as an Energy Supplier* (Stockholm: Swedish Defence Research Agency, 2006).

after the US and Saudi Arabia.[4] From 2004 to 2011, it was in second place after Saudi Arabia, before being overtaken by the US due to the fracking revolution. In September 2019, the US became a net oil exporter—for the first time since records began.[5] Russia remains the world's second-largest oil exporter, supplying about 20 per cent of European oil consumption. As for natural gas, Russia accounts for 20 per cent of global output and holds 25 per cent of proven reserves. Due to the shale gas boom, the US has taken over as the world's top gas producer, but Russia remains the number one exporter, with 15 per cent of the global gas market.[6] It supplies 25 per cent of the gas used by the EU and 33 per cent of the gas that the EU imports. Coal and nuclear power are also important. Russia is the world's sixth-largest coal producer and third-largest coal exporter, with coal exports tripling over the past decade to about US$10 billion per year.

In addition to being a major producer, Russia also serves as a transit country for oil and gas exports to Europe from landlocked Central Asia. The Soviet Union pipeline system connected Kazakhstan, Uzbekistan and Turkmenistan to the Russian Federation network, and it would be two decades before they were able to develop alternative export routes—to China. The 1,800 km long Turkmen–China gas pipeline was opened in 2009, and the same year saw completion of a 2,300 km oil pipeline from Atyrau in Kazakhstan to Alashankou in Xinjiang.[7]

After the Soviet collapse, Russia found itself in the awkward position of being dependent on pipelines transiting Belarus, Lithuania, Latvia and Ukraine to get its oil and gas to Western markets. Starting in the 1990s, it embarked on an ambitious and costly program to build new pipelines to provide alternative export outlets, preferring routes that transited the Baltic and Black Seas, thereby circumventing Russia's ornery neighbours and hostile countries such as Poland (see Table 4.1). Russia built new oil terminals on its Baltic coast and two pipelines to supply them with

---

4    'IEA Atlas of Energy: Oil', International Energy Authority (IEA), accessed 20 August 2020, energyatlas.iea.org/#!/tellmap/-1920537974/0; 'Total Energy Production 2017', US Energy Information Administration (EIA), accessed 20 August 2020, www.eia.gov/beta/international/rankings/#?cy=2015.
5    In December 2018, the US exported slightly more oil than it imported for the first time (both crude and oil products combined). See, Robert Rapier, 'No the US Is Not a Net Exporter of Crude Oil', *Forbes*, 9 December 2018, www.forbes.com/sites/rrapier/2018/12/09/no-the-u-s-is-not-a-net-exporter-of-crude-oil/#248425554ac1.
6    'IEA Atlas of Energy: Natural Gas', IEA, accessed 20 August 2020, energyatlas.iea.org/#!/tellmap/-1165808390/0.
7    Gazprom stopped buying gas from Turkmenistan in 2016 and restarted in April 2019. China buys 40 bcm/y; Russia will buy 6 bcm/y.

crude oil to avoid dependence on the Ventspils terminal in Latvia and Butinge in Lithuania.[8] The Nord Stream gas pipeline across the Baltic to Germany became operational in 2011, adding 55 bcm to Russia's existing 245 bcm export capacity. Construction began on Nord Stream 2 in 2018, but US sanctions delayed work on the project, which as of August 2020 was 94 per cent complete.[9]

**Table 4.1: Key pipeline projects since 2000**

| Year* | Operation |
|---|---|
| 2001 | Baltic Pipeline System (oil) to port of Primorsk on Russia's Baltic coast, second line 2012 |
| | Caspian Pipeline Consortium (oil) from Tengiz, Kazakhstan, to Russian port of Novorossiisk; lead partners Chevron and Lukoil |
| 2005 | Blue Stream (gas) across Black Sea to Turkey |
| 2011 | Nord Stream (gas) under Baltic Sea from Vyborg to Griefswald, Germany; second line added 2012 |
| | Sakhalin–Khabarovsk–Vladivostok (gas), to feed future LNG export plant |
| 2012 | East Siberia – Pacific Ocean (oil) to China |
| 2014 | South Stream (gas) across Black Sea to Bulgaria cancelled, instead new Turkish Stream |
| | Power of Siberia (gas) from Yakutsk to China, construction began |
| 2015 | Ukraine connects reverse flow pipeline to import gas from Poland |
| 2018 | Nord Stream 2 (gas) to Germany, construction began |

* Start of operation, unless otherwise stated.

Russia's success in building these new export pipelines was a major strategic accomplishment of the Putin era. Moscow had the additional goal of deterring Western projects to build new pipelines to bring oil and gas to Europe from the Caspian basin. BP's Baku–Tbilisi–Ceyhan oil pipeline did open in 2005, but more ambitious Trans-Caspian gas projects such as the EU-sponsored Nabucco line have not yet come to fruition. Russia was able to use the ambiguous legal status of the Caspian Sea to block plans to build pipelines across the Caspian to bring Kazakh oil and Turkmen gas to European markets.[10]

---

8    Margarita Balmaceda, *The Politics of Energy Dependency. Ukraine, Belarus and Lithuania Between Domestic Oligarchs and Russian Pressure* (Toronto: University of Toronto Press, 2015), 296.
9    Julia Kuznir, 'The Impact of EU Regulations on Nord Stream 2', *Russian Analytical Bulletin*, 6 June 2019, 9–13; Marco Siddi, 'German Debates and Policies on Russia 2014–17', in *EU Members States and Russia*, ed. Marco Siddi (Finnish Institute of International Affairs, 2018), 28–40.
10    The littoral states signed a convention on 12 August 2018 in Aktau, Kazakhstan, establishing a 15-mile territorial limit, and allowing bilateral agreements on borders between adjacent and opposite countries. It is too early to say whether this will resolve the conflicts.

Russia's energy and metals conglomerates have also aggressively pursued acquisitions of production facilities and distribution networks across Europe, from the Balkans to Britain. The EU tried to use the Energy Charter Treaty (ECT) to mandate third-party access to Russia's pipelines and the 'unbundling' of large energy companies (i.e. the separation of production and distribution companies). Russia signed the ECT in 1994, but never ratified it, and refuses to comply with its mandates.[11] Russia is more dependent on energy exports to the EU than the EU is on Russia as supplier, but Russia has more effective leverage because it is a single actor.[12]

Was the West really in fear of the Russian energy weapon in the 2000s, or was it just an easily evoked threat, a substitute for deeper anxieties— about Russian authoritarianism and imperialism—that could not directly be articulated? After all, Western Europe had been dependent on Soviet oil since the opening of the Druzhba pipeline in 1964, and, despite all the alarms and crises over the next 50 years, at no point was the supply interrupted for political reasons. There were brief disruptions of the gas supply—to Belarus and Ukraine in 2006–07—but these were disputes over the prices in the annual contract, and were limited in time (17 days was the longest interruption) and scope (Bulgaria and Moldova were affected, but none of the major Western customers).[13] Even after the annexation of Crimea, Russian gas continued to flow across Ukraine.[14] In 2018, the Stockholm Arbitration Institute awarded Ukraine US$4.6 billion in compensation from Gazprom for gas transit fees, minus US$2 billion, which Naftohas owed for 5 bcm of gas it had used and not paid for. Soon after, Gazprom appealed the decision and, in 2020, the appeal was rejected.

There is little evidence that Russia gained much from these efforts to wield the 'energy weapon', which often served to alienate the countries on the receiving end and make them seek alternatives to Russia. Trade is a relationship of mutual benefit and dependence between buyer and seller, and use of trade as a 'weapon' can hurt the supplier just as much as the

---

11    Andrey Kazantsev, 'Policy Networks in European–Russian Gas Relations: Function and Dysfunction from a Perspective of EU Energy Security', *Communist and Post-Communist Studies* 45, no. 3–4 (2012): 305–13, doi.org/10.1016/j.postcomstud.2012.07.006.

12    Veli-Pekka Tynkkynen, *The Energy of Russia. Hydrocarbon Culture and Climate Change* (London: Edward Elgar, 2019), 79.

13    Balmaceda, *The Politics of Energy Dependency.*

14    Due to Nord Stream, Russian gas transit across Ukraine had already fallen from 71 bcm in 2011 to 31 bcm in 2014.

customer. The literature on economic sanctions suggest that they are more likely to be effective when they are multilateral, but Russia's efforts have been unilateral. The one exception is their participation in Saudi Arabia's efforts since 2016 to restrain the oil supply (Russia agreed to cut its output by 300,000 b/d).[15] Using energy as a carrot rather than a stick has not proved any more effective. Twenty years of subsidised energy prices for Belarus (amounting to perhaps 10 per cent of GDP) has not produced a loyal and subservient ally.

The concept of an 'energy superpower' is somewhat contradictory, lumping together two quite distinct logics: that of the energy market and that of military superpowers. Despite its vast wealth (and its spiritual role as the birthplace of Islam), we do not think of Saudi Arabia as a world power (it is even unable to prevail in the war in neighbouring Yemen). It is unusual to see a resource-rich country taking on the attributes of a world power: historically, it was the colonised countries and not their imperial masters who were the resource exporters. Typically, resource-rich countries have not used military power to create empires. Rather, it is usually resource-poor countries that create empires in order to acquire more resources. The US itself has a rich resource base, but it was its manufacturing industry and not its resource exports that was the backbone of its rise to superpower status. The US began to import oil in the late 1940s, and it was precisely the search for oil that was (and remains) a contributory factor to its willingness to shoulder the superpower role. Russia, of course, is the grand exception: Tsarist Russia was rich in land and resources and exported commodities such as grain and timber, but it created the world's largest empire. The expansionism of the tsars was driven by a concern for security and prestige rather than a search for resources. Likewise, the USSR's quest for empire was not primarily driven by a need for more resources, but by a combination of security fears and ideological fervour. Putin's Russia seems to be reverting to a similar pattern. Unfortunately, it ended badly both for the tsars and the Soviets.

---

15    James Henderson, 'Russian Oil Production Outlook to 2020', Oxford Institute for Energy Studies, January 2017, www.oxfordenergy.org/publications/russian-oil-production-outlook-to-2020/.

# Russia as a Petrostate: The Domestic Dimension

Even though Russia may not be an energy superpower, it is still a petrostate, heavily dependent on the production and export of energy.[16] For most of the past two decades, hydrocarbons have accounted for 25 per cent of Russia's GDP, 60 per cent of exports and 40 per cent of government revenue.[17] The Russian business cycle was closely tied to fluctuations of the international price of oil, though that relationship has broken down since 2014.[18] The Russian energy giant walks on two legs: oil and natural gas. Externally, oil export revenues are three times larger than those for gas. But, inside Russia, gas accounts for three times as much energy consumption as oil, being used to heat homes and generate 50 per cent of Russia's electricity.[19] Gazprom uses its export revenue to subsidise domestic consumers: in 2017 the export price was US$9.2 mmbtu and the domestic price US$3.8.[20]

Russia has vast untapped oil and gas reserves and it has not yet reached peak oil. However, most of Russia's newly discovered fields are located in permafrost zones and many of them are offshore (notably the Sakhalin deposits and the Shtokman gas field in the Barents Sea). The US$27 billion Yamal gas field, for example, lies north of the Arctic Circle, and LNG will be shipped out on icebreaker tankers (being built in South Korea). Russia doubled its share of global LNG to 8 per cent in 2018 and wants 20 per cent by 2035.[21] The Sakhalin 1 project, which commenced in 2003, needed Exxon advanced 3D seismology and horizontal drilling. Other fields require lengthy new pipelines. These factors substantially increase the extraction costs, meaning that the price of oil will have to stay above US$50 a barrel for

16    Michael Ellman ed., *Russia's Oil and Natural Gas: Bonanza or Curse?* (London: Anthem Press, 2006).
17    Shinichiro Tabata, 'Observations on the Influence of High Oil Prices on Russia's GDP Growth', *Eurasian Geography and Economics* 47, no. 1 (2006): 95–111, doi.org/10.2747/1538-7216.47.1.95.
18    Dmitrii Kuznets, 'Kurs rublia bol'she ne sziazan s kursami na neft' [The rouble exchange rate is no longer linked to oil prices, sanctions are not that terrible], *Meduza*, 30 November 2018, meduza.io/feature/2018/11/30/kurs-rublya-bolshe-ne-svyazan-s-tsenami-na-neft-sanktsii-ne-strashny-proveryaem-slova-ministra-finansov.
19    Susanne Wengle, *Post-Soviet Power. State-Led Development and Russia's Marketization* (Cambridge: Cambridge University Press, 2015), doi.org/10.1017/CBO9781139680479.
20    Natassia Astrasheuskaya, 'Gazprom Takes on Chechnya', *Financial Times*, 11 February 2019.
21    'Russian LNG projects are competitive', *Moscow Times*, 21 March 2019, www.themoscowtimes.com/2019/03/21/russian-lng-projects-are-competitive-shell-executive-a64913.

these projects to be commercially viable.[22] Although oil peaked at US$140 a barrel in 2008, the average oil price over 1997–2007 was US$35 a barrel, and US$80 a barrel in 2008–18. The hefty 60 per cent depreciation of the rouble after 2008 enabled Russia to stay a competitive producer.[23]

Putin embarked on a policy of renationalisation of the oil sector. State-owned Rosneft acquired Yukos in 2003 and Gazprom bought Sibneft in 2004; and the state increased its stake in Gazprom to 50 per cent in 2005.[24] Foreign participation was further restricted: Shell was forced to sell their Sakhalin 2 project to Gazprom in 2006 (under pressure from spurious environmental claims), and in 2013 Rosneft bought TNK-BP for US$56 billion. Rosneft ended up with 40 per cent of the country's oil output. In return, Rosneft has played an active role in Russia's new foreign policy adventurism. For example, it has loaned more than US$1.8 billion to Venezuela, and when the US sanctioned that country in January 2019, Rosneft helped to divert its oil exports to Asia.[25]

The renationalisation campaign saw ownership and control of Russian energy corporations concentrated in the hands of a small circle of individuals close to Putin, such as Igor Sechin (Rosneft) and Aleksei Miller (Gazprom). The Russian state energy companies often use foreign trade intermediaries to siphon off much of the rents from oil and gas exports through a chain of offshore companies. One notorious example is the role of the middleman Rosukrenergo in the sale of natural gas from Russia to Ukraine in the run-up to the crisis of 2009. Rosukrenergo was created in 2004, half owned by Gazprom and half by a Swiss-based entity whose beneficial owner seems to have been the Ukrainian magnate Dmitro Firtash. After the expropriation of Yukos in 2003, its foreign trade activities were transferred to Gunvor, a trading company founded by Putin associate Gennady Timchenko in 1999.[26] Five years later, it had become the world's largest oil trader. By 2007, Forbes was estimating Timchenko's

22    Thane Gustafson, *Wheel of Fortune: The Battle for Oil and Power in Russia* (Cambridge: Harvard University Press, 2012), 466, doi.org/10.4159/harvard.9780674068018.

23    Vitaly Yermakov, 'Russia's Hydrocarbon Rent', Harvard University Davis Center, 9 May 2019.

24    Rosneft also acquired Severnaya Neft in 2003, Yuganskneftegas in 2004, Udmurtneft in 2006 and Bashneft in 2016. See, Nina Poussenkova, 'Rosneft. A Triple A Company' (conference paper, The Russian Corporation, Yale University, 22 May 2009). See also Valerii Panyushkin and Mikhail Zygar, *Gazprom. Novoe Russkoe Oruzhie* [Gazprom: New Russian weapon] (Moscow: Zakharov, 2008).

25    Anatoly Kurmanaev, 'Venezuela's Collapse Frays its Economic Ties with Moscow', *New York Times*, 17 June 2019. www.nytimes.com/2019/06/17/world/americas/venezuela-russia-economy.html.

26    Irina Mokrousova, 'Gennadii Timchenko: ne stolko biznesmen, stol'ko lobbist' [Not so much a businessman, as a lobbyist], *Vedomosti*, 21 January 2012; Catherine Belton and Neil Buckley, 'On the Offensive: How Gunvor Rose to the Top of Russian Oil Trading', *Financial Times*, 14 May 2008.

wealth at US$2.5 billion. Milov argues that gas export pipelines such as Nord Stream were not needed on either national interest or commercial grounds—since Gazprom now has excess export capacity.[27] The pipelines were built to line the pockets of the construction companies owned by Putin cronies Timchenko and Arkady Rotenburg, who together have won two-thirds of Gazprom's construction contracts.[28]

Writing in 2008, I was cautiously optimistic that Russia could beat the resource curse.[29] The Russian economy had doubled in size in the previous seven years, with significant growth in new sectors such as telecoms, retailing and construction. Russia had paid down its foreign sovereign debts (from US$150 billion in 2000 to US$20 billion in 2015), and through the introduction of a sovereign wealth fund in 2004 and conservative fiscal and monetary policies, it seemed to have learned how to cope with the gyrations of global oil markets.

Thirteen years on, the economic picture is far less rosy. The 2008 financial crash hit Russia very hard, and the economy never regained a sustainable growth path.[30] While Russia's foreign reserves meant that it was able to avoid a collapse of the banking system, investment never returned to its pre-2008 levels, GDP growth has averaged less than 2 per cent per year and living standards have stagnated.[31] Complicating the picture was the late 2014 crash, caused by a slump in the world oil price and the post-Crimea sanctions, which furthered dampened Russian growth.

Russia's poor economic performance illustrates one of the central contradictions of the 'energy superpower' model. Resource-dependent economies exhibit the pathologies of the 'resource curse': exposure to global market volatility, driven by shifts in demand and the arrival of new competitors; lack of competitiveness of other sectors due to an overvalued currency; corruption; political authoritarianism; and so on. So an 'energy superpower' finds itself facing economic and political instability at home that erodes its ability to act confidently on the international stage.

---

27   Vladimir Milov, 'Energy Dependence', in *Russia 2030 Scenarios* (Washington, DC: Free Russia Foundation, 2019), 9–20.
28   Neil Buckley, 'Analyst Sackings Will Not Stop Questions for Gazprom', *Financial Times*, 30 May 2018.
29   Rutland, 'Russia as an Energy Superpower'.
30   Torbjorn Becker and Susanne Oxenstierna, eds, *The Russian Economy Under Putin* (London: Routledge, 2019).
31   IMF, 'Russian Federation Staff Report Article IV Consultation', 2 August 2019, www.imf.org/en/Publications/CR/Issues/2019/08/01/Russian-Federation-2019-Article-IV-Consultation-Press-Release-Staff-Report-48549.

# Russia's Evolution over the Past Decade

Two important changes over the past decade have impacted our perception of Russia as an energy superpower.

## The Putin Factor

The consolidation of an authoritarian regime under Vladimir Putin has defied sceptics who initially saw him as a weak, transitional leader—but also defied optimists who posited that Russia's growing middle class and rising young generation (who had no memories of the Soviet system, or even the privations of the 1990s) would demand an open and accountable government. Unfortunately, Putin's determined efforts to marginalise the political opposition, prevent a potential 'colour revolution', reassert state control over the energy sector and limit regional autonomy have all gone much further than most people would have predicted back in 2000. Increasingly, wealth and power have been concentrated in the hands of a small inner circle of Putin cronies.

Putin's decision to return to the presidency in 2012 triggered a large-scale protest movement that was put down by force, and after which the Kremlin turned to a neo-nationalist ideology to bolster its legitimacy. This ideological shift received a boost from the March 2014 annexation of Crimea—which was surprisingly popular. Putin's other military adventures, such as the war in Syria, have been much less popular domestically.

Russia's authoritarian shift has had a deleterious impact on the country's capacity to break out of its hydrocarbon dependency and build a more diverse and globally competitive economy. With Kremlin cronies continuing to engage in asset seizure and even the jailing of rivals, there is little incentive for independent capitalists, both foreign and Russian, to invest in Russian businesses. (Or more exactly, such investments exact a higher risk premium.) A sluggish and crisis-prone economy is not a stable foundation for power projection: the government is tied up in dealing with the latest fiscal or monetary crisis; and stagnant living standards mean that its popular legitimacy is waning and in need of what is delicately called 'manual control' (*ruchnoe upravlenie*)—that is, direct involvement by top government officials to handle local crises.

## Russia's Shift to Hard Power

In 2007, in a speech to the Munich security conference, Putin signalled a new hard line in foreign policy, lambasting the West for abandoning Russia.[32] The shift may have been connected to the Y2008 problem—the fact that Putin would have to step down from the presidency in 2008. (Notably, 2007 was also the first year that photos of the shirtless Putin started to appear.)

Since then, Moscow has shown a new willingness to use military force beyond its borders. Its military interventions in Georgia 2008, Ukraine in 2014, and Syria in 2015 caught Western observers by surprise. Each operation was a success: enemy forces were defeated (without a fight, in the case of Crimea) and Russia's strategic goals were realised. This use of conventional hard power was accompanied by a panoply of techniques of 'hybrid war'—some old, some new. This ranged from the assassination of exiled spies and dissidents to intervention in Western elections through internet troll farms, email hacking and propaganda from the RT international television station.

These successes stand in sharp contrast to Russia's previous track record: humiliating defeats in Afghanistan (1989) and Chechnya (1996), only partly reversed by the bloody but ultimately victorious second Chechen war (1999–2002). The turnaround stemmed in part from the fact that Putin had used some of Russia's surging energy export revenues to rebuild its armed forces. Spending on the Russian military increased threefold in real terms 2000–10, peaking at 4.4 per cent of GDP.[33] The army underwent limited modernisation but was protected from radical reforms, and were rewarded with a prominent place in the regime's patriotic propaganda binge. Of course, the oil and gas companies also indulge in 'petroleum patriotism'.[34]

---

32  Putin was reiterating the 'Primakov doctrine', espoused by Foreign Minister Evgenii Primakov in 1996—that Russia must block the US from exercising global hegemony. Julia Gurganus and Eugene Rumer, 'Russia's Global Ambitions in Perspective', Carnegie Endowment for International Peace, 20 February 2019, carnegieendowment.org/2019/02/20/russia-s-global-ambitions-in-perspective-pub-78067.
33  Susanne Oxenstierna, 'A New Trend in Russia: Defense Spending', in *The Russian Economy Under Putin*, ed. Torbjorn Becker and Susanne Oxenstierna (London: Routledge 2019), 87–105.
34  Doug Rogers, *The Depths of Russia. Oil, Power and Culture after Socialism* (Ithaca: Cornell University Press, 2015), doi.org/10.7591/9781501701573; Peter Rutland, 'Petronation? Oil, Gas and National Identity in Russia', *Post-Soviet Affairs* 31, no. 1 (January 2015): 66–89, doi.org/10.1080/1060586X.2014.952537.

The operation in Syria was risky, since there was a possibility of conflict with US forces operating in the region. As for Donbas, the jury is still out over the wisdom of Russia's intervention. The operation succeeded in establishing a de facto statelet in East Ukraine, but at the cost of driving the rest of Ukraine into the arms of the West and subjecting Russia to quite damaging sanctions, which are still in place seven years later.[35] Apart from the sanctions, the West took other actions to contain Russian expansionism, such as a North Atlantic Treaty Organization (NATO) rapid reaction force for the Baltic. Given that Russia was energetically using hard power, the question of the threat of Russia's energy weapon slipped into second place. The US continues to object to the Nord Stream 2 project, but that is attributed more to its position as a rival gas supplier than a genuine security issue.

Putin's annexation of Crimea caused an immediate 20 per cent boost in his public approval rating—the *Krym nash* ('Crimea is ours') effect. That has faded over time.[36] In October 2014, 67 per cent of poll respondents wanted Russia to be a great power; however, by October 2018, that was down to 49 per cent, behind citizen welfare (51 per cent) (up from 33 per cent in 2014).[37] The top priority was building a developed economy (67 per cent) and living standards (66 per cent). Thus, the main challenge to Putin's embrace of hard power is whether it is politically sustainable on the home front.

# Changes in Global Energy Markets

There have been some revolutionary changes in global energy markets over the past decade that together further undercut Russia's putative role as an energy superpower.

## The Fracking Revolution

The development of 3D and 4D seismology since 1980, plus new horizontal drilling techniques, led to an explosion of oil and gas production in the US. The US shift from an oil importer to an oil exporter was alarming to traditional oil producers, although, thanks to booming demand from

---

35   Richard Connolly, *Russia's Response to Sanctions: How Western Economic Statecraft Is Reshaping Political Economy in Russia* (Cambridge: Cambridge University Press, 2019), doi.org/10.1017/9781108227346.
36   'Approval Ratings', 1 June 2018, www.levada.ru/2018/06/01/rejtingi-odobreniya-2/.
37   Viktor Khamraev, 'Blagopoluchie dorozhe velichiia' [Wellbeing is more precious than greatness], *Kommersant*, 6 November 2018, www.kommersant.ru/doc/3792003.

China and elsewhere, the oil price held up. (In 2013, China became the world's largest oil importer.) Kirill Dmitriyev, head of the state-backed Russian Direct Investment Fund, said that the oil price would have to go below US$40 to drive out US shale producers, but such a price would push Russia into recession.[38] Russia now needs oil at US$50 to balance the budget (down from a US$98 break-even point in 2014).[39]

Gas is a different story: the US gas price toppled from US$13/mmbtu in 2008 to below US$5 since 2010. The decreased demand for LNG imports in the US meant a sharp drop in the price of gas on international markets.[40] Gazprom had to cut prices and faced lawsuits challenging its long-term take-or-pay contracts, obliging it to pay US$3.2 billion in rebates to European customers for 2012 deliveries.[41] In 2012, Gazprom earned US$64 billion from exporting 217 bcm to Europe: in 2016, it earned only US$37 billion, even though its export volume grew to 262 bcm.[42] Gazprom's market cap plunged from US$350 billion in 2008 to less than US$60 billion today. The US is building LNG export facilities and, together with new supplies from Australia and elsewhere, this is putting downward pressure on the long-term gas price. However, while the EU demand for gas is expected to fall from 600 to 500 bcm by 2030, the output of the Norwegian fields will decline from 300 to 200 bcm, so the continent's dependence on gas imports will not shift. The future of gas hinges in large part on policies in response to climate change (see section below). In 2016, the EU settled its longstanding lawsuit against Gazprom, aimed at forcing it to conform to the Energy Charter and allow third-party access to its pipelines.[43]

Russia missed out on the seismology revolution, and has fallen behind in turbines, refining technology and offshore drilling. It urgently needs to import technology through Western oil service companies, but these have been barred by the post-Crimea sanctions. It sees itself locked into an economic war with the US—and one that it is not winning. At the Saint Petersburg Economic Forum in June 2019, Rosneft head Igor

---

38    'Russia Says Oil Price War with US Would be Too Costly', *Reuters*, 23 January 2019, www.reuters.com/article/us-davos-meeting-russia-opec/russia-says-oil-price-war-with-u-s-would-be-too-costly-idUSKCN1PH1A9.

39    Ben Aris, 'Russia's National Projects', *Russia Matters*, 30 May 2109, www.russiamatters.org/analysis/russias-national-projects-economic-reboot-or-mucky-bog.

40    Thiery Bros, 'A New Narrative for Gas in Europe', Harvard University Davis Center, 10 May 2019.

41    Guy Chazan and Neil Buckley, 'A Cap on Gazprom's Ambitions', *Financial Times*, 6 June 2013.

42    Henry Foy, 'Russia's $55 Bn Gamble on China's Demand for Gas', *Financial Times*, 3 April 2018.

43    Rachelle Toplensky, Jack Farchy and Henry Foy, 'Gazprom and Brussels Agree to Settle Long-Running Dispute', *Financial Times*, 26 October 2016.

Sechin said 'the United States uses energy as a political weapon on a mass scale' and accused it of practising 'energy colonialism' with its sanctions on Iran and Venezuela.[44]

## The Rise of China

Alarmists in the West warn of the birth of a new anti-American bloc, forged out of shared authoritarian values and antipathy to America's global leadership role. Sceptics argue that deep differences between Russia and China will prevent them from ever forging a genuine alliance, pointing to factors such as cultural distance, historical rivalry and divergent economic interests.[45] And, even if such an alliance does emerge, Russia would likely be forced into the role of a junior partner.

The 2000s saw increased bilateral trade and, with the opening of a new oil export pipeline in 2009, China overtook Germany as Russia's largest trading partner in 2011.[46] One branch of the East Siberia – Pacific Ocean pipeline goes to Daqing, China, while an extension runs south to the Russian port of Nakhodka for export to Japan and South Korea. Cooperation deepened after the 2008 global financial crisis, which exposed the inadequacy of the Western-led system of global governance.[47] The APEC (Asia-Pacific Economic Cooperation) summit that Vladimir Putin hosted in Vladivostok in 2012 is seen as marking a 'pivot to Asia' (though Putin himself has never uttered that phrase).[48] In May 2015, Putin formally agreed to coordinate the work of the Eurasian Economic Union with China's One Belt One Road initiative—which came to replace the Shanghai Cooperation Organization as the main vehicle for China's engagement with Central Asia.[49]

---

44    Dmitri Zhdanikov, 'Russia's Sechin Accuses US of Using Energy as a Political Weapon', *Reuters*, 6 June 2019, www.reuters.com/article/us-russia-forum-sechin-usa/rosneft-ceo-accuses-us-of-using-energy-as-a-political-weapon-idUSKCN1T70V0.

45    Bobo Lo, *Axis of Convenience: Moscow, Beijing, and the New Geopolitics* (Washington, DC: Brookings Institution, 2008).

46    Peter Havlik, 'Trade Reorientation in Russia: Will China Replace the EU?', WIIW, 10 July 2018, wiiw.ac.at/trade-reorientation-in-russia-will-china-replace-the-eu--n-327.html.

47    Jeff Schubert, 'China's Silk Road and the EAEU', Russian Economic Reform, 5 April 2017, russianeconomicreform.ru/2017/04/chinas-silk-road-and-the-eaeu-in-sco-space/.

48    Stephen Fortescue, 'Russia's "Turn to the East": A Study in Policy Making', *Post-Soviet Affairs* 32, no. 5 (2016): 423–54, doi.org/10.1080/1060586X.2015.1051750.

49    China became less interested in the Shanghai Cooperation Organization as a result of the 2015 decision—after Russian pressure—to admit India and Pakistan. See, Alexander Gabuev and Ivan Zuenko, 'The "Belt and Road" in Russia: Evolution of Expert Discourse from Caution to Euphoria to Disappointment', *Russia in Global Affairs*, 17 January 2019, eng.globalaffairs.ru/number/The-Belt-and-Road-in-Russia-Evolution-of-Expert-Discourse-19915.

Moscow insists on seeing the relationship with China as a partnership of equals. However, China is acutely cognisant of the Soviet collapse and subsequent economic decline. Russia is trying to use military threats to restore a great power status that its demography and level of economic development do not merit. China's economy is five times that of Russia, and is moving ahead not just in low-cost manufacturing but also high-tech sectors. Russian national interests may not be served if they find themselves 'falling into line' behind a rising China.

In 2009, China lent US$25 billion to Rosneft and Transneft to develop Siberian oil supplies, and another US$25 billion loan package was announced in 2015. For many years, Russia was reluctant to allow China equity access to oil and minerals projects, but that started to change in 2013 when CNPC bought 20 per cent of Novatek's Yamal LNG project, which reached full capacity in December 2018. In 2015, Sinopec got permission to buy 20 per cent of oil producer SIBUR, and in 2017 CEFC China Energy bought a 14 per cent stake in Rosneft for US$9 billion. In 2012, work started on the Power of Siberia gas export pipeline that will run 3,200 km from Chayanda to Khabarovsk, where it will link with a pipeline from the gas fields in Sakhalin, and continue to the port of Vladivostok. In May 2014, Russia signed a US$400 billion deal to supply China with 38 bcm of gas for 30 years. The price is not known: China is thought to pay a mere US$9 per mmbtu to Turkmenistan, and it will likely drive an equally hard bargain with Russia.[50]

In the 1990s, China was a major customer for Russian arms, helping to keep Russian defence plants afloat. However, in 2007 Russia denounced China for reverse engineering the Su-27 fighter, which it had been assembling under licence since 1995, and there was a six-year hiatus in arms sales. In March 2013, Moscow relented and agreed to sell China 24 Sukhoi Su-35 fighters (worth US$2 billion) and four Amur-class submarines. In April 2015, Russia sold them 36 S-400 missile defence systems for US$3 billion—which Beijing swiftly deployed to the South China Sea. The two countries have conducted joint peace mission military exercises since 2009 and naval drills since 2012, extending into the Mediterranean in 2014 and the South China Sea in 2016. (Russia came out in support of China after the United Nations Convention on the Law of the Sea ruled against China's position in 2016.)

---

50    Jack Farchy, 'Gazprom's China Contract Offers No Protection Against Low Prices', *Financial Times*, 10 August 2015.

There is also potential for rivalry as Chinese influence expands in the post-Soviet space. The two countries seem to have achieved a stable division of labour in Central Asia, with China taking the lead in economics and Russia handling security issues. China overtook Russia as the region's largest trading partner in 2009. China has growing economic interests in Ukraine. It abstained in the UN vote that condemned Russia's annexation of Crimea (though it did vote for a later IMF loan to Ukraine, over Russian objections). China has also inserted itself into the race to develop the Arctic as a transport route and source of oil and gas supplies, joining the Arctic Council as an observer in 2013.

## The Challenge of Climate Change

Russia reluctantly signed on to the Kyoto and Paris accords, aware that setting a target of 25 per cent carbon emissions reduction from 1990 did not require a substantial policy shift, given the collapse of Russian manufacturing in the 1990s. (As of 2014, Russian emissions were 30 per cent below their 1990 level.) Russia plans to continue making as much money as it can from exporting oil, gas and coal until the last possible moment—using more coal to fuel power plants to free up gas for export. The 2011 Fukushima accident led gas lobbyists in Europe to promote natural gas as the 'cleaner' carbon fuel, encouraging Germany and other countries to switch their power plants from coal to gas for a transitional period, until renewables and storage technology develop to the point where they can provide the bulk of electricity generation.[51] In Germany, Poland and elsewhere, the gas lobby has run into the coal lobby. Since 2005, renewables in Germany have gone from 10 per cent to 40 per cent of power generation, but this has squeezed out gas not coal, which still accounts for 40 per cent.[52] In contrast, the UK has halved electricity generation emissions since 2013, and will phase out coal completely by 2025.

China has established itself as a global leader in solar and wind turbine technology. But rather than invest in conservation or renewable energy, Russia is building more atomic power plants—and has an ambitious

51　Jack Sharples, 'Europe's Largest Natural Gas Producer in an Era of Climate Change: Gazprom', in *Handbook of the International Political Economy of Energy and Natural Resources*, ed. Andreas Goldthau et al. (London: Palgrave, 2018) 154–71, doi.org/10.4337/9781783475636.00019.

52　Tobias Buck, 'Angela Merkl's Tarnished Legacy on the Environment', *Financial Times*, 29 January 2019.

program to export them overseas. Russia has persuaded Hungary and Finland to build plants, though Bulgaria cancelled their contract after a new government came to power in 2016. Tynkkynen argues that generous subsidies for Rosatom's export program are a way to keep the military industry complex happy and share with them some of the spoils from Russia's hydrocarbon economy.[53]

Russian leaders have been complacent about climate change, noting some positive impacts, such as a longer growing season and the opening up of the Arctic for transport and resource extraction. Some prominent Russian scientists are climate change deniers.[54] However, the reality is that climate change will have a severe impact on Russia's ecology and economy, as evidenced by the current droughts and forest fires. The melting of the permafrost will make the maintenance of infrastructure in northern regions a lot more expensive.

Tynkkynen points out that, with its vast forest reserves, Russia has the potential to be a 'green superpower', but the current political and economic system is blocking policies moving the country in that direction.[55] Instead, policy is held hostage by the hydrocarbon elite who are trying to maximise short-run profits. Russia is a particular pernicious example of the potent interconnections between market forces, security concerns and climate change.[56]

## Explaining Russia's Motives

There is a debate over the dynamics behind the role of energy in Russia's foreign policy. Some argue that Russian policy is driven by strategic concerns, with Moscow trying to use energy as a weapon to advance its political agenda.[57] Conversely, there is the argument that Gazprom and the oil companies are merely seeking to maximise profits (subject to

53  Tynkkynen, *The Energy of Russia*.
54  Tynkkynen, *The Energy of Russia*, ch. 6.
55  Tynkkynen, *The Energy of Russia*.
56  Andrea Goldthau, Michael F. Keating and Caroline Kuzemko, 'Nexus Thinking in International Political Economy', in *Handbook of the International Political Economy of Energy and Natural Resources*, ed. Andrea Goldthau, Michael F. Keating and Caroline Kuzemko (London: Palgrave, 2018), 1–23, doi.org/10.4337/9781783475636.
57  Adam Stulberg, *Well Oiled Diplomacy. Strategic Manipulation and Russia's Statecraft in Eurasia* (Albany, NY: SUNY Press, 2008).

political constraints) like any other commercial corporation.[58] There is also a third argument—that bargaining over Ukrainian gas deliveries, or whether to build new export pipelines, is conducted by a narrow circle of individuals with close ties to Putin, who seek to maximise the flow of rents into their personal offshore bank accounts, and use the rhetoric of Russian national interest to disguise their venal machinations.

These three levels of analysis are embedded in three distinct intellectual paradigms that rarely engage directly with each other. They start with very different assumptions about how the world works, and look for very different sorts of empirical evidence to verify their claims.

The geopolitical argument is rooted in deep-seated assumptions about the structural dynamics of the international system. Russia is a Eurasian land empire whose mission is to control as much real estate as possible, extracting the resources from the occupied territories to fund the state that protects and expand said lands. This approach is compatible with the realist school of international relations (IR).

The commercial frame focuses on the micro-dynamics of corporate decision-making, including floating international loans, launching IPOs (initial public offerings) in foreign stock exchanges, concluding agreements with foreign partners and seeking arbitration in international courts. The principal actors in this model are corporate entities answering to a transnational bloc of shareholders, with only a contingent and transactional relationship to any given nation-state. It is congruent with the liberal-institutionalist IR school, and with thinkers (of both right and left) who argue that globalisation has transformed the character of IR. Third, there is the argument that Russia is a kleptocracy, run to benefit the narrow, personal interests of a small group of ruling families. Oligarchic rule is not simply a product of the disruptive transition of the 1990s, but has become an institutionalised organising structure of the Russian political regime, reproducing itself as the rising generation of oligarch children ascend to senior positions. It is journalists who have advanced the kleptocracy argument, through studies of individual oligarchs and money-laundering schemes. Few academics have tried to wrangle this material into a general theory of the functioning of the Russian state.

---

58    Rawi Abdelal, 'The Profits of Power: Commerce and Realpolitik in Eurasia', *Review of International Political Economy* 20, no. 3 (2012): 421–56, doi.org/10.1080/09692290.2012.666214.

Marc Galeotti is the exception.[59] The late Karen Dawisha's work, while influential, does not define what she means by 'kleptocracy', and the empirical material focuses on Putin's cliques in the 1990s.[60]

# A Philosophical Postscript

At the turn of the nineteenth century, Enlightenment philosophers such as Immanuel Kant and Benjamin Constant argued that the surge in trade would lead to a decrease in interstate war, since the benefits of peaceful economic cooperation far outweighed the possible gains from aggressive war. Alas, the next century seemed to disprove that thesis, with several cases where countries went to war with their major trading partner (Germany and France, Germany and Russia, Japan and the US). In the twenty-first century we have seen a remarkable diminution in interstate war; but the economic rise of China has led to a debate over whether that means a war with the US is likely. Economic growth makes war more likely in two respects: increased wealth means more money to spend on military capacity, which can trigger an arms race with rival states; and increased economic interdependency leads to feelings of vulnerability should those resource flows be blocked (such as the US embargo of Japan in 1937). Economic growth mitigates the likelihood of war if powerful domestic lobbies emerge—business interests and/or consumers and voters—with capacity to influence decision-makers in favour of peace. This mechanism seems to work when democracies are competing with other democracies, but not with autocracies.

Russia and China are two autocratic regimes that have experienced two decades of economic growth. China, starting from a lower base, has grown twice as fast as Russia. But while China has not attacked anyone beyond its borders since 1979, Russia has waged three wars. China has significantly expanded its military capacity, but shows no interest in going to war just yet—in part because it is confident that it can achieve its goals without risky military adventures. Russia in contrast has used 'hard power' to defend its interests on its own borders and beyond.

---

59   Marc Galeotti, *We Need to Talk About Putin. How the West Gets Him Wrong* (London: Ebury Press, 2019).
60   Karen Dawisha, *Putin's Kleptocracy. Who Owns Russia?* (New York: Simon & Schuster, 2015).

# 5

# Russian Energy Firms in the Eastern Market

Keun-Wook Paik

Since early 2014, when the Crimean Peninsula was annexed by the Russian Federation and Western sanctions against Russia began to affect its global oil and gas export boundaries,[1] Moscow has had no choice but to prioritise its Asia-Pacific strategy. Russia had laid solid groundwork for its entry into the Asian oil and gas market with completion of the East Siberia – Pacific Ocean (ESPO) oil pipeline in 2009. In 2018, Russia became China's biggest supplier of crude oil, delivering 71.5 mt. In December 2019, the long waited Power of Siberia (POS) 1 gas started to flow; by 2025, it will reach to its full capacity of 38 bcm/y. Russia's independent gas producer, Novatek, transformed the country into an Arctic onshore gas-based liquefied natural gas (LNG) supplier in December 2017 and aims to commission 19.8 mt/y of Arctic LNG by 2023.[2] If the long-delayed Altai gas export to China is materialised during the 2020s,

---

1    'Crimea Profile', *BBC News*, 17 January 2018, www.bbc.co.uk/news/world-europe-18287223; Andrew Chatzky, 'Have Sanctions on Russia Changed Putin's Calculus?', Council on Foreign Relations, 2 May 2019, www.cfr.org/article/have-sanctions-russia-changed-putins-calculus.
2    For background on Sino-Russian oil and gas cooperation during 2014–17, see Keun-Wook Paik, 'Sino-Russian Gas and Oil Cooperation: Entering into an Era of Strategic Partnership', OIES Paper WPM 59, April 2015, www.oxfordenergy.org/wpcms/wp-content/uploads/2015/04/WPM-59.pdf; Keun-Wook Paik, 'Sino-Russian Oil and Gas Cooperation: Where It Stands and How Far Can It Expand?', *Geopolitics of Energy* 38, no. 8 (August 2016): 2–10; Keun-Wook Paik, 'Sino-Russian LNG Trade Perspectives', in *A North Pacific Dialogue on Arctic 2030: Pathways to the Future*, ed. Robert W. Corell et al. (KMI and East-West Centre, 2018), 293–304.

it will guarantee Russia's successful entry into the Asia-Pacific oil and gas market, and Sino-Russian oil and gas cooperation will play a pivotal role in transforming Russia in the 2020s.

This chapter evaluates the performance of Russia's two state-owned flagship oil and gas entities, Rosneft and Gazprom, and the country's biggest independent gas producer, Novatek, with a view to better understanding the achievements and prospects of Sino-Russian oil and gas cooperation.

# Rosneft: Sweet Success in Oil but Unfulfilled Wishes in Gas

Together with Transneft, Rosneft was the driving force behind the ESPO oil pipeline. Completion of the first stage of the pipeline in December 2009 opened the era of Russia's supply of crude oil to the Asian market.[3] Transneft sent 38.3 mt of crude to China in 2018, up 44.5 per cent year on year, according to data by the Central Dispatching Unit (CDU), the statistics arm of Russia's energy ministry. Crude loadings from Kozmino amounted to 30.386 mt in 2019, down 4.2 per cent year on year, according to the CDU data.[4]

As shown in Figure 5.1, in 2018, China's total crude imports were 461.9 mt, of which Russia provided 15 per cent (71.49 mt), followed by Saudi Arabia (12 per cent or 56.73 mt), Iraq and Angola (10 per cent each), Brazil and Oman (7 per cent each), and Iran (6 per cent).

---

3    'Projects Underway', Transneft, accessed 22 August 2020, en.transneft.ru/about/projects/current/.
4    Nadia Rodova, 'Transneft Sees Fast Growth in Arctic, E Siberian Crude Pipeline Flows', Platts S&P Global, 5 April 2019, www.spglobal.com/platts/en/market-insights/latest-news/oil/040519-transneft-sees-fast-growth-in-arctic-e-siberian-crude-pipeline-flows; 'Eastern Siberia–Pacific Ocean Oil Pipeline', Wikipedia, last modified 19 September 2019, en.wikipedia.org/wiki/Eastern_Siberia%E2%80%93Pacific_Ocean_oil_pipeline; 'Russia's Rosneft Aims for $500bn Worth of Energy Deals with China', RT, 29 November 2018, www.rt.com/business/445140-rosneft-china-energy-cooperation/. But the record of 2019 may not be as good as that of 2018. See, Avantika Ramesh, 'Russia's Feb ESPO Blend Crude Oil Exports Down 10 Per Cent on Month', Platts S&P Global, 4 January 2019, www.spglobal.com/platts/en/market-insights/latest-news/oil/010419-russias-feb-espo-blend-crude-oil-exports-down-10-on-month.

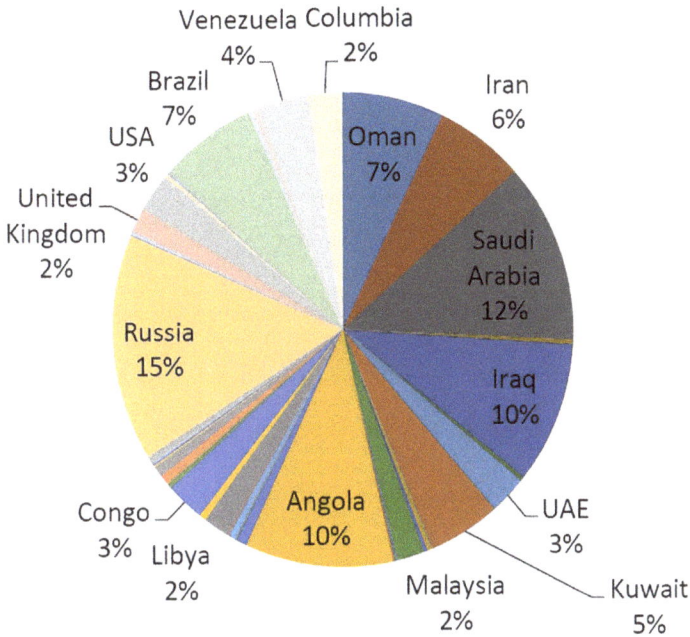

**Figure 5.1: China's crude oil imports by country.**
Source: *China OGP*, 1 February 2019, 6.

According to *China OGP*, an oil industry newsletter issued by Xinhua News Agency, Russia's supply of crude to China has increased significantly since 2000 compared with Saudi Arabia (see Tables 5.1 and 5.2). In 2018, the volume difference between the two countries was as much as 15 mt. Table 5.2 shows that Beijing's initiative to import 20 mt/y of crude via the trunk pipeline from Kazakhstan failed, as the import figure was a mere 1.3 mt in 2018, and this indirectly explains why Beijing is maximising the ESPO crude supply from Russia to cover the collapsed crude supply from Kazakhstan.[5]

5    Tsvetana Paraskova, 'Kazakhstan Looks to Boost Crude Oil Exports to China', Oil Price, 3 July 2019, oilprice.com/Latest-Energy-News/World-News/Kazakhstan-Looks-To-Boost-Crude-Oil-Exports-To-China.html; 'Kazakhstan to Divert Some Oil Flows from Europe to China', 3 July 2019, *Reuters*, www.reuters.com/article/us-kazakhstan-china-oil/kazakhstan-to-divert-some-oil-flows-from-europe-to-china-idUSKCN1TY1W6.

### Table 5.1: China's crude oil imports, 2000–17 (mt/y)

|  | Middle East* | Africa** | Asia-Pacific | Europe | Total*** |
|---|---|---|---|---|---|
| 2000 | 37.65 | 38.47 | 10.61 | 5.05 | 70.27 |
| 2005 | 59.99 | 70.85 | 8.80 | 18.94 | 127.08 |
| 2010 | 112.76 | 70.85 | 8.80 | 25.86 | 239.31 |
| 2015 | 170.16 | 64.46 | 8.31 | 49.85 | 335.49 |
| 2016 | 182.99 | 67.84 | 15.10 | 62.48 | 381.04 |
| 2017 | 182.20 | 82.62 | 14.97 | 73.44 | 419.97 |

* Saudi Arabia recorded 50.54, 51.00 and 52.18 during 2015–17.

** Angola recorded 38.71, 43.75 and 50.43; *** Latin America/Western hemisphere recorded 42.71, 52.63 and 66.73.

Source: *China OGP*, various issues.

### Table 5.2: China's crude oil from Russia and Kazakhstan (mt/y)

|  | Russia | Kazakhstan |
|---|---|---|
| 2000 | 1.77 | 0.65 |
| 2005 | 12.78 | 1.29 |
| 2010 | 15.25 | 10.05* |
| 2015 | 42.43 | 4.99 |
| 2016 | 52.48 | 3.23 |
| 2017 | 59.80 | 2.50** |

Note: In 2018, Russia's crude supply to China reached a record high of 71.5 mt.

* The peak volume was 11.3 mt in 2013.[6] ** Even though not included in this table, the figure of 12.3 mt quoted by *Xinhua Net* is not accurate.[7]

Source: *China OGP*, various issues.

---

6    Paraskova, 'Kazakhstan Looks to Boost Crude Oil Exports to China'.

7    According to PetroChina West Pipeline Co., the China–Kazakhstan pipeline carried a record high 12.3 mt of crude oil into China in 2017. But it is a combination of the total crude from five central Asian republics that passes through the Kazakh–China crude oil pipeline. See, 'Xi Jinping: Persist in Reform and Opening Up, Adhere to High-Quality Development, and Make New and Greater Progress in Accelerating the Construction of a Better Anhui', *Xinhua Net*, 11 January 2018, www.xinhuanet.com/english/2018-01/11/c_136888551.htm; 'Crude Oil Piped from Kazakhstan to China Reaches Record High', *China Daily*, 12 January 2018, www.chinadaily.com.cn/a/201801/12/WS5a584585a3102c394518ed8d.html. As of May 2019, the total crude supply from Kazakhstan to China was 119 mt (CN¥443.8 billion or US$64.2 billion). The supply volume from January–April 2019 was 3.7 mt. See, 'Nearly 120 Mln Tonnes of Crude Oil Piped from Kazakhstan to China', *Global Times*, 31 May 2019, www.globaltimes.cn/content/1152532.shtml. From 2006 to July 2014, the accumulated crude supply volume via the pipeline was 70.22 mt. See, Zhuwei Wang, 'Securing Energy Flows from Central Asia to China and the Relevance of the Energy Charter Treaty to China', Energy Charter Secretariat, 2015, accessed 22 August 2020, energycharter.org/fileadmin/DocumentsMedia/Thematic/China_and_the_ECT_2015_en.pdf.

Russia and Saudi Arabia are engaged in competition to win the biggest market share in China. In late February 2019, during Saudi Crown Prince Mohammed bin Salman's visit to China, Saudi Arabia agreed to form a joint venture with Chinese defence conglomerate Norinco—a refining and petrochemical complex in the north-eastern Chinese city of Panjin worth more than US$10 billion. The partners would form a company called Huajin Aramco Petrochemical Co. as part of a project that would include a 300,000 b/d capacity refinery with a 1.5 mt/y ethylene cracker. Aramco will supply up to 70 per cent of the crude feedstock for the complex, which is expected to start operations in 2024. The investment could help Saudi Arabia regain its place as the top oil exporter to China, a position Russia has held for the last three years.[8] Saudi's initiative suggests that Rosneft's ill-fated partnership with CEFC China Energy was a major setback, and is a strong signal that competition between Saudi Arabia and Russia will be sustained and possibly intensified in the coming years and decades.

## Taas-Yuriakh Saga Exposes the Priority of Rosneft's Asia Strategy

Rosneft changed its stance towards the Beijing Gas Group (BGG) and entered into a blind partnership with CEFC China without proper due diligence: what drove this move? Until 2015, Rosneft had no difficulty in taking advantage of Chinese national oil companies' (NOCs) very generous loans for oil, but the oil price collapse in 2014–15 forced Rosneft to find new ways to raise money. Rosneft chose to work with a Chinese SOE (state-owned enterprise) and the BGG was the ideal choice. The partial equity disposal of Taas-Yuriakh oil and gas assets to BGG was an easy way to raise money. Rosneft had to make a decision between China's BGG and an Indian consortium. In March 2016, BGG was in the final stage of its due diligence for the Taas-Yuriakh asset, but, on 16 March, Rosneft agreed to sell a large stake to Indian state-run energy companies, including a US$1.28 billion share to an Indian consortium.

---

8    Ben Blanchard, 'Saudi Arabia Strikes $10 Billion China Deal, Talks De-radicalisation with Xi', *Reuters*, 22 February 2019, www.reuters.com/article/us-asia-saudi-china/saudi-arabia-strikes-10-billion-china-deal-talks-de-radicalisation-with-xi-idUSKCN1QB15H.

The group of three Indian companies took a combined 29.9 per cent share in Taas-Yuriakh Neftegazodobycha and a 23.9 per cent stake in Vankorneft.[9]

In March 2014, two months before the POS 1 deal in Shanghai, *Reuters* reported that Rosneft wanted to break the monopoly of another state-owned energy champion, Gazprom, to export gas via pipelines. It is worth noting that Rosneft and Novatek had already secured rights to export seaborne LNG, reversing a 2006 law that gave Gazprom a monopoly on gas exports.[10] Two years later, Rosneft's BGG deal revived the pressure towards Gazprom. This touches on the sensitive issue of third-party access to the POS; the assumption is that Rosneft will not give up its attempt to dismantle Gazprom's monopoly of POS 1. The core of the deal is about providing access to independent gas producers when Gazprom is determined to sustain a single export channel. This purpose was recorded in the protocol of the presidential committee that took place in October 2015.[11] Third-party access to the pipeline is a political decision and even Igor Sechin cannot give any assurance on this matter, as the final say has to come from Russian President Vladimir Putin.

Separately from this question of third-party access to POS 1, Rosneft was drawing a bigger picture, as it was aiming to enter into India's downstream market. In August 2017, Rosneft and its partners (Trafigura, a global commodity trading and logistics giant, and UCP Investment Group) completed a US$12.9 billion acquisition of Essar Oil. Reportedly, the new owners, which include Trafigura and UCP Investment Group, will acquire India's largest network of private petrol pumps.[12]

9   'Rosneft Sells 29.9% of Taas-Yuryakh to Consortium of Indian Cos', *Interfax Russia & CIS Oil and Gas Weekly*, 10–16 March 2016, 19–20.
10   'Rosneft Challenges Gazprom Monopoly to Export Russian Pipeline Gas', Reuters, 7 March 2014, www.reuters.com/article/russia-rosneft-gas/update-1-rosneft-challenges-gazprom-monopoly-to-export-russian-pipeline-gas-idUSL6N0M412120140307.
11   Paik, 'Sino-Russian Oil and Gas Cooperation'.
12   'Essar Oil Completes $13 Billion Sale to Rosneft-led Consortium in Largest FDI Deal', *Economic Times*, 22 August 2017, economictimes.indiatimes.com/markets/stocks/news/essar-oil-completes-sale-of-india-assets-to-rosneft-for-12-9-bn/articleshow/60154679.cms; Promit Mukherjee, 'Rosneft Seals First Asian Refinery Deal with Essar Oil Purchase', *Reuters*, 21 August 2017, www.reuters.com/article/us-india-essar-rosneft/rosneft-seals-first-asian-refinery-deal-with-essar-oil-purchase-idUSKCN1B10PL.

Ultimately, Rosneft had to allocate the Verkhnechonskoye field (with C1+C2 reserves, 173 mt of oil and condensate, and 115 bcm of gas)[13] instead of the Taas-Yuriakh field (with 167 mt of oil and condensate, and 181 bcm of gas), which is a part of the Sredne-Botuobinskoye oil, gas and condensate field, to the Indian consortium.[14] The collapse of the value of the rouble placed Rosneft's top management under extreme pressure.[15] This may indirectly explain why the hurried deal with the Indian consortium was prioritised. Besides this, Rosneft wanted to show that Russia's flagship oil firm did not bank on one partner only and to build partnerships with several different players.

Another reason for the allocation of the Verkhnechonskoye field asset to BGG lies in the fact that Russia did not want to upset Beijing, which had offered a US$12 billion loan for gas to Novatek's Yamal LNG project in April 2016. On 29 April 2016, in Beijing, Yamal LNG signed credit agreements with the Export–Import Bank of China (China Exim Bank) and the China Development Bank in the amount of €9.3 billion and CN¥9.8 billion for 15 years. The firm said in a statement that the interest rates for the credit lines were EURIBOR 6M +3.3 per cent per annum for the period of construction and 3.55 per cent after the full commissioning of Yamal LNG, and SHIBOR 6M +3.3 per cent and 3.55 per cent per annum, respectively.[16] However, considering that the gas reserves in the Taas-Yuriakh field are much bigger than that of the Verkhnechonskoye field, Rosneft's decision towards BGG was a face-saving act.

---

13    'Rosneft and Beijing Enterprises Agreed on Joint Operations on Projects in East Siberia', Rosneft, press release, 25 June 2016, www.rosneft.com/press/releases/item/182759/.

14    'Rosneft Sells 29.9% of Taas-Yuryakh to Consortium of Indian Cos'.

15    'Rosneft Profits Fall, Customer Pre-Payments Ease Debt Burden', Reuters, 25 November 2015, www.reuters.com/article/russia-rosneft-results-idUSL8N13K1E120151125.

16    'Yamal LNG Signs Credit Agreements with China Exim Bank, China Development Bank', Russia & CIS Oil and Gas Weekly, 28 April – 4 May 2016, 9; Neil Buckley, 'Sino-Russian Gas Deal: Smoke without Fire', Financial Times, 11 May 2016; James Marson, 'Russian Natural-Gas Project Gets Funding from China: Move Is a Hard-Fought Victory over Western Sanctions', Wall Street Journal, 29 April 2016, www.wsj.com/articles/russian-natural-gas-project-gets-funding-from-china-1461934776.

# Rosneft's Ill-Fated Partnership with CEFC China Energy

Rosneft's misfortune continued. It failed to perform proper due diligence on CEFC China Energy's bid to takeover 14.16 per cent equity of Rosneft with the payment of US$9.1 billion.[17] Unfortunately, the ambitious plan collapsed on 1 March 2018 with the arrest of CEFC China Energy Chairman Ye Jianming, who argued that the Rosneft deal was mainly driven by China's Belt and Road Initiative and had strong support from the government.[18] Rosneft's ill-fated partnership with CEFC China Energy served as indirect confirmation that its honeymoon period with Chinese NOCs for easy financing was over, and there were no private sector alternatives with any real substance. Rosneft had offered an unprecedented discount of ESPO crude supply to Shandong's tea-pot refineries in return for CEFC China Energy's large chunk of equity acquisition. In addition, CEFC China Energy had aimed to penetrate Shandong's gas market by forming an alliance with Qatar and Glencore to take advantage of large-scale LNG supplies at competitive prices. Had this initiative succeeded, Rosneft would have been a major beneficiary of both ESPO crude export and Qatar LNG export to the Shandong province, where no Chinese NOCs had a dominating position. As discussed earlier, Saudi Arabia's low-profile manoeuvring to strike a deal with the Norinco group confirmed Russia's dominant position as the biggest crude supplier to China; this can be effectively challenged at any time and the intensified competition will serve China well, as China's needs for crude supply will be sustained for a considerable period.

---

17 Henry Foy, Max Seddon and Lucy Hornby, 'Russia and China Quietly Build Links', *Financial Times*, 25 September 2017.

18 Andrew Chubb, 'Caixin's Investigation of CEFC and Chairman Ye Jianming', *Southsea Conversations*, 29 March 2018, southseaconversations.wordpress.com/2018/03/29/caixins-investigation-of-cefc-and-chairman-ye-jianming/; 'CEFC's Rosneft Deal Driven By National Strategy—Chairman', *Reuters*, 3 October 2017, uk.reuters.com/article/uk-cefc-china-rosneft/cefcs-rosneft-deal-driven-by-national-strategy-chairman-idUKKCN1C80ZX; Lucy Hornby and Archie Zhang, 'CEFC Chairman Ye Jianming Said to be Detained', *Financial Times*, 1 March 2018; 'Russia's Rosneft Says China CEFC Investigation Not Related to it', *Reuters*, 1 March 2018, www.reuters.com/article/china-cefc-probe-rosneft/russias-rosneft-says-china-cefc-investigation-not-related-to-it-idUSR4N1QG00R; Eric Ng and Xie Yu, 'China Detains CEFC's Founder Ye Jianming, Wiping Out US$153 Million in Value Off Stocks', *South China Morning Post*, 1 March 2018, www.scmp.com/business/companies/article/2135238/chinas-president-orders-arrest-cefcs-founder-ye-jianming-ending.

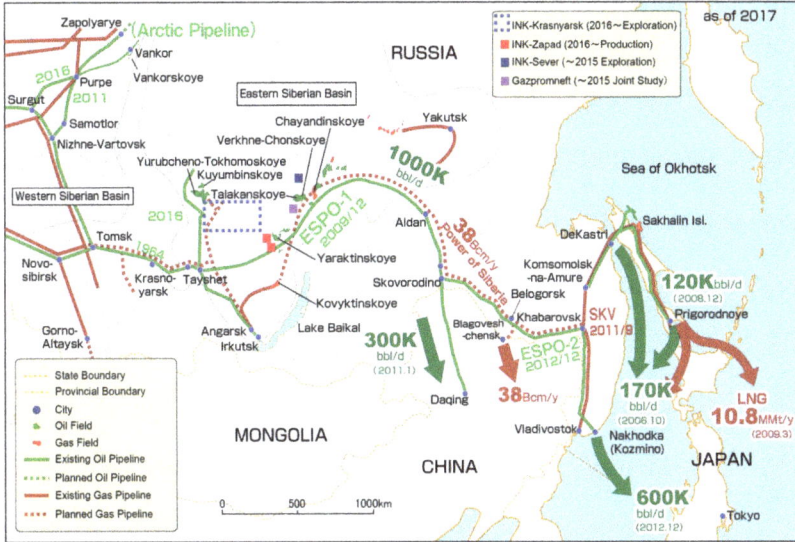

**Figure 5.2: Russia's oil and gas export to Asia.**

Source: Daiske Harada, 'Rising Gas Flow from Russia to East: Current Status, Role of the Arctic Challenges in the future', paper presented at 2018 LNG Congress, Russia. Harada is an officer of the Japan Oil, Gas and Metals National Corporation.

In this context, it is not surprising that Rosneft wanted to switch its obligations to CEFC China Energy from the arm based in China to that based in Singapore, thereby demonstrating its continued commitment to the Chinese firm, despite the failed privatisation deal. Rosneft stated that its board would consider a deal transferring obligations from CEFC China Energy Co. Ltd to CEFC Shanghai International Group (Singapore) Pte Ltd on 25 January 2019. CEFC Shanghai is a CEFC trading arm that receives crude oil supplies from Rosneft and trades them further.[19] The improvised damage control initiative was a minimum requirement to protect Russia's share in China's big oil market.

---

19   Sources familiar with the matter said CEFC would take eight cargoes of ESPO blend crude oil and two cargoes of Urals crude in March from Rosneft, indicating no change in volume for 2019. See, Vladimir Soldatkin and Florence Tan, 'Rosneft Switches Dealing to Singapore Arm of China's CEFC, No Change in Oil Volumes', *Reuters*, 22 January 2019, uk.reuters.com/article/rosneft-china-oil/rosneft-switches-dealing-to-singapore-arm-of-chinas-cefc-no-change-in-oil-volumes-idUKL8N1ZM27I; 'China's CEFC Paid Out Compensation after Rosneft Stake Deal Fell through', *Reuters*, 30 November 2018, uk.reuters.com/article/uk-rosneft-privatisation-cefc/chinas-cefc-paid-out-compensation-after-rosneft-stake-deal-fell-through-idUKKCN1NO1RW; 'Qatar to Take Stake in Russia's Rosneft after Deal with China Falls through', *RadioFreeEurope RadioLiberty*, 5 May 2018, www.rferl.org/a/qatar-takes-20-percent-stake-russia-rosneft-oil-giant-after-deal-with-china-cefc-falls-through/29209725.html.

The most important and urgent task for Rosneft is to identify recoverable oil reserves in its frontier areas to sustain its crude supply capacity to the Asian market. Transneft launched two new pipelines to link green fields in northern and Eastern Siberia to its pipeline network in 2017. The Zapolyarye–Purpe line, with an initial capacity of 25 mt/y (0.5 mb/d) and expansion potential of up to 45 mt/y, runs 488 km across West Siberia, and can deliver crude both westward and eastward. The 700 km Kuyumba–Taishet, with an initial capacity of 8.6 mt/y, runs across East Siberia's Krasnoyarsk and Irkutsk regions to the ESPO pipeline for deliveries to Asian markets and domestic refineries.[20]

Northern Siberia is among Russia's most promising new oil provinces. Lukoil's Pyakyakhinskoye field became the first source of crude for the Zapolyarye–Purpe pipeline, followed by the East Messoyakha field, being developed jointly by Gazprom Neft and Rosneft. Regarding the second pipeline, it is scheduled for expansion to 15 mt/y by 2023, but the actual pace of the work will be dependent on the progress of the Kuyumba field, being developed jointly by Gazprom Neft and Rosneft, and the Yurubcheno–Tokhomskoye field, being developed by Rosneft and the China National Petroleum Corporation (CNPC).[21] It remains to be seen whether new reserves in Russia's Arctic circle will be large enough to sustain the export volume needed for Asia's markets.

In short, Rosneft's export policy towards Asia boils down to the fact that, while China is a very important market for Russia, it is not the only market. That is why Rosneft played the China card and the India card simultaneously. However, the price Rosneft had to pay for its failure to take advantage of the BGG deal in terms of penetrating China's gas market was very high. Without third-party access to the POS 1 gas pipeline, Rosneft's attempt to penetrate China's gas market in the coming decades will be a very tough struggle.

20   Rodova, 'Transneft Sees Fast Growth in Arctic'.
21   Rodova, 'Transneft Sees Fast Growth in Arctic'.

# Gazprom: Starting the POS 1 Gas Supply— No Sign of Altai Gas

Sino-Russian gas cooperation has been a long march with many ups and downs. Gazprom's former CEO Rem Vyakhirev began the process in 1997, but the company delivered no tangible results until May 2014, when the POS 1 gas deal was finally signed.[22] According to the *Financial Times*, Russia's first eastern pipeline is the most striking physical manifestation of Putin's diplomatic pivot towards China in response to deteriorating relations with the West.[23] From December 2019, the pipeline delivered gas at a pilot volume of 5 bcm/y, and is expected to increase to its full capacity of 38 bcm/y by 2024.[24] In the short term, the pipeline's impact on China's LNG imports will not be that significant. It is worth noting that the gas demand from Heilongjiang, Jilin, Liaoning and Hebei (where Beijing and Tianjin are located) provinces will not be large enough to absorb the whole 38 bcm/y. It is fair to say that the 25 bcm/y that comes from the Chayandinskoye field will not face any challenge from the LNG supply to the Bohai gas market, but the remaining 13 bcm of Kovykta gas will be vulnerable when it is extended from Shandong and Jiangsu provinces and Shanghai, as the price will not be that competitive.

From Gazprom's viewpoint, the domestic supplier's challenge to break-up Gazprom's monopoly and open the door for third-party access to POS 1 is the more important issue. To block third-party access for independent gas producers in East Siberia's stranded gas reserves, Gazprom has mapped out its grand supply plan by accelerating the connection of Chayandinskoye gas with Kovykta gas with the 800 km pipeline.

By 2020, Chayandinskoye had some 59 new production wells in addition to the 149 existing wells. Plans had advanced slowly to sell gas containing ethane-propane-butane fractions to China through POS 1. Gazprom will separate ethane-propane-butane and helium from methane at the planned 42 bcm/y Amur Gas Processing Plant from 2021, by which time three

---

22    For the background of Gazprom's export strategy towards China, see Keun-Wook Paik, *Sino-Russian Oil and Gas Cooperation: The Reality and Implications* (Oxford: Oxford University Press, 2012).

23    Henry Foy, 'Russia Takes $55 Bn Punt on Pipeline to Satisfy Chinese Demand for Gas', *Financial Times*, 4 April 2018.

24    'Power of Siberia', Gazprom, accessed 22 August 2020, www.gazprom.com/projects/power-of-siberia/; 'Power of Siberia', Gazprom Export, accessed 4 September 2020, www.gazpromexport.ru/en/projects/transportation/3/.

trains with a combined capacity of 21 bcm/y are due on line, and gas output from Chayandinskoye will have risen to 13.8 bcm/y, as shown in Table 5.3. The firm aims to commission a further three trains in 2022–24.

**Table 5.3: Chayandinskoye and Kovyktinskoye output (bcm/y)**

|  | Chayandinskoye | Kovyktinskoye |
|---|---|---|
| 2019 | 1.5 | - |
| 2020 | 6.9 | - |
| 2021 | 13.8 | - |
| 2022 | 19.2 | - |
| 2023 | 23.6 | 4.9 |
| 2024 | 25.0 | 15.0 |
| 2025 | 25.0 | 25.0 |
| 2045 | 25.0 | 25.0 |
| 2050 | - | 25.0 |

Source: 'Gazprom Prepares for China Exports', *Argus FSU Energy*, 30 May 2019, 1.

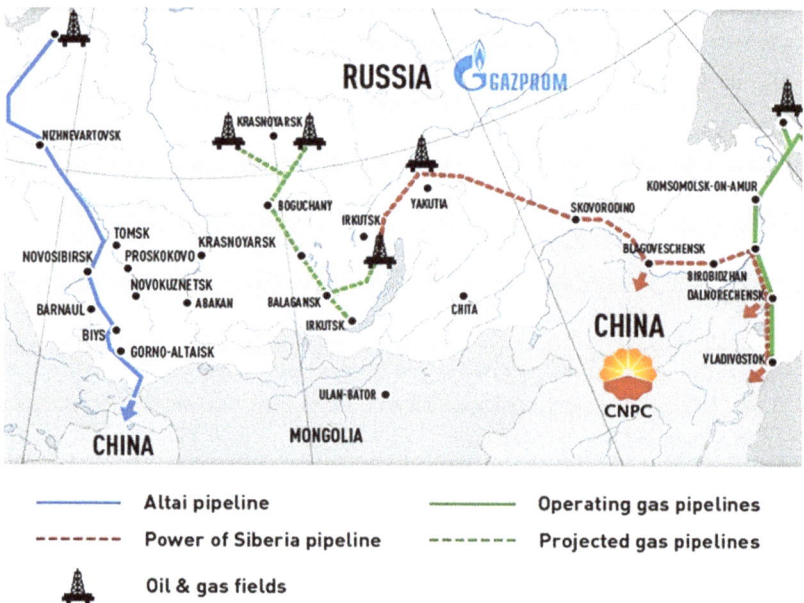

**Figure 5.3: Gazprom's POS 1 and Altai gas to China.**

Source: This map was frequently used by Gazprom to advertise the 2014 POS 1 deal, but it is rarely used now.

Gazprom intended to begin the first seven production wells at Dobycha Irkutsk's Kovykta in 2019, and the firm envisages drilling a further 289 production wells by 2047, eventually rising to a total 514. It will also construct five gas and condensate treatment facilities. Construction of the first three treatment plants began in 2020 and they should be commissioned in 2023–25. Gazprom plans to bring Kovykta on line in late 2022, targeting production at 5 bcm/y in 2023 and reaching a plateau of 25 bcm/y in 2025 that will be maintained until 2045. Almost all of the Kovykta gas will go through the Kovykta–Chayandinskoye 800 km pipeline that should be commissioned in late 2022, with a 48 MW head compressor station at Kovykta.[25] Gazprom will use 1.4 bcm for its own needs over the next 2,000 km through the Yakutia and Amur regions, and another 2.6 bcm will be used for gasification. A total of 44 bcm will be delivered to the Amur Gas Processing Plant with 41 bcm leaving once valuable natural gas components have been taken out. Of this, 1 bcm will be sent to the Amur Gas Chemicals Complex, 1 bcm will be sidelined for gasification in Amur and another 1 bcm for the needs of the Zeyskaya compressor station.[26]

Gazprom's other main task is the long-delayed POS 2 or Altai gas pipeline development. Since the May 2014 POS 1 breakthrough, Gazprom has paid little more than lip-service to the Altai gas pipeline development. Had Turkmenistan proceeded with the D Line construction, it would have been impossible for Gazprom to strike the Altai gas deal with CNPC. The delayed construction of the D Line enabled Gazprom to explore a fast tracked Altai gas line.

In May 2018, according to figures from pipeline officials in Kazakhstan, deliveries through the three existing strands of the 2,000 km (1,242 mile) cross-border network will rise by nearly a third from the 38.7 bcm supplied to China in 2017. The planned volumes of 51.37 bcm would be

---

25  'Gazprom Outlines Kovykta Plans', *Argus FSU Energy*, 18 October 2019, 1.

26  'Gazprom Considering Possibility of Increasing Gas Exports to China Via Power of Siberia up to 48 bcm per Year', *Interfax Russia & CIS Oil and Gas Weekly*, 29 November – 5 December 2018, 30. See, 'Amur Gas Processing Plant', Gazprom, accessed 22 August 2020, www.gazprom.com/projects/amur-gpp/. For Sibur Amur GCC (Gas Chemicals Complex), see 'Growth Projects', Sibur25, accessed 22 August 2020, www.sibur.ru/en/about/investments/16906/. See also 'Sinopec Signs Agreement to Take Stake in Amur Petchems Project in Russia', HIS Markit, accessed 22 August 2020, ihsmarkit.com/research-analysis/sinopec-signs-agreement-to-take-stake-in-amur-petchems-project.html; Dina Khrennikova, 'Russia's Largest Chemicals Company Is Plowing Ahead with Saudi, China Deals', *Bloomberg*, 21 February 2019, www.bloomberg.com/news/articles/2019-02-21/russias-sibur-revives-project-plans-in-china-saudi-arabia.

perilously close to the Central Asian Gas Pipeline's (CAGP) rated capacity of 55 bcm per year. The constraint could have serious consequences for China's huge investments over the past decade in Turkmenistan.[27] The Central Asian capacity problem would force China to deepen its growing reliance on LNG imports as the country is seeking to reduce pollution from coal. From the start of imports in 2010 until 2019, the CAGP's A, B and C lines carried 203.2 bcm to China, nearly equal to the country's total consumption in 2016. The scheduled imports from Central Asia in 2018 included 38.7 bcm from Turkmenistan, 7.6 bcm from Uzbekistan and more than 5 bcm from Kazakhstan.[28]

Beijing has wanted to introduce a new 1,000 km (621 mile) D Line to China since 2013, but the plan has been subject to repeated delays. The new D Line from Turkmenistan through Uzbekistan, Tajikistan and Kyrgyzstan would carry 25–30 bcm/y to China's western border. But, despite official target dates for completion—initially in 2016 and then in 2020—the most recent reports suggest that it will be commissioned no sooner than the end of 2022. Although the new line would diversify China's routes and avoid excessive reliance on transit through Kazakhstan, it would not diversify supplies. Equally important is the apparent failure to coordinate the expansion of the CAGP with the explosion in China's gas demand during the winter of 2017, when the National Development and Reform Commission (NDRC) ordered a ban on coal-fired heating in 28 northern cities. To make matters worse, CAGP volumes dropped by half at the end of January 2018 due to 'frequent equipment failures' in Turkmenistan, according to a CNPC statement at the time. The outages highlighted China's dependence on Central Asian gas. In 2017, Turkmenistan's gas production fell 7.1 per cent to 62 bcm, marking the first annual decline since 2009.[29]

---

27    Michael Lelyveld, 'China Nears Limit on Central Asian Gas', *Radio Free Asia* (RFA), 25 June 2018, www.rfa.org/english/commentaries/energy_watch/china-nears-limit-on-central-asian-gas-062 52018100827.html; Dominique Patton, 'Central Asia—China Gas Pipeline to Hit Maximum Capacity—PetroChina', *Reuters*, 12 November 2018, www.reuters.com/article/china-gas-petrochina-idAFL4N1XN3DF.

28    Lelyveld, 'China Nears Limit on Central Asian Gas'; Patton, 'Central Asia—China Gas Pipeline'.

29    Lelyveld, 'China Nears Limit on Central Asian Gas'.

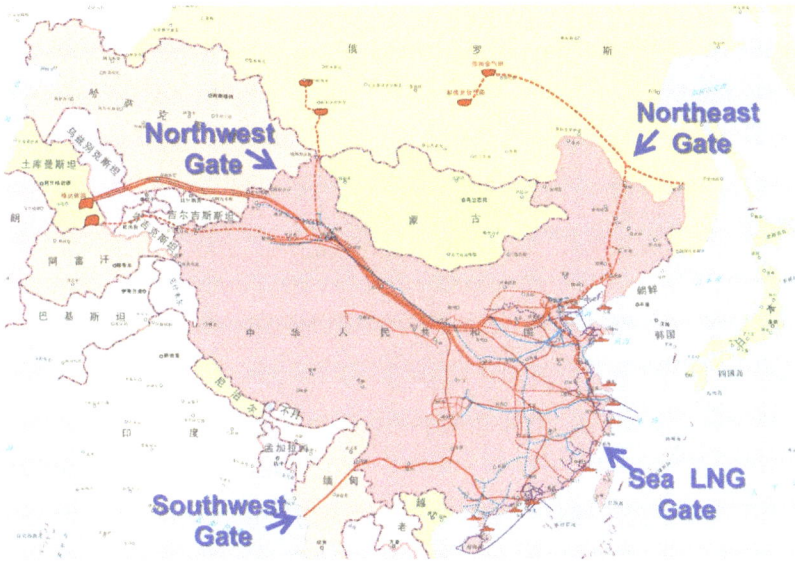

**Figure 5.4: China's gas imports by pipeline and LNG.**
Source: China National Petroleum Corporation.

Turkmenistan's failure to supply sufficient gas to China revived the chances for West Siberian gas. However, CNPC and Gazprom have made no announcements about Altai gas, despite Chinese President Xi Jinping commenting on Altai gas at the Vladivostok Economic Forum in September 2018.[30] Interfax reported Nur Bekri, Director of China's NDRC NEA (National Energy Administration), as stating that:

> We expect in the end, China will receive 30 bcm of gas from the western route … in time, and given supplies from the eastern route (38 bcm) as well as LNG, overall Russian gas supplies might rise to 80 bcm.[31]

---

30   Witold Rodkiewicz and Michal Bogusz, 'The Eastern Economic Forum in Vladivostok. In the Shadow of Russian-Chinese Cooperation', OSW, 14 September 2018, www.osw.waw.pl/en/publikacje/ analyses/2018-09-14/eastern-economic-forum-vladivostok-shadow-russian-chinese-cooperation; Michael Lelyveld, 'China, Russia May Vie for Turkmenistan's Gas', RFA, 6 May 2019, www.rfa. org/english/commentaries/energy_watch/china-russia-may-view-for-turkmenistans-gas-050620 19104507.html.
31   'Task Set to Sign Contract on Gas Supply to China Via Western Route before End of Year— Kozak', *Interfax Russia & CIS Oil and Gas Weekly*, 13–19 September 2018, 9–13.

Ultimately, the market provider will dictate the terms and conditions of pipeline gas supply. If no breakthrough on the Altai line is made, Beijing will have no choice but to maximise the supply of LNG, including Russia's Arctic LNGs.

The target supply time and competitive pricing of Novatek's Arctic LNG 2 to markets like Shandong, Jiangsu and Shanghai, with prices that could be substantially lower than LNG supplied from Qatar, Australia and the US, makes it Gazprom's main competition for its Altai line; in the end, price will be the biggest issue. If Novatek finds a way to duplicate the scale of its Arctic LNG 2 (19.8 mt/y) by 2025–26, it will deliver a massive challenge to Gazprom's POS 2 or Altai gas supply to China. Despite considerable talk and deal making, it is not clear whether or when the POS 2 will be built.

There is another difficult task facing Gazprom in the Baltic area. Gazprom and Shell's flagship LNG project was derailed in April 2019, forcing Gazprom to prove its capacity to perform with a Russian partner. Gazprom agreed to work with RusGazDobycha to build an LNG plant at the Russian Baltic port of Ust-Luga, a decision that forced Shell to stop the project with Gazprom.[32] This is because RusGazDobycha's unheralded arrival was accompanied by changes to the configuration of the project, which Shell did not feel comfortable with.[33] No explanation has been provided for why Gazprom brought RusGazDobycha into the Baltic LNG project, and questions remain about how seriously Shell's departure will affect the project's price competitiveness. The outcome should be known during the first half of 2020s.

---

32   The plant will process 45 bcm/y of gas with a high ethane content from the deeper Achim and Valazhin formations in West Siberia's Nadym-Pur-Taz area. The plant foresees 25 bcm of the processed gas being used to produce 13 mt/y of LNG, 4 mt/y of ethane and 2.2 mt/y of LPG, with the remaining 20 bcm/y going into Gazprom's network. The Ust-Luga plant will have two 6.5 mt/y LNG trains, commissioned in 2023 and 2024, with the same deadlines for ethane and LPG production startup, respectively. Gazprom estimates the facilities will cost over ₽700 billion (US$10.7 billion). See, 'Gazprom Agrees New Baltic LNG project', *Argus FSU Energy*, 4 April 2019, 4.

33   Dmitry Zhannikov and Olesya Astakhova, 'Arrival of Putin's Judo Partner Squeezed Shell Out of LNG Project—sources', *Reuters*, 11 April 2019, uk.reuters.com/article/us-gazprom-shell-exit-exclusive/exclusive-arrival-of-putins-judo-partner-squeezed-shell-out-of-lng-project-sources-idUKKCN1RN2K5; 'Gazprom Drilling Company Named its Owners', Rus Letter, 13 January 2018, rusletter.com/articles/gazprom_drilling_company_named_its_owners; 'Arkady Rotenberg and Gennady Timchenko Will Share with Gazprom the Most Expensive', Rus Letter, 29 March 2019, rusletter.com/articles/arkady_rotenberg_and_gennady_timchenko_will_share_with_gazprom_the_most_expensive; 'Russia's Baltic LNG: Gazprom Stays, Shell Quits, Rotenberg Brothers Enter the Game', Warsaw Institute, 25 April 2019, warsawinstitute.org/russias-baltic-lng-gazprom-stays-shell-quits-rotenberg-brothers-enter/.

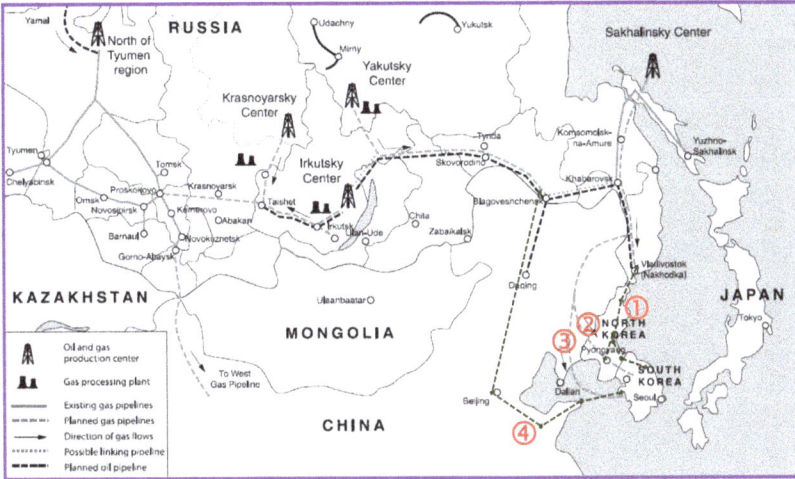

**Figure 5.5: Pipeline gas supply options to the Korean Peninsula.**
Source: Gazprom and Russian Petroleum Investor, 2018.

The export of Sakhalin offshore gas via the Sakhalin–Khabarovsk–Vladivostok gas pipeline is another area of difficulty for Gazprom. If timely development can be guaranteed, Sakhalin offshore gas can be allocated either to China's Jilin province or the Korean Peninsula during the second half of the 2020s. However, if the first Sakhalin line's 8 bcm/y gas is not available for the second Sakhalin line's third train expansion (5.4 mt/y), there will be only 5.5 bcm/y from Kirinsky in 2021, and then 8 bcm/y from South Kirinksy by 2023. (The plateau of 21 bcm/y will be reached by 2033–34).[34] If Gazprom aims to supply 10 bcm/y or 7 mt/y of Sakhalin offshore gas to the Korean Peninsula, the earliest this could occur would be in second half of the 2020s. Separate from the volume supply issue is price. Authorities in Seoul have repeatedly advertised that imported gas from the pipeline gas will be 30 per cent cheaper than LNG, but this is somewhat misleading.[35] The cost of producing the offshore gas will be high. Unless Putin decides to make a political gesture, the price of this gas will not be 30 per cent cheaper than LNG.

---

34 'Gazprom Prioritises China-focused Projects', *Argus FSU Energy*, 21 March 2019, 3; 'Crunch Time for Sakhalin 2 Third Train', *Argus FSU Energy*, 13 December 2018, 6; 'China Gas Talks Move up a Gear', *Argus FSU Energy*, 20 September 2018, 1.
35 Jeanne Choi, 'Development in Russian-Asian Energy Cooperation. Interview with Keun-Wook Paik', National Bureau of Asian Research (NBR), 26 July 2018, www.nbr.org/research/activity.aspx?id=884.

In short, the start of POS 1's gas supply at the end of 2019 to northern China's gas market will not affect LNG supply that significantly. The greater impact will come from Novatek's Arctic LNG 2—but only if the price is competitive. The introduction of POS 2 is another factor that will affect China's LNG imports in the coming decades.

Before discussing the impressive performance of Novatek's Arctic onshore gas-based LNG exports, it is worth noting where China's gas expansion stands at present. In 2018, China's gas demand reached 280.4 bcm (or 196.3 mt) and the country imported 90.1 mt of gas, of which 53.9 mt was LNG and 36.2 mt came by pipeline, according to data by the General Administration of Customs. This solidified China's position as the world's biggest importer of natural gas. In 2017, the figure was 38.3 mt of LNG and 30.4 mt of piped gas. LNG demand growth slowed to 40.8 per cent year on year in 2018 compared with 46.4 per cent in 2017. In contrast, Chinese pipeline imports increased by 20.3 per cent year on year in 2018 compared with 8.8 per cent in 2017. China's gas demand in 2019 was projected to be 308 bcm.[36] In 2019, China's total gas imports were projected to be 143 bcm, a 14 per cent increase from 2018, which is equivalent to 124 bcm or 90.39 mt (a 32 per cent increase from 2017).[37]

During the LNG2019 conference in Shanghai, CNOOC Vice President Li Hui said that China was expected to import 57 bcm of pipeline gas in 2019 and 63 bcm in 2020. He added that China's piped offtake would surge in the early 2020s, reaching 121.8 bcm by 2025 and 126 bcm in 2030, representing a 121 per cent increase from the 2019 figure.

36    Chen Aizhu and Henning Gloystein, 'China Gas Demand to Surge in 2019, but Maybe Not Enough to Sop Up LNG Glut', *Reuters*, 8 April 2019, www.reuters.com/article/us-china-gas-beijinggas/china-gas-demand-to-surge-in-2019-but-maybe-not-enough-to-sop-up-lng-glut-idUSKCN1RK0BW; 'Cold Snap Boosts Gas Demand but Slowdown Beckon', *Argus China Petroleum*, January 2019, 13; 'China's Imports of Crude Oil, Natural Gas Surge in 2018', *China Daily*, 21 January 2019, www.chinadaily.com.cn/a/201901/21/WS5c458568a3106c65c34e5a7c.html; Tsvetana Paraskova, 'Breakneck LNG Demand Surge in China Is History', Oil Price.Com, 2 February 2019, oilprice.com/Energy/Gas-Prices/Breakneck-LNG-Demand-Surge-In-China-Is-History.html#.

37    In 2018, China paid an average price of US$6.14 mmbtu for its pipeline purchases, which was considerably cheaper than the US$9.58 mmbtu average it paid for LNG. See, Colin Shek, 'China's Slowing Economy to Drag on Gas Demand Growth', *Interfax Energy*, 17 January 2019, interfaxenergy.com/gasdaily/article/33847/chinas-slowing-economy-to-drag-on-gas-demand-growth (site discontinued).

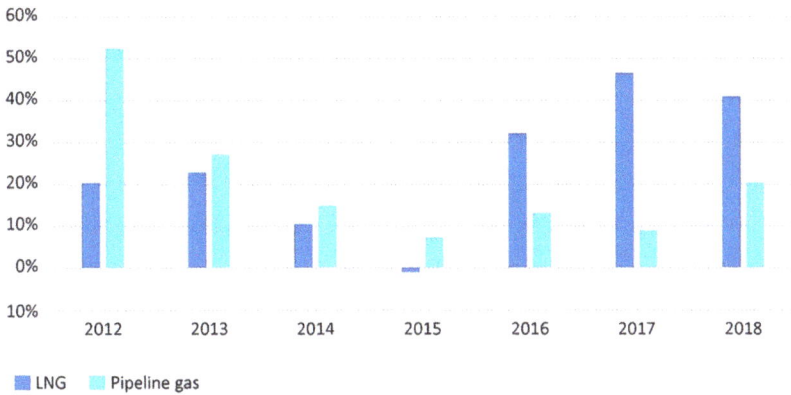

**Figure 5.6: Chinese LNG and pipeline gas import growth.**

Source: Colin Shek, 'LNG Expands Dominance of China's Gas Import Mix', *Interfax Gas Daily*, 28 January 2019.

China's LNG imports reached 50 bcm in 2019, rising only slightly to 50.8 bcm in 2020. CNOOC expects imports to rise slowly in the second half of the 2020s, reaching 83 mt (116.2 bcm) in 2025 and 88.6 mt (124 bcm) in 2030. This would equate to growth of 48 per cent between 2019 and 2030.[38]

In 2018, China's pipeline gas imports recorded 52 bcm.[39] Pipeline gas growth was even stronger in 2019, as Kazakhstan agreed in October 2018 to double exports to China to 10 bcm in 2019. CNPC's research arm ETRI (Economic and Technology Research Institute) has predicted that pipeline imports will hit 65 bcm in 2020 and will double to 130 bcm by 2030. An executive from PetroChina stated at LNG 2019 that China's LNG imports could hit 110 bcm, equivalent to 80 mt/y, by 2025.[40] According to executives at CNOOC and CNPC, the volume of pipeline gas projected to be imported by 2030 is between 126 and 130 bcm/y; this is in line with the volume Bernstein projected with only one pipeline— Altai gas or D line—as shown in the Table 5.4. If both pipelines are introduced, it will scale down China's LNG import volume in 2030.

---

38    Colin Shek and Tang Tian, 'China's Piped Imports to Surpass LNG Shipments in Long Run', *Interfax Energy*, 5 April 2019, interfaxenergy.com/article/34099/chinas-piped-imports-to-surpass-lng-shipments-in-long-run (site discontinued).

39    'China's LNG Imports Could Reach 110 Bln Cubic Meters by 2025: CNPC', *Reuters*, 3 April 2019, www.reuters.com/article/us-shanghai-lng-conference-cnpc/chinas-lng-imports-could-reach-110-bln-cubic-meters-by-2025-cnpc-idUSKCN1RF0UG.

40    Shek and Tian, 'China's Piped Imports'.

## Table 5.4: China's long-term gas supply demand projection

| Year (bcm) | 2021E | 2022E | 2023E | 2024E | 2025E | 2026E | 2027E | 2028E | 2029E | 2030E |
|---|---|---|---|---|---|---|---|---|---|---|
| **Demand** | 374 | 407 | 435 | 461 | 484 | 506 | 529 | 553 | 578 | 604 |
| **Domestic supply** | 189 | 200 | 211 | 222 | 234 | 246 | 259 | 273 | 288 | 303 |
| **Non-shale** | 162 | 170 | 178 | 186 | 192 | 201 | 211 | 222 | 234 | 243 |
| **Shale** | 27 | 30 | 33 | 36 | 42 | 45 | 48 | 51 | 54 | 60 |
| Imports | | | | | | | | | | |
| **Pipeline** | **74** | **79** | **89** | **98** | **98** | **98** | **98** | **98** | **98** | **98** |
| Central Asia – A & B | 30 | 30 | 30 | 30 | 30 | 30 | 30 | 30 | 30 | 30 |
| Myanmar | 5 | 5 | 5 | 5 | 5 | 5 | 5 | 5 | 5 | 5 |
| Central Asia – C | 25 | 25 | 25 | 25 | 25 | 25 | 25 | 25 | 25 | 25 |
| East Siberia | 14 | 19 | 29 | 38 | 38 | 38 | 38 | 38 | 38 | 38 |
| **LNG** | **87** | **87** | **87** | **87** | **87** | **87** | **87** | **87** | **87** | **87** |
| **Additional imports** | **35** | **41** | **49** | **55** | **66** | **75** | **85** | **95** | **105** | **116** |
| Central Asia – D | 10 | 18 | 30 | 30 | 30 | 30 | 30 | 30 | 30 | 30 |
| West Siberia | | | | | | 10 | 15 | 20 | 25 | 30 |
| LNG | 15 | 23 | 19 | 25 | 36 | 35 | 40 | 45 | 50 | 56 |
| Total imports | 186 | 207 | 224 | 239 | 251 | 260 | 270 | 280 | 290 | 301 |
| Imports % of demand | 50% | 51% | 52% | 52% | 52% | 51% | 51% | 51% | 50% | 50% |
| **Total LNG bcm** | **102** | **110** | **106** | **111** | **123** | **122** | **127** | **132** | **137** | **143** |
| **Total LNG (MTPA)** | **74** | **79** | **77** | **81** | **89** | **88** | **92** | **95** | **99** | **103** |

E = estimate

Source: Bernstein Research, 'Global LNG: Lower for Longer. Peak Supply Meets Slowing Asian LNG Demand Growth', 22 July 2019.

Nonetheless, China's LNG expansion will continue, as CNOOC will still go ahead with a major expansion of its regasification capacity in the next decade. CNOOC will have 80 mt/y of regasification capacity by 2030, according to CNOOC Chairman Yang Hua. The company currently operates 45.2 mt/y of regasification capacity across 10 terminals and has long-term supply contracts for 24.8 mt/y of LNG. It imported 26.4 mt of LNG and supplied 51.1 bcm of gas in 2018, accounting for 18 per cent of China's gas supply. CNOOC will expand the capacity of its existing LNG terminals in Tianjin, Shanghai and Fujian provinces between 2019 and 2030 while building two new terminals at the provinces of Jiangsu and Fujian.[41] CNOOC's role in China's LNG expansion is pivotal; that it bought 10 per cent equity in Novatek's Arctic LNG 2 project was a bold but unsurprising move.

## Novatek: Arctic Onshore LNG Becomes a Real Game Changer

With most of the Western media's attention focused on the US shale revolution and the US's related LNG export capacity expansion during the 2010s, little attention was paid to Novatek's Yamal LNG development. In December 2017, with the official opening of Yamal LNG's operation at Sabetta, the Western world saw that Novatek had managed to deliver the project on time and on budget.[42] The same month, Novatek CFO Mark Gyetvay confirmed the firm's plan to create a major LNG production centre in the Russian Arctic Zone to rival Qatar, Australia and the US.[43] This Arctic onshore gas-based LNG export initiative signalled Russia's

---

41   Shek and Tian, 'China's Piped Imports'.

42   'Ceremony of First Tanker Loading Under the Yamal LNG Project', President of Russia, 8 December 2017, en.kremlin.ru/events/president/news/56338; 'Yamal LNG Project Reaches Full Production Capacity', *Xinhua News*, 12 December 2018, www.xinhuanet.com/english/2018-12/12/c_137666821.htm; Vladimir Soldatkin and Oksana Kobzeva, 'Russia Offers to Sell Gas to Saudi Arabia from Yamal LNG', *Reuters*, 8 December 2017, www.reuters.com/article/us-russia-lng-novatek/russia-offers-to-sell-gas-to-saudi-arabia-from-yamal-lng-idUSKBN1E22HR; Keun-Wook Paik, 'The Arctic as a Future Global Natural Gas Supply Hub', in *A North Pacific Dialogue on Arctic Futures: Emerging Issues and Policy Responses*, ed. Robert W. Corell, Jong Deog Kim, Yoon Hyung Kim and Oran R. Young (KMI and East-West Centre, December 2016), 239–51, www.eastwestcenter.org/sites/default/files/filemanager/pubs/pdfs/Arctic2016/2016arctic-01frontmatter.pdf.

43   Henry Foy, 'Novatek Widens Arctic LNG Ambitions', *Financial Times*, 13 December 2017; 'Exclusive Interview: Novatek CFO Mark Gyetvay', Riveria, accessed 22 August 2020, www.rivieramm.com/opinion/exclusive-interview-novatek-cfo-mark-gyetvay-54658.

strong desire to become a major player—perhaps even a game changer—in the coming years. The role of Novatek will be decisive in transforming Russia into a competitively priced global supplier of LNG.

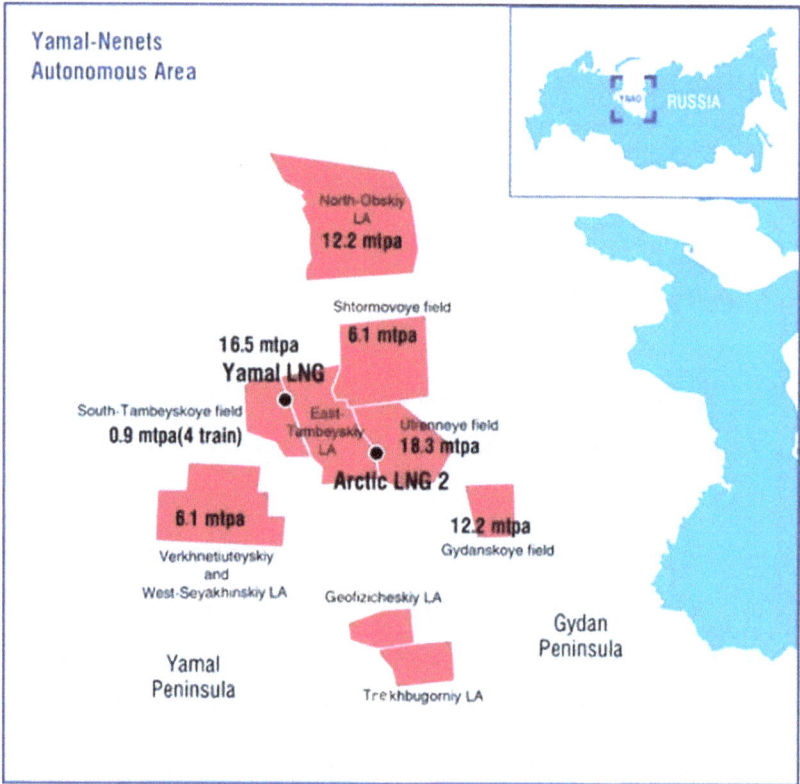

**Figure 5.7: Novatek's Yamal and Gydan peninsulas' gas reserves.**

Note: Yamal LNG: 16.5 mt + 0.9 mt = 17.4 mt/y; Gydan LNG: 18.3 mt + 12.2 mt + 12.2 mt + 6.1 mt + 6.1 mt = 54.9 mt/y.

Source: 'Transforming into a Global Gas Company', Novatek, Strategy Presentation, released 12 December 2017, www.novatek.ru/en/investors/strategy/.

In December 2017, Novatek released its ambitious 2030 plan, which envisages the potential capacity of LNG production in the Gydan Peninsula alone will reach 55 mt/y by 2030. In April 2019, Argus projected that Novatek's LNG capacity in Russia's Arctic region could reach 43.3 mt by around 2026, of which 17.4 mt/y would come from Yamal, 19.8 mt/y from Arctic 2 and 6.1 mt/y from Ob LNG. If a possible 1.8 mt/y from Novatek's Cryogas-Vysotsk LNG on the Baltic Sea is added, the total capacity would reach 45.1 mt/y. However, considering that Novatek's initial 2030 target was 57 mt/y, this still leaves a gap of

11.9 mt/y: clearly another large LNG project is needed.[44] In June 2019, Novatek released a revised plan, *Expanding Our Global LNG Footprint, from 2018 to 2030: Energy Affordability, Security & Sustainability*, which stipulated that the firm's LNG production capacity in 2024–25 would be 39 mt/y, and that this figure would increase to 57–70 mt/y in 2025–30.[45]

**Table 5.5: LNG cost breakdown by origin and destination (US$/mmbtu)**

|  | US | Australia | Yamal LNG | Arctic LNG 2 |
|---|---|---|---|---|
| Extraction | 3 | 3.8 | 0.8 | 0.8 |
| Liquefaction | 2.5 | 4.9 | 4.1 | 2.5 |
| Transport to Europe | 0.9 | 2.1 | 1.1 | 1.1 |
| Transport to Asia | 2 | 0.7 | 2.8 | 2.8 |
| Total to Europe | 6.4 | 10.8 | 6 | 4.4 |
| Total to Asia | 7.5 | 9.4 | 7.7 | 6.1 |

Source: 'Arctic LNG 2 to be 23% More Competitive than US LNG in Supplies to Asia— Novatek', *Interfax*, 5 September 2018.

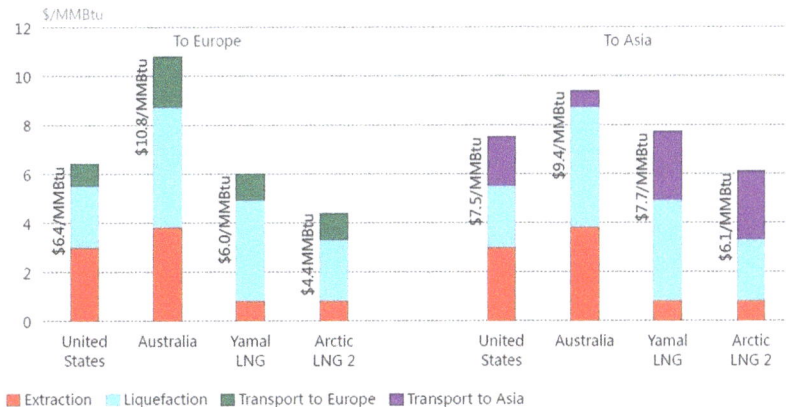

**Figure 5.8: LNG cost breakdown by origin and destination.**
Source: *Interfax Natural Gas Daily*, 7 September 2018, 4.

---

44 'Novatek Plans New Yamal LNG Plant', *Argus FSU Energy*, 18 April 2019, 5; Atle Staalesen, 'Novatek Makes Big Discovery in Gulf of Ob', *Barents Observer*, 11 October 2018, thebarentsobserver. com/en/industry-and-energy/2018/10/novatek-makes-big-discovery-gulf-ob; Atle Staalesen, 'Novatek Announces 3rd LNG Project in Arctic', *Barents Observer*, 23 May 2019, thebarentsobserver.com/en/ industry-and-energy/2019/05/novatek-announces-3rd-lng-project-arctic.
45 'Transforming into a Global Gas Company', Novatek, Strategy Presentation, released 12 December 2017, www.novatek.ru/en/investors/strategy/; Mark Gyetvay, 'Expanding Our Global LNG Footprint from 2018 to 2030: Energy Affordability, Security & Sustainability', Novatek, Presentations, 3 June 2019, www.novatek.ru/en/investors/presentations/.

On 27 February 2019, during the IP Week Conference in London, Novatek CFO and Deputy Chairman Mark Gyetvay stated that Novatek was able to deliver LNG to Europe for US$3.15mmbtu compared to US$7–8 mmbtu for US producers. He added that Novatek was extracting gas at a cost of US$0.1 mmbtu versus US$3mmbtu in the US, and liquefying gas for US$0.5 versus US$3 in America.[46] But this figure was not reported by the media. Gyetvay concluded that the firm could deliver LNG to Asia for US$3.6 mmbtu, a shockingly low figure. The liquefaction figure shown in Table 5.5 does not support this figure, even though it confirms Russia's LNG price competitiveness. Time will tell whether Novatek can prove they have the capacity to produce LNG with such a low cost. If it succeeds, it will be the game changer in the 2020s.

**Table 5.6: LNG project competitiveness in US$/mmbtu, high-income market test—Japan, Korea, Taiwan or China (JKC) 2025 (US$/mmbtu)**

|  | Gas Supply | Liquefaction | Shipping | Total |
|---|---|---|---|---|
| Qatar | 2.00 | 1.69 | 1.10 | 4.79 |
| Russia | 0.50 | 4.52 | 0.49 | 5.51 |
| Nigeria | 2.63 | 1.88 | 2.44 | 6.95 |
| US GOM (New) | 2.25 | 2.25 | 2.55 | 7.05 |
| Western Canada | 2.54 | 3.50 | 1.13 | 7.17 |
| Mozambique | 2.54 | 3.79 | 1.53 | 7.86 |
| US GOM (Existing) | 3.52 | 3.10 | 2.55 | 9.17 |

Source: Claudio Steuer, 'Outlook for Competitive LNG Supply', *Petroleum Review*, July 2019, 21.

The successful implementation of Arctic LNG 2 will guarantee Russia's transformation into the game changer of global LNG supply in the 2020s. During the first half of 2019, Novatek made a number of important announcements, and the preparation work for FID (financial institutions duty) on Arctic LNG 2 was completed. The first announcement occurred on 5 March 2019, when Total SA, a French oil and gas company, signed a purchase and sales agreement for a 10 per cent equity stake in Arctic LNG 2. Total SA issued the letter of intent at the 22nd Saint Petersburg International Economic Forum in May 2018. The following year, during the 23rd Saint Petersburg International Economic Forum, Novatek

---

46    Dmitry Zhdammikov, 'Novatek, Shell See Russian Gas Keeping Edge in Europe Over US', *Reuters*, 28 February 2019, www.reuters.com/article/us-russia-novatek-sanctions/novatek-shell-see-russian-gas-keeping-edge-in-europe-over-us-idUSKCN1QG21K.

announced that it had sold a 20 per cent stake in its Arctic LNG 2 project to two Chinese companies, CNPC's upstream arm CNODC and China's biggest LNG buyer CNOOC, on the same terms as Total SA.[47]

In March 2019, after talks with Saudi Arabia's Energy Minister Khalid al-Falih, Novatek CEO Mikhelson reconfirmed that the firm was prepared to consider selling a stake of up to 30 per cent in the Arctic LNG 2 project to Saudi Aramco if it was offered good terms. The deal with CNPC and CNOOC was clear confirmation that Novatek would brook no delaying tactics. As for the payment structure, Mikhelson added that:

> Around 40 per cent – 45 per cent is the first payment, and over 12 months the next payment to Novatek. Plus, there is the relatively large share the partners will be contributing to the Arctic LNG 2 charter capital.[48]

A third announcement occurred on 29 June 2019 when Novatek signed a deal with Mitsui & Co. and Japan Oil, Gas and Metals National Corporation (JOGMEC) for 10 per cent equity sales in the Arctic LNG 2 project. The deal will supply 2 mt/y of LNG to Japan—about one-tenth of total capacity.[49] It is clear that Russia wants closer cooperation with Japan and China in developing natural gas reserves; at the same time, establishing more buyers in Asia will help insulate its companies against additional Western sanctions. Japan's acquisition of the remaining 10 per cent equity not only opened the door for Novatek's FID before the end of 2019, but also makes it likely that Arctic LNG 2 will achieve its 2023 production schedule deadline.

Considering that both Saudi Aramco and South Korea failed to take part in the Arctic LNG 2 project, and Novatek has increased the 2030 target production capacity from 57 mt/y to 70 mt/y, an accelerated second Arctic LNG 2 (with 19.8 mt/y) looks increasingly likely.[50] It is no longer Novatek's

47    'NOVATEK and TOTAL Sign Sale Agreement for Arctic LNG 2 Stake', Novatek, 5 March 2019, www.novatek.ru/en/press/releases/index.php?id_4=3058; 'Novatek Sells Stake in Arctic LNG to Chinese Firms on Same Terms as Total Deal', *Reuters*, 26 April 2019, uk.reuters.com/article/us-russia-gas-novatek/novatek-sells-stake-in-arctic-lng-to-chinese-firms-on-same-terms-as-total-deal-idUKKCN1S21G8.

48    'Novatek Expects Binding Agreement with Fourth Partner in Arctic LNG 2 to be Signed in H1', *Interfax Russia & CIS Oil and Gas Weekly*, 6–11 June 2019, 13–15.

49    Tomoyo Ogawa, 'Russia Looks for Asia LNG Buyers to Blunt Western Sanctions' Bite', Nikkei Asian Review, 14 July 2019, asia.nikkei.com/Business/Energy/Russia-looks-for-Asia-LNG-buyers-to-blunt-Western-sanctions-bite2.

50    'Novatek to Revise LNG Production Strategy Soon, Raise Target from 57 Mln to 70 Mln Tonnes by 2030—Mikhelson', *Interfax Russia & CIS Oil and Gas Weekly*, 21–27 February 2019, 18–19.

initiative alone, as the Russian state is fully supportive. In early March 2019, Interfax reported that Putin had ordered Russian Energy Minister A. Novak to study a number of proposals from Vladimir Litvinenko, rector of Saint Petersburg Mining University, concerning the development of the Russian LNG sector. According to Litvinenko, the unique geographical positions of the Yamal and Gydan peninsulas with respect to the Atlantic and Pacific sales markets, Russia's no less unique gas resource base and expertise, and the accumulated competencies of Novatek, allowed for a confident scaling of LNG production up to 140 or 150 mt/y.[51] In light of this, Novak claimed at the International Arctic Forum in Saint Petersburg on 9 April 2019 that Russian LNG production could reach 73 mt/y by 2025, and 100 to 120 mt/y by 2035.[52] Russia's aim is to become one of the four major global LNG suppliers in the coming decades.

There are two factors Russia must consider if it wishes to expand its LNG operations on the Gydan Peninsula. The first is the availability of financing and the second is the timely provision of competitively priced icebreaking tankers. Saudi Arabia had been exploring the possibility of participating in Novatek's Arctic LNG 2 project since December 2017; it was considering taking a 30 per cent equity stake in the project.[53] However, in April 2019, Chinese NOCs—CNODC under CNPC and CNOOC—took 20 per cent,[54] and then, in June (during the G20 meeting in Osaka), Mitsui & Co. and JOGMEC took up the remaining 10 per cent equity in the project.[55] Subsequently, Saudi Arabia's offer to purchase 30 per cent equity in the Arctic project with an investment of US$5 billion was vetoed by Novatek, which saw no reason to continue to provide a substantial discount to encourage Saudi Arabia's entry.

It is worth noting that, instead of prioritising the Arctic LNG 2 deal, Saudi Arabia shopped around. In mid-July 2019, Interfax reported that Saudi Aramco had expressed interest in other liquefied gas projects in Russia, including Baltic LNG with Gazprom and Far Eastern LNG with

51    'Putin Orders Energy Ministry to Study Idea of Arctic National Project with Production of up to 150 Mln Tonnes of LNG a Year—Source', *Interfax Russia & CIS Oil and Gas Weekly*, 28 February – 6 March 2019, 7–8.

52    'Moscow Steps Up LNG Ambitions', *Petroleum Argus*, 12 April 2019, 10.

53    Soldatkin and Kobzeva, 'Russia Offers to Sell Gas'.

54    Nastassia Astrasheuskaya, 'Russia's Novatek to Sell Stake in Arctic Gas Project to Chinese Partners', *Financial Times*, 25 April 2019.

55    Dina Khrennikova and Ilya Arkhipov, 'Mitsui, Jogmec to Invest $3 Billion in Novatek's Arctic LNG Plant', *Bloomberg*, 29 June 2019, www.bloomberg.com/news/articles/2019-06-29/mitsui-jogmec-to-invest-3-billion-in-novatek-s-arctic-lng-2.

Rosneft.[56] Saudi Arabia was attempting to use these LNG supply options as bargaining chips against Novatek, but the tactic backfired. Saudi Arabia will doubtless explore all options before the second Arctic LNG 2 project commences development in the early 2020s. No doubt, financing from Saudi Arabia and China will be necessary for the rapid expansion of Russia's Arctic onshore gas-based LNG exports in the 2020s and 2030s.

Another important factor is the construction of an icebreaking fleet. In 2014, Russia's state-owned shipping company Sovcomflot placed its first order for a US$316 million LNG carrier. South Korean shipbuilder Daewoo Shipbuilding & Marine Engineering Co. Ltd (DSME) was commissioned to construct an ice-class tanker, known as Arc7, the first of its kind in the industry. This vessel kicked-off a US$5 billion new-build program, which will see 15 icebreaking LNG carriers built (Table 5.7).[57]

As shown in Table 5.7, the first carrier's delivery was made in November 2016 and a total of 11 carriers were in operation as of May 2019. According to *China Daily*, the first direct shipment of LNG from Russia's Arctic region was delivered to PetroChina's Rudong terminal in Jiangsu province on 19 July 2018.[58] The second LNG tanker bound for Asia, *Eduard Toll*, which departed on 27 June 2018, arrived at CNPC's Rudong LNG terminal on 7 July. It is worth noting that, on 13 November 2018, Novatek Gas & Power Asia Pte. Ltd, a subsidiary of Novatek, delivered the first shipment of LNG to CNOOC.[59] In 2018, a total of four tankers were sent eastwards. On 29 June 2019, the *Vladimir Rusanov*, an Arc7-classed LNG tanker, left the port of Sabetta and, by 5 July, was in the Chukchi Sea close to the Bering Strait, according to Refinitiv Eikon shipping data. This marked the first voyage of the 2019 summer season across the Northern Sea Route (NSR). In 2018, four such tankers were sent eastwards.[60] The *Rusanov* transited the ice-covered part of the route in just six days, setting

56  'Saudi Aramco Interested in LNG Projects in Russia, Including Baltic LNG with Gazprom, Far Eastern LNG with Rosneft', *Interfax Russia & CIS Oil and Gas Weekly*, 11–17 July 2019, 4.

57  'DSME to Build 1st ARC7 Ice-Class Tanker for Yamal', Offshore Energy, 17 March 2014, worldmaritimenews.com/archives/106699/dsme-to-build-1st-arc7-ice-class-tanker-for-yamal/; 'DSME Launches World's First Icebreaking LNG Carrier', Maritime Executive, 18 January 2016, www.maritime-executive.com/article/dsme-launches-worlds-first-icebreaking-lng-carrier.

58  'LNG from Arctic Reaches Jiangsu', *China Daily*, 20 July 2018, www.ecns.cn/business/2018-07-20/detail-ifywhfmh2714619.shtml.

59  'NOVATEK Shipped First LNG Cargo to CNOOC', Novatek, 13 November 2018, www.novatek.ru/en/press/releases/index.php?id_4=2804.

60  Sabina Zawadzki, 'Arctic Sea Route Opens for the Summer with First Yamal LNG Cargo', *Reuters*, 5 July 2019, www.reuters.com/article/russia-arctic-lng/arctic-sea-route-opens-for-the-summer-with-first-yamal-lng-cargo-idUSL8N246304.

a new record for independent passage via the NSR without icebreaking support and with cargo on board. The net voyage time from Sabetta to the destination port (Tianjin) in China was completed in a record 16 days.[61] Separately, on 26 June 2019, Novatek announced that Yamal LNG had shipped the first cargo of LNG to Japan in accordance with the long-term offtake agreement with Total SA. The cargo was unloaded at the Tobata LNG terminal.[62]

**Table 5.7: List of 15 icebreaking LNG carriers**

| Vessel name | Stage | Operator/Commencement of operation |
|---|---|---|
| *Chris. de Margerie* | In operation | Sovcomflot/November 2016 |
| *Boris Vilkitsky* | In operation | Dynagas/November 2017 |
| *Fyodor Litke* | In operation | Dynagas/November 2017 |
| *Eduard Toll* | In operation | Teekay/CLNG/December 2017 |
| *Vladimir Rusanov* | In operation | MOL/CSLNG/January 2018 |
| *Rudolf Samoylovich* | In operation | Teekay/CLNG/August 2018 |
| *Vladimir Vize* | In operation | MOL/CSLNG/October 2018 |
| *Georgiy Brusilov* | In operation | Dynagas/December 2018 |
| *Boris Davydov* (DSME 2428) | In operation | Dynagas/January 2019 |
| *Nikolay Zubkov* (DSME 2429) | In operation | Dynagas/February 2019 |
| *Nikolay Evgenov* (DSME 2430) | In operation | Teekay/CLNG/May 2019 |
| *Vladimir Voronin* (DSME 2431) | Sea trials | Teekay |
| *Nikolay Urvantsev* (DSME 2432) | Sea trials | MOL |
| *Georgiy Ushakov* (DSME 2433) | Due 29 January 2020 | Teekay |
| *Yakov Gakkel* (DSME 2434) | Wet dock | Teekay |

Note: CLNG = China LNG Shipping; MOL = Mitsui OSK Lines; CSLNG = China COSCO Shipping.

Source: Mark Gyetvay, 'Expanding Our Global LNG Footprint from 2018 to 2030: Energy Affordability, Security & Sustainability', Novatek, Presentations, 3 June 2019, www.novatek.ru/en/investors/presentations/; Sabina Zawadzki, 'Two Arc7 Arctic LNG Tankers Start Sea Trials to Join Yamal Fleet', *Reuters*, 18 June 2019, www.reuters.com/article/lng-yamal-shipping/table-two-arc7-arctic-lng-tankers-start-sea-trials-to-join-yamal-fleet-idUSL8N23P141; 'Ice-Breaking LNG Carrier for Yamal LNG Project Named Vladimir Vize', MOL, 12 September 2018, www.mol.co.jp/en/pr/2018/18060.html; 'Christophe de Margerie Class Icebreaking LNG Carriers', Ship Technology, accessed 22 August 2020, www.ship-technology.com/projects/christophe-de-margerie-class-icebreaking-lng-carriers/.

---

61  'LNG Carrier "Vladimir Rusanov" Opens the Northern Sea Route 2019 Navigation Period', *Port News*, 25 July 2019, en.portnews.ru/news/280799/.
62  'Yamal LNG Shipped First LNG Cargo to Japan', Novatke, 26 June 2019, www.novatek.ru/en/press/releases/index.php?id_4=3268&from_4=2.

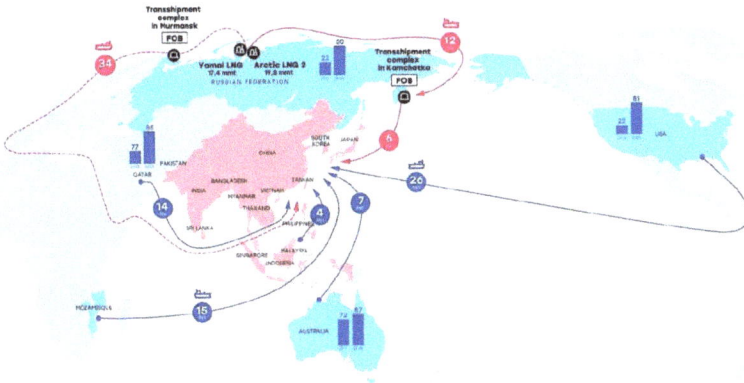

**Figure 5.9: Novatek's LNG logistics to Asia.**

Source: Mark Gyetvay, *Expanding Our Global LNG Footprint from 2018 to 2030: Energy Affordability, Security & Sustainability* (Novatek, 2019).

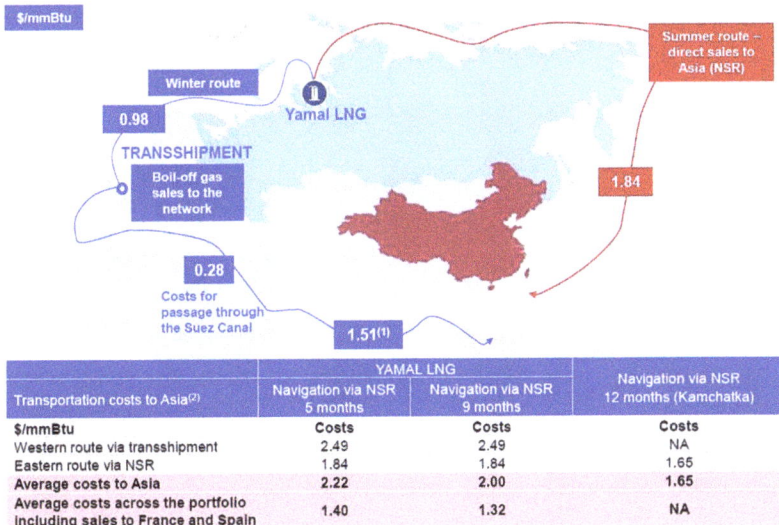

| Transportation costs to Asia[2] | YAMAL LNG | | Navigation via NSR 12 months (Kamchatka) |
|---|---|---|---|
| | Navigation via NSR 5 months | Navigation via NSR 9 months | |
| $/mmBtu | Costs | Costs | Costs |
| Western route via transshipment | 2.49 | 2.49 | NA |
| Eastern route via NSR | 1.84 | 1.84 | 1.65 |
| Average costs to Asia | 2.22 | 2.00 | 1.65 |
| Average costs across the portfolio including sales to France and Spain | 1.40 | 1.32 | NA |

(1) including costs for passage through the Suez Canal
(2) NOVATEK

**Figure 5.10: LNG transportation costs: East versus West routes.**

Source: 'Transforming into a Global Gas Company: From 2018 to 2030'. Novatek, 12 December 2017.

In an effort to overcome a potential shortage of LNG carriers and other logistical challenges, Novatek partnered with Sovcomflot (Russia's largest shipping company) in ordering four new Arc7 LNG carriers, and contracted TechnipFMC, a UK-based company that provides complete project life cycle services, to engineer, procure, supply, construct and commission Arctic LNG 2's new facility on the Gydan Peninsula.[63]

Experts calculate that Novatek will require another 5 to 10 Arc7 carriers in addition to its existing fleet of 15 carriers.[64] Mikhail Grigoriev of Arctic consultancy Gecon explained that this would allow it to maintain a continuous flow of LNG to Europe and Asia. Experts caution that only the 120 MW Leader Class nuclear icebreaker, which is more than twice as powerful as any other nuclear icebreaker, will be capable of keeping the route open. That icebreaker, however, has yet to progress past initial discussion stages and would not be available until 2027 at the earliest.[65]

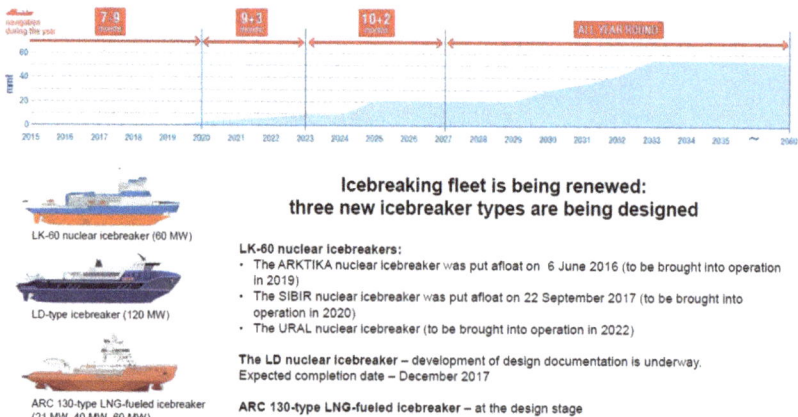

**Icebreaking fleet is being renewed:**
**three new icebreaker types are being designed**

LK-60 nuclear icebreaker (60 MW)

**LK-60 nuclear icebreakers:**
- The ARKTIKA nuclear icebreaker was put afloat on 6 June 2016 (to be brought into operation in 2019)
- The SIBIR nuclear icebreaker was put afloat on 22 September 2017 (to be brought into operation in 2020)
- The URAL nuclear icebreaker (to be brought into operation in 2022)

LD-type icebreaker (120 MW)

The LD nuclear icebreaker – development of design documentation is underway. Expected completion date – December 2017

ARC 130-type LNG-fueled icebreaker (21 MW, 40 MW, 60 MW)

**ARC 130-type LNG-fueled icebreaker** – at the design stage

**Figure 5.11: LNG transit via Northern Sea Route subject to icebreakers commissioning.**

Source: Mark Gyetvay, 'Expanding Our Global LNG Footprint from 2018 to 2030: Energy Affordability, Security & Sustainability', Novatek, Presentations, 3 June 2019, www.novatek.ru/en/investors/presentations/.

---

63    Malte Humpert, 'Novatek Signs Contract for Construction of Arctic LNG 2, Orders New LNG Carriers', *High North News*, 21 May 2019, www.highnorthnews.com/en/novatek-signs-contract-construction-arctic-lng-2-orders-new-lng-carriers; 'Novatek's Yamal LNG to Face Logistical Challenges during Winter Months', *High North News*, 5 October 2018, www.highnorthnews.com/en/novateks-yamal-lng-face-logistical-challenges-during-winter-months.

64    'Novatek Allowed to Operate Foreign LNG Carriers on Northern Sea Route', *High North News*, 21 March 2019, www.highnorthnews.com/en/natural-gas-company-novatek-was-granted-exemption-new-law-banning-foreign-flagged-oil-and-gas.

65    'Novatek Allowed to Operate Foreign LNG Carriers on Northern Sea Route'.

Novatek is confident that it can shift the majority of its LNG exports from Europe to Asia by 2023. Mikhelson stated:

> If Atomflot provides us with a speed of seven to eight knots, we have no doubt that we will make a transit point on Kamchatka by 2022. We are very clearly oriented that 80–85 per cent [of LNG], no matter what they say, will be delivered to the East.[66]

While the original 15 carriers were constructed by South Korea's DSME, the Russian Government aims to construct subsequent vessels at the Zvezda shipbuilding complex in the Russian Far East, in cooperation with DSME.[67] In April 2019, Sovcomflot placed an order for an additional Arc7 carrier to be built by Zvezda by 2023, to coincide with the opening of Arctic LNG 2. On 21 May, Novatek, Sovcomflot and Zvezda agreed on the construction of an additional four vessels, at a unit cost of US$375 million for delivery by 2025. This order would potentially close Novatek's projected shortage of Arc7 carriers. However, unit costs are around US$50 million or 15 per cent higher than in South Korea.[68] The price difference—up to 20 per cent—will be covered through subsidies from the Russian state budget.[69] The Russian Government is willing to pay the price to improve its shipbuilding capacity.

Novatek was much faster than the Russian Government in taking a pragmatic but bold stance, opening the door for China Offshore Oil Engineering Company (COOEC), a subsidiary of CNOOC, to play a major role in the Yamal LNG project. On 9 April 2016, COOEC delivered the first key module of the project to the Russian client, marking China's first export of the key LNG modules. COOEC ultimately built 36 core modules for Yamal LNG, mastering this technology

---

66  Humpert, 'Novatek Signs Contract'.

67  'Novatek Allowed to Operate Foreign LNG Carriers on Northern Sea Route'.

68  'Sovcomflot Moored at Arctic LNG', *Kommersant*, 20 May 2019, www.kommersant.ru/doc/3974775.

69  'Sovcomflot Moored at Arctic LNG'; 'Zvezda Shipyard Signs Contract with Sovcomflot to Build Arctic Gas Carrier for Arctic LNG 2 Project', *Port News*, 10 April 2019, en.portnews.ru/news/275342/; 'Sovcomflot Approves LNG-Fueled Tanker Orders at Zvezda Shipyard', Offshore Energy, 29 July 2019, www.lngworldnews.com/sovcomflot-approves-lng-fueled-tanker-orders-at-zvezda-shipyard/; 'Zvezda Shipyard Started Serial Production of Aframax Tankers', Zvezda, 21 November 2018, www.sskzvezda.ru/index.php/en/contact/9-news-en/195-zvezda-shipyard-started-serial-production-of-aframax-tankers.

through participation in the project. This breakthrough is in line with Beijing's plan for China to move up the chain in manufacturing ocean engineering equipment.[70]

In early June 2019, Novatek, together with China SOSCO Shipping Co. Ltd, Sovcomflot and the Silk Road Fund, signed an agreement in respect of the Maritime Arctic Transport LLC.[71] The agreement confirms that the four parties aim to establish a long-term partnership providing for the joint development, financing and implementation of year-round logistics arrangements for shipping hydrocarbons from the Arctic Zone of the Russian Federation to the Asia-Pacific region, as well as organising transit cargo traffic along the NSR between Asia and Western Europe.

The Japanese shipbuilding company with the greatest involvement in the Yamal LNG project is Mitsui OSK Lines (MOL). MOL, in cooperation with the China Ocean Shipping Company (COSCO), aimed at taking ownership of four of the project's icebreaker tankers, with the first of these, *Vladimir Rusanov*, entering operation in January 2018.[72] Based on their Yamal experience, it is not surprising that MOL formed an alliance with JOGMEC to purchase a 10 per cent equity stake in Arctic LNG 2.

Unlike China and Japan, South Korea failed to take part in the Arctic LNG 2 project despite the MOU between Kogas and Novatek in June 2018.[73] South Korea's somewhat naive approach to the NSR shipping business explains the difficulties Russia faces in gaining entry to the Asian gas market. Had South Korea decided to take 10 per cent equity in the Arctic LNG 2 project, it would have opened the door for DSME to build the extra icebreaking tankers needed for Arctic LNG 2 project. Diversification of LNG supply and optimal price is Korea's highest

---

70   'COOEC Delivers 36 Core Modules of Yamal LNG Project on Time', Euro Petrole, 21 August 2017, www.euro-petrole.com/cooec-delivers-36-core-modules-of-yamal-lng-project-on-time-n-i-15307; Xu Yihe, 'Chinese Yards Back in the Fray for Arctic LNG 2',*Upstream*, 8 May 2019, www.upstream online.com/hardcopy/1774834/chinese-yards-back-in-the-fray-for-arctic-lng-2; Li Yulong, Kong Linghao and Liu Jia, 'Yamal LNG Project and Made-in-China Equipment Going Globally', *China Oil & Gas*, no. 3 (2016): 13–17; Zheng Xin and Zhang Min, 'Top-end Oil-gas Equipment Next', *China Daily*, 17 April 2017, www.chinadaily.com.cn/business/2017-04/17/content_28953838.htm; 'Milestone Is in the Pipeline', *China Daily Europe*, 23 April 2017.
71   'NOVATEK, COSCO SHIPPING, Sovcomflot and Silk Road Fund Sign an Agreement in Respect of Maritime Arctic Transport LLC', Novatek, 7 June 2019, www.novatek.ru/en/press/releases/index.php?id_4=3243&from_4=2.
72   James D. Brown, 'Japan and the Northern Sea Route', *Shingetsu News*, 5 March 2018, shingetsunewsagency.com/2018/03/05/japan-northern-sea-route/.
73   Choi, 'Development in Russian-Asian Energy Cooperation'.

priority, as President Moon Jae-In's administration is determined to move away from coal and nuclear to renewable energy and gas.[74] Novatek CFO Mark Gyetvay warned during an interview with *JoongAng Daily*[75] that DSME's easy ride for the US$5 billion worth of icebreaking LNG tankers then under construction would not be repeated if there was no financial contribution for Arctic LNG 2 from South Korea. However, all is not lost. Even though the Arctic LNG 2 project's funding procedure is closed, there is no harm in South Korea exploring the possibility of securing 5–9.9 per cent of equity by diluting Novatek's 60 per cent equity to 50.1–55 per cent. Novatek's expectation of participation by South Korea in its Arctic LNG projects is purposefully done.

Russia's old and ambitious dream of becoming the swing oil and gas supplier for Europe and Asia may no longer be a pipedream. As the POS 1 gas started to flow at the end of 2019, Russia witnessed the first tangible results of exporting piped gas to China. It remains to be seen whether and when the Altai gas or POS 2 will follow.

Russia's dominance in the European gas market has brought increased pressure to bear from the US. According to Rystad Energy, Russian gas delivered to Europe has a low break-even price of around US$5 per mmbtu. This compares to a long-run marginal cost of between $6.00 and $7.70 mmbtu for US LNG.[76] The hard line US stance towards Russia is very likely to trigger Gazprom's compromise on the Altai gas deal. Ironically, the US's strategy of using Qatar LNG to balance Russia's dominance in Europe's gas market could unintentionally help Russia's ambition of becoming a swing gas supplier. In September 2018, Qatar said it would invest €10 billion (US$11.6 billion) to strengthen its ties with Germany over the next five years, including the possible creation of an LNG terminal.

---

74  Keun-Wook Paik, 'South Korea's Energy Policy Change and the Implications for its LNG Imports', OIES Paper, 27 June 2018, www.oxfordenergy.org/wpcms/wp-content/uploads/2018/06/South-Koreas-Energy-Policy-Change-and-the-Implications-for-its-LNG-Imports-NG132.pdf.
75  Author assisted with this interview in October 2017 and the article was published in early December 2017. See, Kim Sang-jin, 'First Export of LNG from Arctic … The Global LNG Market Is Also Changing', MNNews, accessed 22 August 2020, mnews.joins.com/article/22184683?cloc=joongang#home.
76  'Could LNG from the US Pose a Short-Term Challenge to Russian Gas in Europe?', Rystad Energy, 5 February 2019, www.rystadenergy.com/newsevents/news/press-releases/Could-LNG-from-the-US-pose-a-short-term-challenge-to-Russian-gas-in-Europe/.

In January 2019, Deputy US Energy Secretary Dan Brouillette, speaking in Doha, confirmed that the US was talking with Doha about supplying Europe with LNG, as it wanted Germany and other countries to import Qatari and US gas rather than Russian gas, which accounted for 60 per cent of German gas imports. Brouillette said he had discussed the issue with Qatar's Minister of State for Energy Affairs Saad al-Kaabi, who was also chief executive of Qatar Petroleum (QP)—majority owner of the Golden Pass LNG terminal, with Exxon Mobil and ConocoPhillips holding smaller stakes. Brouillette added that Qatari investments in the Golden Pass, and in US export facilities, enabled the US to get natural gas to Europe. He acknowledged that LNG would cost more than piped gas but said that LNG supplies from Qatar and other countries would help diversify supply sources to Europe.[77] Qatar's LNG cooperation with the US has been carefully managed to ease the pressure of a blockade by its regional neighbours, Saudi Arabia, Arab Emirates (UAE), Bahrain and Egypt, since 2017.[78] In this context, it is understandable why Russia is so keen on Saudi Arabia's participation in the Gydan Peninsula's LNG development scheme. Russia's desire to make Saudi Arabia its strategic partner and LNG buyer is a direct response to Qatar's alliance with the US.

Wood Mackenzie projected that LNG imports to Japan would fall by 12 per cent to 72.8 mt/y by 2022, while China's import volumes would rise by 37.5 per cent to 74.1 mt/y. The firm added that Japanese imports would remain above 70 mt/y through much of the 2020s, while LNG demand was declining. The country would remain the second-largest LNG consumer in the world until at least 2040, with demand exceeding 60 mt/y.[79] It took only two decades for China to become the biggest LNG importer, and it looks very likely that China will become the price setter of global LNG supply. The expansion of LNG in China will be fundamentally affected by the supply of pipeline gas to China.

---

77    Rania El Gamaland Eric Knecht, 'US Wants Qatar to Challenge Russian Gas in Europe—US Official', *Reuters*, 14 January 2019, www.reuters.com/article/usa-energy-gulf-idUSL8N1ZE1XG.
78    Linah Alsaafin, 'Qatar Has Moved on Two Years Since Blockade, Analysts Say', *Aljazeera*, 5 June 2019, www.aljazeera.com/news/2019/06/qatar-moved-years-blockade-analysts-190604215831200.html.
79    David Rowlands, 'Wood Mackenzie: China Could Overtake Japan as Top LNG Importer by 2022', LNG Industry, 23 July 2019, www.lngindustry-com.cdn.ampproject.org/c/s/www.lngindustry.com/regasification/23072019/wood-mackenzie-china-could-overtake-japan-as-top-lng-importer-by-2022/amp/.

CNOOC has warned that China's LNG imports will grow much more slower than its piped imports during 2019–30. CNOOC VP Li Hui said at the LNG 2019 conference that China is expected to import 57 bcm of pipeline gas in 2019 and 63 bcm in 2020. The figure will be 121.8 bcm by 2025 and 126 bcm in 2030, representing a 121 per cent increase from 2019. In the meantime, China's LNG imports will reach 60 mt in 2019— equivalent to 84 bcm after regasification—and then rise to 70.7 mt in 2020. CNOOC expects imports to rise slowly in the second half of the 2020s, reaching 83 mt (116.2 bcm) in 2025 and 88.6 mt (124 bcm) in 2030. This would equate to a growth of 48 per cent between 2019 and 2030. CNPC ETRI has predicted that pipeline imports will hit 65 bcm in 2020 and will double to 130 bcm by 2030.[80]

China's leaders' preference for pipeline gas is well known and this will definitely be strengthened if the Hormuz Strait crisis and South China Sea's territorial disputes are intensified. An executive from PetroChina said at LNG 2019 that China's LNG imports could hit 110 bcm, equivalent to 80 mt/y, by 2025. CNPC's projection of 130 bcm/y by 2030 indicates that China may not take both Altai gas and Central Asian D Line gas. In other words, only one, either Altai or D Line, will be chosen.[81] If Altai gas instead of D Line is chosen, it will transform Russia into an effective swing gas supplier between the European and Asian markets in the coming decades. Russia's long-term dream of becoming a swing supplier of both oil and gas between the European and Asian markets will then be a reality. Although a blessing for Russia, this would be a nightmare for both Western Europe and the US.

In short, the coming decade will witness no slowdown of ESPO crude supply to the Asian oil market and increasing supplies of both pipeline gas and LNG. Sino-Russian oil and gas cooperation will play the pivotal role in opening the era of Russia's Asia-Pacific policy.

---

80   Shek and Tian, 'China's Piped Imports'.
81   Shek and Tian, 'China's Piped Imports'.

# Part 3: Australia's Asia-Pacific Energy Interests

# 6

# Unpacking Australia's Energy Strategy for the Region

John Blackburn

A classic assumption related to Australian fuel security, quoted in the *Australian* in January 2019, is revealing: 'The Energy Department said Australia's low supplies were not a serious concern as there had never been a serious interruption to Australia's supply'.[1] Using that logic, perhaps you should cancel your house insurance if you have never had a fire. National security decisions should not be left to economists. Not everything can be monetised, nor rationalised, by a cost–benefit analysis.[2] Our understanding and comprehension of 'risk' is influenced by our assumptions—as individuals, as societies and as governments. We often assume our logistic chains are reliable as they appear to be working—until they don't.

The discipline of logistics is not well understood beyond logistics specialists: it is difficult and multifaceted and, certainly from a military perspective, takes second place behind the platforms. For a government, the challenge of logistics is central to getting our economic and security settings right; however, it is often neglected and frequently left to the market to sort out.

---

1    Primrose Riordan, 'Red Light Flashing over Fuel Security', *Australian*, 6 January 2019.
2    The folly of this approach is addressed in part in Binyamin Applebaum, *The Economists' Hour: False Prophets, Free Markets and the Fracture of Society* (New York: Little, Brown and Co., 2019).

# Australia's Fuel Security

Having identified concerns in Australia's supply chains, I was fortunate to obtain sponsorship from the NRMA to conduct three studies into fuel security to determine the extent of the problem.[3] These investigations focused on supply lines, from source to port to the movement of supplies around the country, trying to understand supply chain risks.

It is worth considering the analysis that underpinned the 2011 National Energy Security Assessment (NESA)—the last one conducted in Australia. Only two scenarios were used with respect to fuel security. The first was a repeat of the 1970s Middle East oil embargo and the second was the outage of a Singapore refinery for 30 days. No consideration was given to potential problems in the South China Sea, supply chains being disrupted by conflict or the implications of critical points of failure within the domestic supply chain. Here begins part of Australia's challenge.

How does the rest of the developed world view fuel security? Interestingly, considerably more seriously than does Australia. A 2013–14 review of stockholdings and comparison with other developed countries found that the Australian Government was the only fuel-importing country in the developed world that had none of the following: public-owned oil/fuel stocks; mandated commercial stock holdings; or government control of, or participation in, the country's oil/fuel markets.

Figure 6.1 illustrates a number of converging trends in Australia's fuel outlook. Australia's crude oil resources are small by world standards and depleting at a faster rate than they are being replenished by discovery. Australia's transport fuels import dependency grew from around 60 per cent in 2000 to over 90 per cent by 2013. Between 2012 and 2015, there was a 42 per cent loss in Australia's refining capacity when three refineries were closed leaving a total of only four refineries in country. When asked what the minimum number of refineries should be in Australia to ensure sufficient fuel security and resilience, the Department of Resources, Energy and Tourism responded that a 'zero' refining capacity in Australia would be acceptable, as it would be cheaper to import refined

---

3    The three NRMA liquid fuel security reports can be accessed online, see 'Australia's Liquid Fuel Security Part 1', 'Australia's Liquid Fuel Security Part 2' and 'Benchmarking Australia's Transport Energy Policies', Presentations/Interviews/Reports, JBCS, accessed 23 August 2020, www.jbcs.co/#/reports/.

fuels from Asian refineries. Further, Australia has not met its stockholding obligations of 90 days of 'net imports' under the International Energy Agency (IEA) members agreement since 2011.

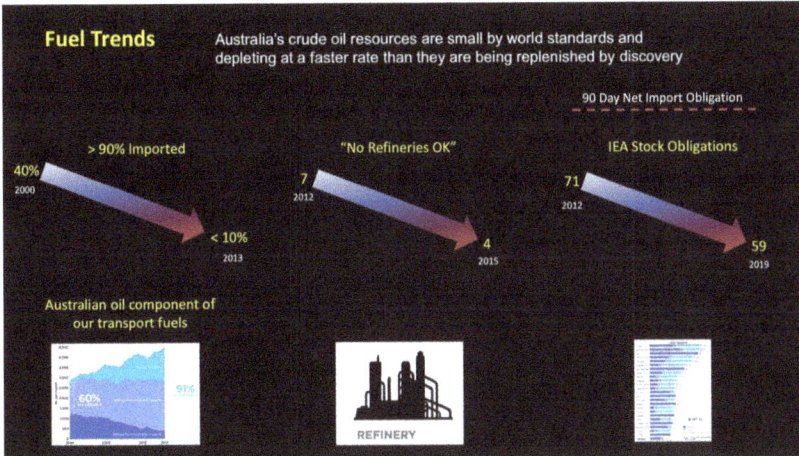

**Figure 6.1: Australian fuel market trends.**

Source: The figures and trends used to compile this graphic were extracted from John Blackburn's NRMA liquid fuel security reports. See, 'Australia's Liquid Fuel Security Part 1', 'Australia's Liquid Fuel Security Part 2' and 'Benchmarking Australia's Transport Energy Policies', Presentations/Interviews/Reports, JBCS, accessed 23 August 2020, www.jbcs. co/#/reports.

In June 2016, in response to pressure from other IEA member countries, the Australian Government committed to purchasing 'tickets' (i.e. options to buy oil stocks for release to the market) between 2018–20, and promised full compliance with IEA stockholding obligations by 2026—some 15 years *after* Australia first failed to meet its membership obligations. The government did subsequently enter into a ticketing contract with the Netherlands for approximately three days of net import stocks to be held for release to the market should collective IEA action be required in the event of an oil supply disruption. So, the first purchase of 'government stocks' was for an option to purchase oil tickets in a foreign country. This had little impact on Australia's domestic fuel security.

Despite this latest action, Australia, with only 59 days holdings as at July 2019, remains the only country out of 28 member countries that fails to meet its 90-day net oil import stockholding levels. The world's ninth-largest energy producer is the lowest and only non-compliant stockholder in the IEA.

In 2015 the Australian Government's *Energy White Paper* (EWP) made the following statements:

> Australia is endowed with vast energy resources. We have had decades of readily available and low-cost energy to meet domestic and export demand …

> Our guiding principle is that markets should be left to operate freely, without unnecessary government intervention …

> The Australian Government continues to monitor and identify emerging risks to energy supplies … through the periodic National Energy Security Assessment. [Yet, this has clearly not happened.][4]

Interestingly, the 2015 EWP did not refer to electricity supply security, perhaps because the 2011 NESA had noted that 'improved reliability for electricity supply is expected as current new infrastructure investments replace ageing network infrastructure'.[5] Unfortunately, that improved reliability proved wanting when, in 2016, Australians were confronted with a statewide electricity system blackout in South Australia.

In 2015, a Senate Inquiry into Australia's Transport Energy Resilience and Sustainability explored supply chains and global and domestic risks to transport energy security and resilience.[6] The importance of realistic scenario modelling was pursued by the committee, despite testimony from an industry lobby group that national security scenarios were 'not appropriate' for use in assessing fuel supply chain risks; the implication being that only market factors, forces and fluctuations, could undermine our fuel security in Australia. Perhaps this was an ambit claim by an industry group to minimise the risk of government regulation or control for national security purposes?

The first recommendation of the 2015 Senate Inquiry was:

> The committee recommends that the Australian Government undertake a comprehensive whole-of-government risk assessment of Australia's fuel supply, availability and vulnerability. The assessment

4    Department of Industry and Science, *Energy White Paper 2015*, April 2015, i, 5, apo.org.au/sites/default/files/resource-files/2015-04/apo-nid54017.pdf.
5    Department of Resources, Energy and Tourism, *National Energy Security Assessment December 2011*, 2011, 55, www.energy.gov.au/sites/default/files/national-energy-security-assessment-2011_0.pdf.
6    Senate Standing Committee on Rural and Regional Affairs and Transport, *Australia's Transport Energy Resilience and Sustainability Report*, June 2015, www.aph.gov.au/Parliamentary_Business/Committees/Senate/Rural_and_Regional_Affairs_and_Transport/Transport_energy_resilience/Report.

should consider the vulnerabilities in Australia's fuel supply to possible disruptions resulting from military actions, acts of terrorism, natural disasters, industrial accidents and financial and other structural dislocation. Any other external or domestic circumstance that could interfere with Australia's fuel supply should also be considered.[7]

The government rejected that recommendation on the grounds that the issues were adequately addressed in the NESA process. As mentioned above, as yet there has been no update to the 2011 NESA.

The 2015 Senate Inquiry also recommended that:

The Australian Government develop and publish a comprehensive Transport Energy Plan directed to achieving a secure, affordable and sustainable transport energy supply. The plan should be developed following a public consultation process. Where appropriate, the plan should set targets for the secure supply of Australia's transport energy.[8]

No action was taken by the government on this recommendation.

In 2018, as part of the *Energy Policies of IEA Countries* series, the *Australia 2018* review was released.[9] The review made the following observations: while Australia is well endowed with natural resources, energy security risks across several sectors have increase; the signs of stress in the Australian energy system have grown and energy policy governance in Australia is very complex and fragmented; Australia is increasingly exposed to new challenges for maintaining security of energy supply. Therefore, an updated NESA remains critical. Significantly, Australia is the only IEA country that is a net oil importer and relies solely on the commercial stockholding of industry to meet its obligation. All IEA countries have two obligations; Australia meets neither obligation. This is problematic given that the country's oil stocks are at an all-time low, and the country has no strategic oil stocks and has not placed any stockholding obligations on industry.

---

7    Senate Standing Committee on Rural and Regional Affairs and Transport, *Australia's Transport*.
8    Senate Standing Committee on Rural and Regional Affairs and Transport, *Australia's Transport*.
9    International Energy Agency, *Energy Policies of IEA Countries, Australia 2018 Review*, 2018.

The IEA review concluded that Australia's oil security policy is based on ensuring the operation of an efficient and flexible oil market. Accordingly, the country's liquid fuels market is largely unregulated during business-as-usual. 'However, it is less clear how the country would respond in the event of a serious oil supply disruption leading to market failure.'[10] These observations and conclusions do not reflect a coherent approach to energy security nor energy policy in this country.

In March 2018, the Parliamentary Joint Committee on Intelligence and Security published an Advisory Report on the Security of Critical Infrastructure Bill 2017.[11] The first recommendation of that report was:

> That the Department of Home Affairs, in consultation with the Department of Defence and the Department of the Environment and Energy, review and develop measures to ensure that Australia has a continuous supply of fuel to meet its national security priorities. As part of developed measures, the Department should consider whether critical fuel assets should be subject to the Security of Critical Infrastructure Bill 2017.[12]

The response to that recommendation was due in December 2018, but the Department of Energy failed to deliver.

On 4 April 2019, 12 months after the Joint Committee's report, the Department of Energy published their interim *Liquid Fuel Security Review* report.[13] The interim report was a positive step in the right direction; however, it revealed how little analysis had been conducted by successive governments with respect to how our supply chains work and the risks we face in a rapidly changing global environment. The authors deduced the following:

> Fuel shortages are not something that most Australians have experienced …
>
> Australia manages fuel differently from other countries …

---

10    International Energy Agency, *Energy Policies of IEA Countries, Australia 2018 Review*, 53.
11    Parliamentary Joint Committee on Security and Intelligence, *Advisory Report on the Security of Critical Infrastructure Bill 2017*, March 2018, parlinfo.aph.gov.au/parlInfo/download/committees/reportjnt/024155/toc_pdf/AdvisoryreportontheSecurityofCriticalInfrastructureBill2017.pdf;fileType=application%2Fpdf.
12    Parliamentary Joint Committee on Security and Intelligence, *Advisory Report*.
13    Department of the Environment and Energy, *Liquid Fuel Security Review Interim Report*, April 2019, www.energy.gov.au/publications/liquid-fuel-security-review-interim-report.

Australia is heavily reliant on imports of liquid fuels, and this is unlikely to change …

Australia is an energy superpower, but not when it comes to oil …

Australia needs to keep pace with global trends, otherwise we risk being left behind with ageing infrastructure and potentially more limited supply of oil …

Burdensome administrative requirements of the Liquid Fuels Emergency Act are likely to delay an effective Government response in an emergency. [This is a serious issue—in other words, we do not have an effective legal framework through which government can respond rapidly to a fuel supply emergency.] …

There is no overarching understanding of the whole liquid fuel market in Australia and how different parts interact with each other. [The Department is now developing a model of the fuel market and its supply chains.] …

Australia is potentially exposed to potential fuel supply disruption in Asia and the Middle East. While it is extremely unlikely, ongoing tensions in the Middle East may affect oil production. [Recent developments in the Middle East would suggest that this assessment was somewhat optimistic.][14]

The report discussed further work that needed to be done and estimated that the final report would be delivered to government in the second half of 2019 (some 12 months late). By that time, the 2015 NESA would be four years overdue, making the only 'current' NESA eight years old.

In August 2019, Minister for Energy and Emissions Reduction Angus Taylor announced that the government was negotiating to buy millions of barrels of oil from America's fuel reserve under an emergency strategy to lower the risk of Australia plunging into an economic and national security crisis. In June 2020, the strategic fuel reserve deal was inked. In doing this, Taylor was trying to meet our obligations as a member of the IEA. However, this obligation does not mean holding 90 days of diesel and 90 days of unleaded and 90 days of jet fuel. The 90-day figure is an accounting measure. For example, we hold about 22 days of diesel stocks according to government statistics; however, diesel stocks have been as low as 12 days in the past couple of years.

---

14    Department of the Environment and Energy, *Liquid Fuel Security*.

Will this 'deal' make any real difference to our energy security, given that we import more than 90 per cent of all our transport fuels as either oil or refined product? Unfortunately, it will not. What we are seeing here is marketing instead of real action and a clever accounting move to avoid having to address our real fuel security problem.

In 2021 we have three refineries (soon to be two) while we used to have 100 Australian-flagged ships, we now have only four flagged ships capable of international trade, and these are liquefied natural gas (LNG) carriers.

Paying for US oil stocks, which will stay in the US, is a move to try to meet the IEA measure set in the 1970s. A lot has changed since then. The security of our fuel supplies has become much more complex and a move to count oil in a foreign country as our own will do little for our domestic energy security. We only have four oil refineries and, as at August 2019, while we used to have 100 Australian-flagged ships, we now have only four flagged ships capable of international trade, and these are liquefied natural gas (LNG) carriers. We depend completely on foreign-owned ships to bring oil and fuel to Australia.

# Australia's Absent Energy Security Policy

The world, the economy and governments have all changed considerably since the last NESA, and yet no update has been conducted to reflect the current environment nor help shape government energy and security policy. Successive governments have committed to developing a new NESA—initially in 2015, then each year until 2019. Yet, in 2021, we are still yet to see an updated NESA. Australia lacks a contemporary and relevant assessment of our energy security, including analysis of a full range of future threat scenarios. We need a contemporary and relevant assessment of our energy security, including analysis of a full range of future risk scenarios.

Can the market forces so confidently spruiked by government and industry actually provide for energy security? The simple answer is 'no, they cannot'. The lowest price has become the default target. We want more 'stuff' and we want the cheapest 'stuff', but what is the real cost of the lowest price if we fail to consider the resilience and security aspects of the supply chain? Especially given Australia's poor track record in fuel security, we must ask ourselves this question. The answer is that the real cost is poor resilience, increased vulnerability and inadequate security.

# Implications for Australia's Gas Energy Sector

So far, this chapter has addressed our fuel security. Given that the book focuses on Russian energy strategy and implications for Australia, it is worth considering the approach of successive Australian governments to energy policy with respect to the gas energy sector.

The 2011 NESA noted that 'the longer term role for gas … will be dependent on the interplay between carbon pricing policy, technological developments … and—importantly—gas prices'.[15] The carbon price policy did not survive the transition to the Abbot government in 2014, and gas price rises over the past few years have been the subject of much public debate and blame shifting. It is clear that the 2011 NESA was based on assumptions that were invalid within three years.

Australia is currently being touted as the largest global exporter of LNG. Has the government assessed the emerging risks to that trading position? What assumptions has our government made? What scenarios are being considered for the NESA of the 2020s? While we await an updated NESA, it is worth noting that the Australian Government is now considering a gas reservation policy in reaction to current domestic gas prices, despite refusing to consider this approach over the past decade.

In addition, and with respect to further investment in this sector, the economic impacts of the July 2019 change in the Petroleum Resources Rent Tax (PRRT) for future projects are yet to be seen.[16] These changes are long overdue given the paltry amounts of PRRT collected over the past 20 years.

---

15 Department of Resources, Energy and Tourism, *National Energy Security Assessment December 2011*, 34.
16 See, Australian Government, *Treasury Laws Amendment (2019 Petroleum Resources Rent Reforms No. 1) Act 2019*, accessed 23 August 2020, www.legislation.gov.au/Details/C2019A00043.

As well as these Australian policy changes, the impact of Russian gas exports into the Asia-Pacific could be significant for Australian LNG exporters. In a June 2019 report, the chief economist of the Department of Industry noted that LNG spot prices were forecast to remain low, as additions to global capacity outstripped increases in global demand.[17]

With 96 per cent of Australian LNG currently being exported to the Asian market, Russian gas exports to that same market, which are expected to be at prices significantly lower than Australian LNG, could have a major impact on the Australian LNG industry.[18] Russia's proven gas reserves are significantly greater than Australia's, as highlighted in Figure 6.2.

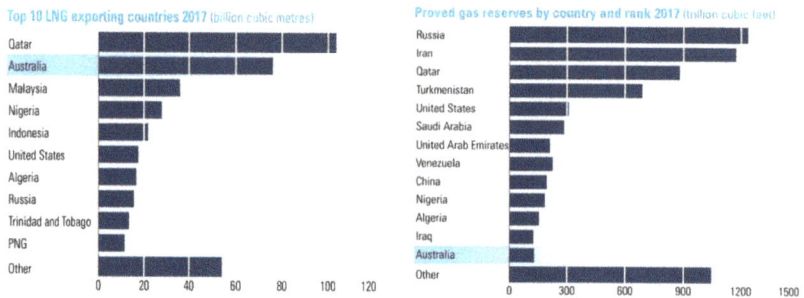

**Figure 6.2: LNG exporting countries and proved gas reserves.**
Source: Australian Petroleum Production and Exploration Association Limited, *Key Statistics 2019*, 2, 11, accessed 23 August 2020, www.appea.com.au/wp-content/uploads/2019/06/APPEA_Key-Statistics_2019.pdf.

The combination of proposed gas reservation policies, a change in the PRRT, the spectre of lower-priced Russian gas exports to the Asian market and the significantly larger proven Russian gas reserves could auger badly for future investment in the Australian LNG market. We await the delayed NESA to find out.

One positive indicator for the Australian gas market is the national hydrogen strategy that is expected to be released in early 2020. The production of 'green' hydrogen from renewable electricity and water has significant potential as a large-scale export industry, energy storage

---

17    Department of Industry, Innovation and Science, Office of the Chief Economist, *Resources and Energy Quarterly*, June 2019, 54, www.industry.gov.au/data-and-publications/resources-and-energy-quarterly-june-2019.
18    Australian Petroleum Production and Exploration Association Limited, *Key Statistics 2019*, accessed 23 August 2020, www.appea.com.au/wp-content/uploads/2019/06/APPEA_Key-Statistics_2019.pdf.

medium, source of renewable NH3 and adjunct to our methane gas supply zero emissions transport energy source that could significantly improve our energy security by reducing the reliance on imported fossil fuels. It remains to be seen whether the strategy encompasses the full range of potential benefits of a domestic and export hydrogen industry, and provides appropriate market incentives to build a resilient industry base that benefits the Australian economy more that the first 20 years of the PRRT.

The reality is that energy security, like national security, can only be addressed with consistent nonpartisan political support. This is sadly absent in Australia, where energy policy has been the subject of political battles at the expense of our nation's security. There is no energy security strategy and there is no coherent energy policy. Energy security is about much more than a 'reliable' and cheaper electricity supply.

There are significant issues with our energy systems today that should concern us all. Energy security is a vital component of national security and an increased level of government control and leadership with respect to energy security is warranted.

In 2021, Australia does not have a national security strategy. We need one that integrates all aspects of national power and includes an energy security plan. Without such strategies, policies and plans, we navigate a rapidly changing world, facing backwards and reacting to events after they have occurred.

# 7

# Future of Russian Coal Exports in the Asia-Pacific

## Stephen Fortescue

Russia is a major coal producer and an up-and-coming supplier of coal to the Asia-Pacific region (APR). In 2017, Russia was the world's sixth-largest producer, with a 5.3 per cent share (Australia was fourth with 6.2 per cent), and third-largest exporter, with an 18 per cent share (Australia was first with 41.1 per cent).[1] In 2018, Russia exported around 120 mmt to the APR. As a rough point of comparison, in the 12 months between 2016 and 2017, Australia exported 379 mmt, overwhelmingly to the APR. Russia has serious ambitions to strengthen its position in this region.

This chapter reviews progress in Russia's development of an APR-oriented coal export industry and evaluates prospects for further development. No attempt is made to describe or analyse demand issues. The focus is on the availability of coal and the capacity to get it to market. This chapter also asks whether an APR export strategy is commercially sustainable and what might be the cost to the Russian state of trying to make it so. While not systematically, Australia's coal export industry is used as a comparator.

---

1    'Coal of Russia and the World: Production, Consumption, Export, Import', Central Dispatch Office of the Fuel and Energy Complex, 27 September 2018, cdu.ru/tek_russia/issue/2018/7/499/.

As noted in mid-2018 by Russian Minister for Energy Aleksandr Novak, the major targets set in the *Program for the Development of the Coal Industry of Russia for the Period to 2030*, approved in 2014 and referred to in what follows as the Program,[2] had been or were set to be achieved well ahead of schedule.[3] Table 7.1 shows the Program forecasts for 2020, 2025 and 2030, with actual figures for 2018. It can be seen that output approached the 2025 target in 2018, that total exports exceeded it and that exports to the APR approached it.

**Table 7.1: Forecasts in the *Program for the Development of the Coal Industry of Russia for the Period to 2030*, with outcome in 2018 (mmt)**

|  | 2018 actual | 2020 actual | 2025 forecast | 2030 forecast |
|---|---|---|---|---|
| Output | 439.3 | 401.6 | 450 | 500 |
| • Coking | 98.3 | 92.3 | 158 | 200 |
| • Thermal | 341.0 | 309.3 | 292 | 300 |
| Exports | 193.2 | 195.6 | 180 | 205 |
| • Coking | 16.3 | 21.6 | 45 | 60 |
| • Thermal | 176.9 | 174.0 | 135 | 145 |
| Exports to APR | 120.8* | 120.8 | 95 | 120 |

*Calculated from Table 7.3. There might be some exports from regions not included in that table.

Source: *Programma razvitiia ugol'noi promyshlennosti Rossii na period do 2030 goda* [Program for development of Russia's coal industry for the period to 2030], approved by government directive no. 1099-r, 21 June 2014, 9; Igor' Gennadievich Tarazanov, 'Itogi raboty ugol'noi promyshlennosti Rossii za ianvar'-dekabr' 2018 goda' [Results of the work of the coal industry in Russia for January–December 2018], *Ugol'* 3 (2019): 64–79, doi.org/10.18796/0041-5790-2019-3-64-79.

The stronger than predicted performance led Novak to undertake a revision of the Program, taking the end date out to 2035. In June 2020, the new Program was approved by the Russian government.[4] At an August 2018 meeting, Novak reported that the ministry had arrived at new output forecasts, in consultation with coal companies, of 560 mmt in 2025

---

2    *Programma razvitiia ugol'noi promyshlennosti Rossii na period do 2030 goda* [Program for development of Russia's coal industry for the period to 2030], approved by government directive no. 1099-r, 21 June 2014.
3    'Meeting of the Commission on the Development Strategy of the Fuel and Energy Complex and Environmental Safety', President of Russia, 27 August 2018, kremlin.ru/events/president/news/58382.
4    Sergey Sukhankin, 'Coal Strategy 2035: Is Russia Preparing for the Last War?', *Eurasia Daily Monitor* 17, 109 (2020), jamestown.org/program/coal-strategy-2035-is-russia-preparing-for-the-last-war/.

(the Program had forecast 450) and 590 mmt in 2030 (the Program had forecast 500). He estimated that exports to the APR in 2018 would be around 100 mmt (Table 7.1 suggests higher), and that that figure could be doubled to 207 mmt in 2025.[5]

Twelve months later, as the revised Program was being drawn up, Novak reported two forecasts for output by 2035: 550 or 670 mmt. He noted that coal companies were predicting 770 mmt, but that the ministry had decided to be more cautious.[6] The newspaper *Kommersant* claimed to have seen more detailed figures, which forecast exports at 322–92 mmt, of which 214–20 mmt would be exported to the APR.[7]

There is clearly a struggle underway between optimistic coal producers and more cautious government planners, the suspicion being that the former are making ambit claims in order to maximise government commitment to infrastructure provision, on which more below.

**Table 7.2: Output by selected regions as forecast in the *Program for the Development of the Coal Industry of Russia for the Period to 2030*, with outcomes in 2013 and 2018 (mmt)**

|  | 2013 actual | 2018 actual | 2020 actual | 2030 forecast |
|---|---|---|---|---|
| Kuzbass | 203.6 | 255.3 | 232.1 | 178 |
| East Siberia | 88.6 | 79.4 | 74.6 | 162 |
| Russian Far East | 33.1 | 74.1 | 78.9 | 122 |

Source: *Programma razvitiia ugol'noi promyshlennosti Rossii na period do 2030 goda* [Program for development of Russia's coal industry for the period to 2030], approved by government directive no. 1099-r, 21 June 2014, 16; Igor' Gennadievich Tarazanov, 'Itogi raboty ugol'noi promyshlennosti Rossii za ianvar'-dekabr' 2018 goda' [Results of the work of the coal industry in Russia for January–December 2018], *Ugol'* 3 (2019): 64–79, doi.org/10.18796/0041-5790-2019-3-64-79.

---

5    'Meeting of the Commission on the Development Strategy of the Fuel and Energy Complex and Environmental Safety'.

6    'Meeting with Leaders of Coal Mining Regions'.

7    Natal'ia Skorlygina and Evgenii Zainullin, 'Vse budet narubis' [All will be chopped], *Kommersant*, 23 August 2019.

**Table 7.3: Exports to the Asia-Pacific from selected regions as forecast in the *Program for the Development of the Coal Industry of Russia for the Period to 2030*, with outcomes in 2013 and 2018 (mmt)**

|  | 2013 actual | 2018 actual | 2030 forecast |
|---|---|---|---|
| Kuzbass | 35.0 | 79.06* | 27.0 |
| East Siberia | 12.7 | 12.50** | 20.0 |
| Russian Far East | 10.9 | 29.24** | 46.0 |

*Calculated from Natal'ia Skorlygina and Anatolii Dzhumailo, 'Velikii ugol'nyi put' [The great coal route], *Kommersant*, 26 July 2018.

**These figures are for total exports from the region. It is assumed that all exports go to the APR. See, Igor' Gennadievich Tarazanov, 'Itogi raboty ugol'noi promyshlennosti Rossii za ianvar'-dekabr' 2018 goda' [Results of the work of the coal industry in Russia for January–December 2018], *Ugol'* 3 (2019): 64–79, doi.org/10.18796/0041-5790-2019-3-64-79.

Source: *Programma razvitiia ugol'noi promyshlennosti Rossii na period do 2030 goda* [Program for development of Russia's coal industry for the period to 2030], approved by government directive no. 1099-r, 21 June 2014, 17.

As is evident from Tables 7.2 and 7.3, the forecasts set in 2014 saw a decline in Kuzbass output and exports to the APR, to be made up for by new capacity in the Russian Far East (RFE) and East Siberia. So far, this has not happened—Kuzbass has massively exceeded forecasts already and the RFE and East Siberia could well struggle to meet the targets. We have no figures on what the Russian Ministry of Energy sees as the contribution of different regions into the future. But figures that *Kommersant* claimed in July 2018 to have been agreed between the Kemerovo regional administration (Kemerovo being the core administrative region of the Kuzbass) and local coal companies predict exports of 126.5 mmt from the region to the APR in 2025 (from output of 394.6 mmt).[8] The Program did not provide forecasts for exports by region in 2025, but the new figure is considerably above the Program's forecast of 27 mmt from Kuzbass in 2030. If it were to be achieved, other regions would have to contribute 80.5 mmt to meet Novak's prediction of 207 mmt of APR exports by 2025. The Program had an 8 mmt contribution from neighbouring Khakasia and 19 mmt from 'others', presumably from Arctic deposits to be briefly described below, by 2030.[9] The RFE and East Siberia were slated

8    Natal'ia Skorlygina and Anatolii Dzhumailo, 'Velikii ugol'nyi put' [The great coal route], *Kommersant*, 26 July 2018.
9    Export forecasts are not available, but Khakasia's output in 2030 is predicted to be 46 mmt. See, Dmitrii Lysenko, Dmitrii Akatov and Natal'ia Skorykh, 'Faktory i tendentsii razvitiia ugeldobyvaiushchei promyshlennosti Respubliki Khakasiia' [Factors and trends in the development of the coal mining industry in the Republic of Khakassia], *Ugol'* 5 (2019): 28–30, doi.org/10.18796/0041-5790-2019-5-28-30.

to provide 66 mmt, making a non-Kuzbass total of 93 mmt. Thus, if the recent Kuzbass predictions have any basis in reality, the share of APR exports of other regions is expected to be less than were forecast in 2014. If current trends are maintained, East Siberia and RFE might reach their targets, but further analysis is undertaken below to determine whether those trends can indeed be maintained, and, in particular, sufficiently so to make up the gap if Kuzbass fails to perform as forecast.

There are two implications of the unforeseen continued dominance of Kuzbass coal. First, that the expected increase in the share of coking coal forecast in 2014 will not materialise, given the predominance of thermal coal in Kuzbass output; and, second, that coal being exported to the APR has to be shipped further by rail than would be the case if more coal were coming from East Siberia and the RFE. These are matters to which we will return. But first some consideration must be given to the sustainability of the Kuzbass expansion, and the reasons for, and chances of, reversal of relatively poor East Siberian and RFE performance.

# Kuzbass

Kuzbass is a large topic that cannot receive the attention due in the space available here. Kuzbass coal is like West Siberian oil: despite constant predictions of the peak having been reached, output continues to increase. One hesitates to bet against the positive trend continuing. Nevertheless, not everyone is optimistic. Kopytov and Shaklein express scepticism about the region's reserves data, which are based on exploration done in the Soviet period, as well as doubts about the sustainability, on social and environmental grounds, of the open-cut mining on which big increases in output depend.[10] In what admittedly sounds like lobbying for underground mining (one author being a professor in the Department of Underground Structures and Mines at Kuzbass State Technical University), they call for the development of new technology to enable more intensive underground recovery. Plakitkina and Plakitkin also see Kuzbass as close

10   A. I. Kopytov and S. V. Shaklein, 'Napravlenie sovershenstvovaniia strategii razvitiia ugol'noi otrasli Kuzbassa' [Approach to improving the Kuzbass's coal industry's development strategy], *Ugol'* 5 (2018): 80–86.

to the limit on both production and environmental dimensions (while also noting the poor performance of East Siberia).[11] As a consequence, their scenarios for future coal output show a decline to 2025.

There have long been strong social and environmental pressures on Kuzbass coal, with mine explosions leading to a program to close dangerous pits, and atmospheric pollution leading to calls—including from Aman Tuleev, the long-time governor of Kemerovo region—for a moratorium on granting new mining licences.[12] Tuleev, however, was replaced in April 2018 by Sergei Tsivilev, a mine owner from outside the region, while scepticism was warranted given the new owner, limited mining activity stemmed more from production issues in the Kuzbass coal zone.

# Russian Far East

The situation in the RFE is examined by region.

## Sakhalin

Table 7.4 shows significant increases in output and exports from a low base since 2012. Over the period, an increasing share of output has been exported, to virtually 100 per cent, a consequence of the gasification of the domestic regional market. In 2017, the main destinations for Sakhalin coal were South Korea (3.432 mmt), China (1.979 mmt) and Philippines (807 tmt).[13] (Table 7.5 shows Russia's export markets more generally.) Beyond a vague claim in 2017 by then governor Kozhemiako that exports could reach 20 mmt/y sometime in the future, no recent estimates of future regional output or exports have been found.[14]

11    L. S. Plakitkina and Iu. A. Plakitkin, 'Novye tsenarii razvitiia ekonomiki Rossii: aktualizirovannye prognozy razvitiia dobychi uglia v period do 2025 goda' [New scenarios for the development of the Russian economy: Updated forecasts for the development of coal mining in the period up to 2025], *Ugol'* (2018): 66–71, doi.org/10.18796/0041-5790-2018-5-66-71.

12    Igor' Lavrenkov, Tat'iana Kosacheva and Anatolii Dzhumailo, 'Kuzbass prikroet dostup v nedra' [Kuzbass will cover access to raw materials], *Kommersant*, 18 December 2017.

13    'Coal Industry', Governor and Government of the Sakhalin Region, accessed 24 August 2020, sakhalin.gov.ru/index.php?id=162.

14    'The Governor of Sakhalin Expects an Increase in Investment in the Coal Industry', Union State, 9 April 2017, ria.ru/20170904/1501704458.html.

**Table 7.4: Output and exports from Sakhalin (mmt)**

|        | 2012 | 2016 | 2017 | 2018 |
|--------|------|------|------|------|
| Output | 4.1  | 6.97 | 7.65 | 10.8 |
| Exports| 1.92 | 4.65 | 7.53 | 10   |

Source: 'Coal Industry', Governor and Government of the Sakhalin Region, accessed 24 August 2020, sakhalin.gov.ru/index.php?id=162; 'Vneshnetorgovyy oborot Sakhalinskoy oblasti v 2012 godu sostavil 17,8 mlrd' [The foreign trade turnover of the Sakhalin region in 2012 amounted to $ 17.8 billion], Sakhalin.Biznes, 1 April 2013, sakhalin.biz/en/news/finance/82458.

**Table 7.5: Russian coal export destinations, 2018, top five worldwide and other Asian destinations (mmt)**

| Rank | Destination | Deliveries 2018 | % change on 2017 |
|------|-------------|-----------------|-------------------|
| 1 | South Korea | 29.182 | +11.7 |
| 2 | China | 27.591 | +7.6 |
| 3 | Japan | 18.277 | +3.9 |
| 4 | Ukraine | 14.206 | +53.2 |
| 5 | Germany | 13.835 | +42.1 |
| 9 | Taiwan | 9.308 | +6.1 |
| 11 | India | 4.492 | +24.8 |
| 15 | Malaysia | 3.134 | +2.3 |
| 17 | Vietnam | 2.649 | +15.3 |
| 26 | Hong Kong | 1.161 | -2.3 |
| 27 | Philippines | 1.063 | +8.9 |
| 28 | Thailand | 0.970 | −30.9 |

Source: Igor' Gennadievich Tarazanov, 'Itogi raboty ugol'noi promyshlennosti Rossii za ianvar'-dekabr' 2018 goda' [Results of the work of the coal industry in Russia for January–December 2018], *Ugol'* 3 (2019): 76, doi.org/10.18796/0041-5790-2019-3-64-79.

The dominant producer is VGK (Vostochnaia gornorudnaia kompaniia), which, according to some sources, has squeezed out other producers through its influence over the licensing process.[15] It operates the Solntsevskii and Boshniakovskii open-cut mines.[16] Solntsevskii produced 7.51 mmt in 2018 of which it exported 7.47 mmt, an increase of

---

15 'Misevra Can Get More Boshnyakovsky Coal', *Business Newspaper*, 5 December 2016, biznes-gazeta.ru/?id=location.view&obj=d1b0855b88ac30e0c6855d800550691e.
16 VGK's ownership of the latter is claimed in 'Misevra Can Get More Boshnyakovsky Coal', but confirmation has not been found.

55.1 per cent on 2017.[17] Boshniakovskii produced 901,000 metric tons in 2017 and 880,300 metric tons in 2018. Export figures have not been found. Claimed maximum capacity of the mine is 1 mmt/y for 10 years.[18] VGK wants to reach 10–12 mmt/y peak capacity for the two mines combined.[19]

The only other Sakhalin miner of any note is Gorniak-1, based in Nevel'sk. One source claims that it exported nearly 800,000 metric tons (of 1.367 mmt dug) in 2017, up significantly from 138,000 metric tons in 2015 and 293,000 metric tons in 2016. Peak output is put at 3 mmt.[20] Another source states Gorniak-1 exported 1.36 mmt in 2018, down 1.7 per cent on the 2017 figure.[21]

None of Sakhalin's ports are deepwater, meaning that coal is loaded by lighter into carriers standing offshore, seriously increasing shipping costs. There has been talk of building a 10 mmt/y deepwater terminal at the current port of Shakhtersk, as well as a deepwater port in the south of the island, at Il'inskoe.[22] The fate of the latter is tied to the recurring grand scheme of building a bridge to Sakhalin from the mainland. As will be discussed further below, the bridge would mainly carry coal from the mainland through Sakhalin and on to APR markets. The new port would at the same time improve logistics for Sakhalin miners, although in the end their output potential and ambitions are so limited that improved logistics will not turn them into major exporters.

## Khabarovsk

The only producer in the Khabarovsk region is Urgalugol', owned by the Kuzbass giant SUEK. As Table 7.6 shows, the company steadily increased output until 2017, with a decline in 2018. Throughout, it has consistently

---

17   Igor' Gennadievich Tarazanov, 'Itogi raboty ugol'noi promyshlennosti Rossii za ianvar'-dekabr' 2018 goda' [Results of the work of the coal industry in Russia for January–December 2018], *Ugol'* 3 (2019): 64–79, 76, doi.org/10.18796/0041-5790-2019-3-64-79.

18   'Boshnyakovsky Coal Mine was the First to Receive the Status of a Regional Investment Project', Sakhalin.Info, 22 June 2017, sakhalin.info/news/134516.

19   Anatolii Dzhumailo, 'VGK aktiviziruet ugol' [VGK is activating coal], *Kommersant*, 3 September 2015.

20   Natalia Golubkova, 'General Director of LLC "Gornyak-1": Russian Railways Policy Does Not Meet the Requirements of the State and Business', Sakhalin.Info, 13 April 2008, sakhalin.info/news/150205.

21   Tarazanov, 'Itogi raboty ugol'noi promyshlennosti', 76.

22   Dzhumailo, 'VGK aktiviziruet ugol'.

been unable to meet targets. The difficulty appears to be exhaustion of existing deposits and delays in scaling up the new Pravoberezhnaia open-cut mine (the company mines both open-cut and underground: the 2015 output was divided into 2.43 mmt open-cut and 3.167 mmt underground). The new mine, which opened in November 2017, is designed to reach a maximum capacity of 3 mmt/y in 2021.[23] The company's coal is of poor quality and requires enrichment in a plant that cost ₽7 billion.[24] The company has a major market in the domestic power generation sector; in 2013, it exported 2.937 of 4.639 mmt of output.[25] More recent export data have not been found, but predicted peak exports are put at 15 mmt/y.[26] That would require a very substantial increase in output—the company CEO sees 10 mmt/y as the output target for the near future.[27]

**Table 7.6: Output of Urgalugol', forecast and actual (mmt)**

|          | 2004 | 2010 | 2013 | 2015 | 2016 | 2017 | 2018 | 2019 |
|----------|------|------|------|------|------|------|------|------|
| Forecast | N/A  | 5.6  | N/A  | N/A  | 9.1  | N/A  | 8    | 8.1  |
| Actual   | 2.6  | 2.7  | 4.64 | 5.6  | 6.6  | 6.5  | 6.14 | N/A  |

Source: 'Urgalugol Will Work for the Export of Electricity', *Kommersant*, 22 March 2007, kommersant.ru/doc/752351; Stephen Fortescue, 'Russia's Economic Prospects in the Asia-Pacific Region', *Journal of Eurasian Studies* 7, 1 (2016): 49–59, 55, doi.org/10.1016/j.euras.2015.10.005; 'On Supplementing the List of Investment Projects Planned for Implementation in the Far East', Russian Government, 5 September 2017, government.ru/docs/29123/; V. B. Artem'ev, 'SUEK—itogi 2017 goda' [SUEK—results of 2017], *Ugol'* 3 (2018): 4–13, 13, doi.org/10.18796/0041-5790-2018-3-4-13; Igor' Gennadievich Tarazanov, 'Itogi raboty ugol'noi promyshlennosti Rossii za ianvar'-dekabr' 2018 goda' [Results of the work of the coal industry in Russia for January–December 2018], *Ugol'* 3 (2019): 66, doi.org/10.18796/0041-5790-2019-3-64-79.

---

23   V. B. Artem'ev, 'SUEK—itogi 2017 goda' [SUEK—results of 2017], *Ugol'* 3 (2018): 4–13, 11, doi.org/10.18796/0041-5790-2018-3-4-13.

24   Irina Sergeeva, 'Prostaia arifmetika AO "Uralugol"' [Simple arithmetic of JSC 'Urgalugol'], *DV Kapital*, 18 December 2018, dvkapital.ru/companies/khabarovskij-kraj_18.12.2018_13748_prostaja-arifmetika-ao-urgalugol.html.

25   Stephen Fortescue, 'Russia's Economic Prospects in the Asia-Pacific Region', *Journal of Eurasian Studies* 7, 1 (2016): 49–59, 55, doi.org/10.1016/j.euras.2015.10.005.

26   'The Working Settlement of Chegdomyn Is the "Heart" of the Coal Mining Industry of the Khabarovsk Territory', Ministry of Economic Development of the Khabarovsk Territory, 25 February 2018, minec.khabkrai.ru/events/Novosti/2975.

27   Sergeeva, 'Prostaia arifmetika AO "Uralugol"'.

## Primor'e and Amur

The major coal companies in the Primor'e and Amur regions, Primorskugol' and Amurugol', traditionally produced almost exclusively for the domestic power generation market. The former produced 3.6 mmt and the latter 3.53 mmt in 2018.[28] Primorskugol' began exporting in 2016 and, in 2017, exported 467,800 metric tons.[29] No export data on Amurugol' are available. A new field in the Amur region, at Sugodinsko-Ogodzhina, started production in 2020 with an output of 10 mmt/y to be reached by 2022, and a maximum capacity of 20 mt/y.[30] The project is owned by Dmitrii Bosov, of whom we will hear more below. There are occasional references to a Chinese-connected venture, Primor'e-Suchan-ugol', with plans to revive the closed mine at Partizansk (expected annual output of 500,000 metric tons, with reserves of 15 mmt).[31]

## Northern RFE

There is talk of greenfield projects in Magadan and Kamchatka.[32] But it is in even more remote Chukotka that actual mining activity can be found. The Beringovskii mine is on the Pacific coast of Chukotka; its core shareholder is the Australian Tigers Realm Coal Company, with a 14.4 per cent investment by the Russian Direct Investment Fund. It is a coking coalmine, unlike the thermal coalmines further south. The first coal was mined in January 2017, with 217,400 metric tons dug that year. From January to October 2018, 433,150 metric tons were dug. Early shipments were to domestic ports along the coast, with the first export shipment being 100,000 metric tons to China. In 2017–18, 259,000 metric tons

---

28  Tarazanov, 'Itogi raboty ugol'noi promyshlennosti', 66.
29  Kompaniia, 'Primorskugol'' v iubileinyi god professional'nogo prazdnika Den' shakhtera: 70 let radi sveta i tepla!' [Primorskugol' in the jubilee year of the industry holiday miner's day: 70 years producing light and warmth!], *Ugol'*, 3 (2018): 21–26, 22.
30  'Sugodinsko-Ogodzhinskoe Field: The Largest Coal Deposit in the Far East Region', Vostok Coal, accessed 1 April 2021, vostokcoal.ru/assets/sugodinsko-ogodginskoe-mestorozhdenie/.
31  'A Free Port Resident Will Create a Coal Cluster in Primorye with Investments of 4 Billion Rubles', TASS, accessed 24 August 2020, tass.ru/vef-2017/articles/4544606.
32  'CJSC North-Eastern Coal Company', EMCO, accessed 24 August 2020, eastmining.ru/pred priiatiia/severo-vostochnaia-ugol-naia-kompaniia/; Nicholas Trickett, 'Is Russia's Asia Outreach Bearing Fruit?', *Diplomat*, 6 April 2017, thediplomat.com/2017/04/is-russias-asia-outreach-bearing-fruit/.

were exported.[33] Port facilities are extremely primitive,[34] but there are plans for modernisation to take capacity to an eventual 10 mmt/y.[35] Even when the port is modernised, it will be closed by ice eight months a year with icebreakers required for some of the summer period.[36]

While RFE coal has shown growth in recent years, forecasts of future growth and exports, particularly at the level of individual producers, are modest—something like 50 mmt/y at peak capacity. Further gasification might allow greater exports of Primorskugol' and Amurskugol' output, but that would not be enough to make RFE a significant contributor to APR exports.[37]

## East Siberia

The figures for East Siberia are also modest. There are established producers: Vostsibugol', owned by Oleg Deripaska's En+, and Yakutugol', owned by the steelmaker Mechel. The former produces thermal coal primarily for the power stations of Deripaska's Irkutsk Energy Company. However it also exports. In 2017, it met its export target of 1.1 mmt and was looking for 2 mmt in 2018.[38] Yakutugol' supplies Mechel's steel plants, but also exports coking coal from the Neriungri area in south Yakutia. The mines are not far from a rail line with a direct link to the Baikal–Amur Mainline (BAM). However, the deposits are depleted, as can be

---

33 A. Ignat'eva and O. Bakhtina, 'Ugol' Chukotki! Dlia morskogo porta Beringovskii razrabotaiut predlozhneiia po sozdaniiu infrastruktury' [Chukotka coal! Proposals for the creation of infrastructure will be developed for the seaport of Beringovsky], Neftegaz.ru, 30 October 2018, neftegaz.ru/news/transport-and-storage/197408-ugol-chukotki-dlya-morskogo-porta-beringovskiy-razrabotayut-predlozheniya-po-sozdaniyu-infrastruktur/.

34 'Beringovsky Commercial Sea Port', Basov-Chukotka, accessed 24 August 2020, basov-chukotka.livejournal.com/384644.html.

35 'On Major Projects for the Development of Transport Infrastructure in the North of Russia', Russian Government, 17 April 2017, government.ru/news/27387/.

36 'During the Navigation Period of 2018, Beringpromugol Plans to Export 500 Thousand Tons of Coal to the Countries of the Asia-Pacific Region', Neftegaz.ru, 23 July 2018, neftegaz.ru/news/coal/199812-v-period-navigatsii-2018-g-beringpromugol-planiruet-eksportirovat-v-strany-aziatsko-tikhookeanskogo/. For an essentially positive Australian analysis of the project, see 'Tigers Realm Coal Ltd on Track at Amaam Coal Operations', Proactive, 10 July 2017, proactiveinvestors.com.au/companies/news/180570/tigers-realm-coal-ltd-on-track-at-amaam-coal-operations-180570.html.

37 Curiously, there were no RFE representatives at a meeting Putin hosted in August 2019 of regional leaders from coal-producing regions, see 'Meeting with Leaders of Coal Mining Regions'.

38 Galina Volynets, 'Vytianuli iz medvezh'ego ugla' [Vostsibugol intends to double coal exports in 2018, using new open-pit mines], Izvestiia, 20 April 2018, interfax-russia.ru/Siberia/special.asp?id=885635&sec=1737interfax-russia.ru/Siberia/special.asp?id=885635&sec=1737.

seen in output and export data. In 2018, output, at 6.985 mmt, was down 16.3 per cent, and exports, at 3.233 mmt, were down 27.9 per cent on 2017.[39]

Mechel has a new coking coalmine in the area, at El'ga. It was due to reach its Stage 1 output target of 11.7 mmt/y in 2017, yet, in 2018, managed only 4.9 mmt, of which 1.74 mmt were exported. Those figures represented increases of 18.6 per cent and 12.4 per cent on the previous year, so at least the trend is upward.[40]

Other East Siberian operations are also in the early stages of development. The Apsat mine, owned by SUEK and producing coking coal, is situated about 50 km from the Novaia Chara station on BAM north-east of Lake Baikal. It was opened in 2012. With a planned capacity of 5 mmt/y by 2021, in 2013 it produced 652,000 metric tons, of which 462,100 metric tons were exported.[41] In 2017, it produced 661,000 metric tons and, in 2018, 619,000 metric tons.[42] The deposit has been described as 'difficult' and clearly there are problems getting it anywhere near planned capacity.

Elegest, in the Tuva region and owned by Ruslan Baisarov's TEPK, has a planned peak output of 15 mmt/y by 2024, and yet, with construction of a spur line not yet begun, no coal has been mined or shipped.[43]

The company Kolmar, which operates in the Neriungri area of Yakutia, is interesting, not least because it is part owned by the well-connected Gennadii Timchenko—not that one would know it from descriptions of its ownership arrangements by company executives. Its current chief beneficial owner and board chair is Anna Tsivileva, the wife of Sergei Tsivilev, a founding and majority shareholder who transferred his interest when he was appointed governor of Kemerovo region.[44] It has two underground operations producing coking coal. The Denisovskii mine was half finished when Kolmar took over in 2003, with plans to invest US$450 million to expand output to 2.4 mmt/y. An enrichment plant was opened in May 2018. The Inaglinskii mine is a greenfield operation, with an original

---

39  Tarazanov, 'Itogi raboty ugol'noi promyshlennosti', 66, 76.
40  Tarazanov, 'Itogi raboty ugol'noi promyshlennosti', 66, 76.
41  Fortescue, 'Russia's Economic Prospects in the Asia-Pacific Region', 55.
42  Tarazanov, 'Itogi raboty ugol'noi promyshlennosti', 66.
43  Volynets, 'Vytianuli iz medvezh'ego ugla'.
44  Anna Tsivileva, 'Osnovnoi benefitsiar 'Kolmar grup': kachestva nashego uglia unikal'ny' [The core beneficiary of Kolmar group: The quality of our coal is unique], *Vedomosti*, 1 November 2018.

target of 6 mmt/y by 2016 and then ultimately 10.5 mmt/y.[45] In practice, in 2016, the company produced across the two mines 3.7 mmt, in 2017 4.5 mmt and in 2018 4.59 mmt (divided 2.768 mmt and 1.821 mmt between Denisovskii and Inaglinskii, respectively). In 2018, 1.635 mmt were exported, an increase of 18.1 per cent on the previous year.[46] In a November 2018 interview, Tsivileva set a target for exports of 60–70 per cent of output.[47] She did not explain the slow progress, but made a virtue of the small scale of operations and exports, noting that the company has more flexibility in serving the needs of fussy steelmakers than Australia's bulk shippers.

Clearly, the East Siberian producers are struggling to hit their targets, as relatively modest as they are. Whether that is a sign of them being unattainable or simply a matter of more time being required is not easy to determine. On the one hand, deposits are routinely described as being difficult geologically and topographically; on the other, there have been funding and economic circumstances causing delays. The projects are owned either by smaller operators with limited access to funding or by bigger operators for whom they do not appear to be a high priority. There is no reason to believe that these circumstances will change.

If it is unlikely that Eastern Siberia and RFE will increase their share of coal exports to the APR, we must return to the implications of the continuing and, indeed, increasing reliance on Kuzbass coal.

The first—that such a circumstance reinforces the dominance of thermal coal in Russian output and exports—can be dealt with relatively quickly. The failure of coking coal to meet Program forecasts can be seen in Table 7.2, as well as the accounts of individual coking coal projects above. Coking coal prices are more than double those for thermal coal, and coking coal is likely to be more resistant to climate change–driven declines in demand.[48] A coal industry so reliant on thermal coal is less profitable and resilient than one with the coking coal presence originally predicted.

45    Fortescue, 'Russia's Economic Prospects in the Asia-Pacific Region', 55.
46    Tarazanov, 'Itogi raboty ugol'noi promyshlennosti', 68.
47    Tsivileva, 'Osnovnoi benefitsiar 'Kolmar grup'.
48    Tarazanov, 'Itogi raboty ugol'noi promyshlennosti', 75.

# Transport

The second implication of the continued reliance on Kuzbass coal—the greater distance of Kuzbass from APR markets compared to East Siberia and RFE—is a more complicated issue. There are three stages in getting Russian coal to APR markets: from mine to main transport corridor, in this case the Trans-Siberian and BAM rail lines; along those two main lines; and then through a port on the RFE coast.[49]

## Spur Lines

Spur lines, which can run several hundred kilometres through very difficult terrain, have been the subject of endless debate and negotiation, at the core of which has been the question of whether they are infrastructure or part of the project. The government has generally taken responsibility for infrastructure, including the not insignificant cost of electricity connections and approach roads to ports. But the government (or sections of it) has baulked at paying for multibillion-rouble spur lines. Mechel went ahead and spent US$2 billion on the 316 km line from its El'ga mine to Ulak on the BAM. When the company hit serious financial difficulties, the fact that it had paid for the line itself was presented as an argument by its supporters for a government bailout (which entailed half the company being sold to Gazprombank). The line remains as a limit on the capacity of the mine, and Mechel is negotiating a funding arrangement with the government to expand it, as well as considering selling out of the project altogether.[50] TEPK hung out for government money for the 410 km, ₽192.4 billion Elegest line. A concession agreement was reached in late

---

49   It should be noted that a significant percentage of coal is exported across a land border—72.4 of 132.5 mmt of exports shipped by rail in 2018. See, Tarazanov, 'Itogi raboty ugol'noi promyshlennosti', 77. Most of this is presumably across European borders, although Zabaikal'sk and for some reason Port Astaf'eva are also listed as land border points (the former is on the Russian–Chinese border east of Mongolia and the latter is a port near Nakhodka). Shipments directly through Zabaikal'sk to China average around 150,000 metric tons a month (e.g. in January 2017, 168,000 metric tons, and February 2019 130,000 metric tons). See, 'Transportation through the Border Crossing Zabaikalsk in January Increased by 13.8%—up to 1.4 Million Tons', TASS, 15 February 2017, tass. ru/transport/4021986; 'FGK Transshipments on the Border with China Doubled', *Logirus*, 25 March 2017, logirus.ru/news/transport/peregruzki_fgk_na_granitse_s_kitaem_vyrosli_vdvoe.html.

50   Ol'ga Adamchuk, Vitalii Petlevoi, Polina Trifonova, "Mechel' ishchet sposob snizit' raskhody na zhelznuiu dorogu do El'ginskogo mestorozhdeniia' [Mechel is looking for a way to cut expenditure on the rail line to the El'ga deposit], *Vedomosti*, 8 October 2018; Vitalii Petlevoi, Ol'ga Adamchuk, Artur Toporkov, Polina Trifonova, 'Mechel mozhet rasstat'sia s glavnym proektom' [Mechel might say goodbye to its main project], *Vedomosti*, 19 February 2019; Vitalii Petlevoi, 'Gazprombank nashel pokupatelia na 49 % v odnom iz krupneishikh ugol'nykh proektov' [Gazprombank has found a buyer for 49% of one of the biggest coal projects], *Vedomosti*, 23 August 2019.

2017, with a large part of the funding to come from bonds issued by Gasprom's assets manager 'Leader' (Lider).[51] In 2020, the project entered an active planning phase with an update provided noting trains would run by 2023.[52]

## Ports

At the other end of the transport chain are coal-loading ports. All the main coal exporters have, or are in the process of building, coal terminals on the RFE seaboard. In an earlier study, I noted that announced expansion plans in the middle of the current decade matched the forecast levels of exports to the APR.[53] But that was when forecast exports in 2030 were 110 mmt/y. The Ministry of Energy's forecast is now 207 mmt/y by 2025. In 2018, Russian Railways estimated that, by 2026, RFE port capacity would stand at 172 mmt/y—50 mmt/y more than required.[54] If the Russian Ministry of Energy is more cautious than coal producers in its forecasts, Russian Railways is even more so, as it struggles to serve the needs of producers. Coal and coke exports through RFE ports increased steadily from zero in 2006 to 42 mmt in 2011 and 82 mmt in 2016.[55] Russian Railways data show shipments through RFE ports of coal alone of 61.93 mmt in 2015, 63.99 mmt in 2016, 70.96 mmt in 2017 and 73.38 mmt in 2018.[56]

Turning to individual ports, SUEK has a terminal at Vanino, east of Khabarovsk. In 2017, it shipped around 20 mmt, with its most recent plan to ship 40 mmt/y by 2024.[57] Pos'et, south of Vladivostok, is owned by Mechel. It had a capacity of 4.5 mmt/y in 2015; in 2016, it shipped

51    Natal'ia Skorlygina, 'Dobycha uglia pod garantii biudzheta' [Coal output guaranteed by the budget], *Kommersant*, 19 April 2018.
52    Railfreight, 'This is Russia's most ambitious railway project: Line to Siberia', 17 March 2020, www.railfreight.com/railfreight/2020/03/17/this-is-russias-most-ambitious-railway-project-line-to-siberia/.
53    Fortescue, 'Russia's Economic Prospects in the Asia-Pacific Region', 57.
54    Natal'ia Skorlygina, Dmitrii Kozlov, Anastasiia Vedeneeva, 'BAM vyezhaet na ugle' [BAM lives on coal], *Kommersant*, 15 August 2018.
55    Dar'ia Beloglasova, 'Dal'nevostochnye porty pochti vosstanovili gruzooborot posle krizisa' [Far Eastern ports have nearly restored throughput after the crisis], Vedomosti, 5 September 2017.
56    Igor' Gennadievich Tarazanov, 'Itogi raboty ugol'noi promyshlennosti Rossii za ianvar'-dekabr' 2016 goda' [The results of the work of the coal industry in Russia for January–December 2016], *Ugol'* 3 (2017): 36–50, 48, doi.org/10.18796/0041-5790-2017-3-36-50; Tarazanov, 'Itogi raboty ugol'noi promyshlennosti', 76.
57    'JSC "Daltransugol": 150 Million by Sea in 15 Years', Armur Media, 14 May 2019, amurmedia. ru/news/812204.

7 mmt and, in 2018, 9 mmt, with expansion plans to 12 mmt/y.[58] Nakhodka-Vostochnyi, owned by Kuzbassrazrezugol', shipped 22.8 mmt in 2015 and 24.2 mmt in 2018.[59] A third terminal was built to take capacity to 39 mmt/y by 2020.[60] The Sakhalin port at Shakhtersk and Port Beringovskii in Chukotka have already been mentioned.

Coal ports under development include Kolmar's Vaninotransugol' terminal at Vanino. Construction began in June 2017, with the original plan to have a capacity of 12 mmt/y by 2019 and 24 mmt/y by 2021.[61] The latter target was later moved out to 2024, and it was only in August 2018 that tenders were called for infrastructure for the first stage.[62] Construction of SDS's Sukhodol loader across the Ussuri Bay from Vladivostok began in mid-2018, with plans to operate at 20 mmt/y by 2021–22.[63] Dmitrii Bosov's Vostokugol' has two port projects underway. The first, Port Vera in Primor'e region, is to have a capacity of 20 mmt/y by 2022.[64] In 2019, the company was fined by the environmental protection agency for operating the incomplete terminal without measures to control coal dust.[65] The other, the Sever terminal at Vostochnyi near Nakhodka, was originally begun by the conglomerate Summa, but ownership was transferred in mid-2019 after Summa's owners were arrested. The planned capacity is 20 mmt/y by 2025.[66]

58   'Site Map', Mechel, accessed 24 August 2020, mechel.ru/sector/logistics/poset.
59   Anastasiia Vedeneeva and Anatolii Dzhumailo, 'Na Dal'nem Vostoke zhdut ugol'', *Kommersant*, 17 August 2016; '"Vostochny Port" Increased the Volume of Coal Transshipment in 2018 by 4.3%', Regnum, 11 January 2019, regnum.ru/news/2550586.html.
60   'The Third Stage of the Specialized Coal Production and Transfer Complex', Vostport, accessed 24 August 2020, vostport.ru/business/third-stage/.
61   '"Kolmar" Will Buy Gondola Cars for 6 Billion Rubles for the Transport "Daughter"', TASS, accessed 24 August 2020, tass.ru/pmef-2018/articles/5227384.
62   'Rosmorport Is Again Looking for a Contractor for the Port Infrastructure, Where Kolmar Is Building a Coal Terminal', Y2K24, 30 August 2018, www.bairdmaritime.com/ship-world/port-world/rosmorport-wraps-up-phase-one-of-construction-at-vanino-coal-export-terminal/.
63   'Port "Sukhodol" in Primorye Will Build a Closed Terminal for Transshipment of Coal', PrimaMedia, 14 June 2018, primamedia.ru/news/703049/.
64   'Port Vera', VostokUgol, accessed 3 September 2020, vostokcoal.ru/assets/porte-vera/.
65   'Rosprirodnadzor Found Violations in the Coal Port under Construction in Podyapolsky', VL.RU. News, 4 March 2019, newsvl.ru/society/2019/03/04/178651/. Coal dust pollution at RFE loaders has become a major issue, raised even with Putin at his 2017 'Direct Line' with the public. See, Anastasiia Vedeneeva and Natal'ia Skorlygina, 'S shumom i s pyl'iu' [Noise and dust], *Kommersant*, 6 July 2017.
66   Dmitrii Dzhumailo, '"Rostekh" nashel zamenu Kitaiu' ['Rostekh' found replacement for China], *Kommersant*, 30 July 2018; Anastasiia Vedeneeva, 'Plius utilizatsiia vsei strany' [Recycling the whole country], *Kommersant*, 19 August 2019.

We see steadily increasing capacity at established ports. They handle primarily Kuzbass coal. Progress at new ports being built for new mines in East Siberia has been slower. The projected capacity of the three major established ports—Vanino, Pos'et and Nakhodka-Vostochnyi—is 92 mmt/y. The maximum projected capacity of the startup ports—Kolmar (24 mmt), Sukhodol (20 mmt), Vera (20 mmt) and Sever (20 mmt)—is 84 mmt/y. The two combined is 176 mmt, almost precisely the 172 identified by Russian Railways above (even if the company believes 50 mmt/y will be excess to requirements). It is, however, short of Novak's expectation that 207 mmt will be exported to the APR by then.

## Trans-Siberian/BAM

While spur lines and ports are not without their issues, most focus has been on problems with the middle link in the chain—mainline rail capacity for the long haul from Kuzbass to the RFE seaboard. As indicated in Table 7.7, it is 5,500 km from Kuzbass to Vanino and 6,100 km to Primor'e ports. Note that the average distance from an Australian coalmine to port is 206 km.[67]

**Table 7.7: Distances from coal-producing regions to Shanghai ('000 km)**

| Route | Distance |
|---|---|
| Newcastle–Shanghai | 9,500 |
| Mezhdurechensk (Kuzbass)–Vanino | 5,500 |
| Mezhdurechensk–Primor'e | 6,100 |
| Neriungri–Vanino | 2,100 |
| Vanino–Shanghai | 3,000 |
| Primor'e–Shanghai | 2,000 |

The expansion of mainline capacity was vigorously debated in the middle years of the decade, with the economic ministries and the RFE policy block fighting against the coalminers and Russian Railways. The economic block did not want to spend the money and expressed scepticism over projected load projections; the RFE policy block wanted the money spent on manufacturing and hi-tech development in the RFE, not a resource-oriented policy in which the RFE was no more than a transit point. Russian

---

67  National Energy Resources Australia (NERA), *Coal Industry Competitiveness Assessment*, December 2016, 17, www.nera.org.au/Publications-and-insights/Attachment?Action=Download&Attachment_id=150.

Railways, although a supporter of expansion, was very wary about taking on commitments it could not afford.[68] The coalminers won. To make sense of the expansion figures bandied about is extremely difficult, and what follows is a very simplified summary.

After considerable discussion about how much capacity should be added, a figure of 66 mmt/y was agreed upon, from a base figure of around 90 mmt/y and at a cost of ₽562 billion (around US$13.5 billion at the then exchange rate).[69] Russian Railways was confident that the program could be completed on schedule in 2020, although some commentators were sceptical.[70] Almost as soon as the initial expansion plan got underway there was talk of a second stage, again with extensive discussion of what the target capacity should be. It was eventually decided that a further 55 mmt/y would be added at a cost of ₽622 billion (around US$10.4 billion when the amount was announced, in October 2017). In the obscure wording of Russian Railways' long-term development plan, the money would be spent on:

> Increasing the transit and carrying capacity of the shipment infrastructure of the Kuzbass, BAM and Trans-Siberian mainlines in order to achieve the forecast level of loads by 2025, including achieving a transit capacity of BAM and the Trans-Siberian mainlines of 180 mt by 2024 and ensuring shipments in the eastern direction of 210 mt by 2025.[71]

It is not stated that these capacities are specifically for coal; however, in August 2018, Novak referred to the second expansion program as adding 180 mmt/y specifically for coal, and then declared that a further increase had been negotiated, to 210 mmt/y eastwards by 2025, of which 195 mmt would be coal.[72] Clearly, the expectation is that coal will make up a very

---

68    Stephen Fortescue, 'Russia's "Turn to the East": A Study in Policy Making', *Post-Soviet Affairs* 32, no. 5 (2016) 423–54, 436–39, doi.org/10.1080/1060586X.2015.1051750; Fortescue, 'Russia's Economic Prospects in the Asia-Pacific Region', 57–58.

69    Fortescue, 'Russia's Economic Prospects in the Asia-Pacific Region', 57.

70    Natal'ia Skorlygina, 'Nad BAMom sgushchaiutsia uchastki' [The sections are gathering over BAM], *Kommersant*, 16 July 2019.

71    'Dolgosrochnaia programma razvitiia otkrytogo aktsionernogo obshchestva "Rossiiskie zhelznye dorogi" do 2025 goda' [Long-term program for the development of the limited liability company Russian railways to 2025], approved by government decree no. 466-r, 19 March 2019, Appendix 8, 10–11.

72    'Meeting of the Commission on the Development Strategy of the Fuel and Energy Complex and Environmental Safety'.

large proportion of the eastward movement of freight. There are claims that the figures are way short of what coalminers will need, matched by counterclaims that the coalminers' estimates are exaggerated.[73]

Given the importance of Kuzbass coal to APR export targets, it is not only Trans-Siberian/BAM capacity that is a restraint. The coal has to get to the mainline in the first place. For that reason, considerable attention has been paid to the capacity of the rail line from Kuzbass to the main lines at Taishet. In Russian Railways' long-term program, ₽70.58 billion is allocated to expanding the capacity of that line (with at least ₽37 billion having already been allocated).

The significance of the rail capacity issue was brought home in 2018–19, when, as prices fell in the West but remained steady in the East, miners sought to push ever more coal eastwards. Russian Railways was not able to handle the load. It issued warnings that it could offer only a 1.2 per cent increase in shipments in 2019, when the 2018 figure was down on 2017 because of delays caused by weather and trackwork.[74]

Promises are regularly made that the situation will improve after 2020. The commitment is there and progress is being made. But rail capacity appears likely to remain a serious restraint on expansion of coal exports to the APR, particularly as long as the major source of supply is Kuzbass. If East Siberian mines eventually contribute their hoped-for supply, that would also entail pressure on the network, albeit over shorter distances.

The issue is serious enough that alternatives have been sought. In 2018–19, Russian Railways encouraged miners to increase shipments westwards, including through offering discounts on Western routes.[75] It was even suggested that the Asian price premium was such that shipping from Kuzbass through European ports and by sea to the Pacific would still be profitable.[76] The mining companies were not impressed, and wanted offsetting guarantees of access eastwards.[77]

---

73    Skorlygina and Dzhumailo, 'Velikii ugol'nyi put'.

74    Natal'ia Skorlygina, 'Ugol' bol'she ne gruzit" [No more threat from coal], *Kommersant*, 23 January 2019; Tarazanov, 'Itogi raboty ugol'noi promyshlennosti', 76.

75    Skorlygina, 'Ugol' bol'she ne gruzit".

76    Evgenii Zainullin, 'Ugol'shchiki snizhaiut dobychu planov' [Coal miners reduce plan output], *Kommersant*, 24 June 2019.

77    Natal'ia Skorlygina and Evgenii Zainullin, 'Zheleznye dorogi ishchut garanta' [Railways looking for a guarantee], *Kommersant*, 18 July 2019.

A particularly imaginative approach to the Western solution has been proposed by Dmitrii Bosov—to develop coal deposits in the Taimyr region and ship them from a coal terminal at the Arctic port of Dikson. Theoretically, with the expected opening of the Northern Sea Route (NSR) for regular commercial shipping, deliveries eastwards should be possible. However, distance (Dikson is much closer to Murmansk than it is to the Pacific), to say nothing of remaining ice problems, make eastwards deliveries an unlikely commercial proposition. With a claimed output of 23 mmt/y, the project is being pushed in terms of its contribution to Putin's goal of having 80 mmt/y of traffic along the NSR by 2024.[78] On that basis, it has been included in the Ministry of Transport's draft plan for the NSR and dredging work commissioned.[79]

There are more straightforward approaches to alleviating the rail bottleneck problem. One is the Severomuissk tunnel, to the north-east of Lake Baikal. Russian Railways is clearly not enthusiastic about dealing with the bottleneck there by building a second tunnel. It claims that it would cost ₽261 billion, take 10 years to build, and could not be begun before 2025. Bosov has stepped forward to claim that he can build it for ₽45–51 billion and complete it in five years. His spokesperson has said that all the preparatory work has been done and construction can start immediately to take the capacity of the tunnel from 16 mmt/y to 100 mmt/y. In return for building it, Bosov wants priority access.[80] In August 2019, there were reports that Russian Railways was proposing rule changes to allow priority access to customers who had invested in increasing capacity, which could well be a response to Bosov's proposal. Opposition to such a rule change is likely to be fierce.[81] Experts claim the money would be better spent on more straightforward improvements to the current tunnel and other bottlenecks along the main lines.[82]

---

78    Anastasiia Vedeneeva, 'Shire Sevmorput' [Wider than the North Sea route], *Kommersant*, 10 April 2019.

79    'Decisions Following the Meeting on the Development of the Arctic', Russian Government, 19 December 2019, government.ru/orders/selection/401/35123/. Kuzbass coal companies are also backing a proposal to build a coal loader at Indiga on the Arctic Ocean in the Nenetsk Autonomous Region. Like Dikson, Indiga is much closer to Murmansk than the APR. See, Anatolii Dzhumailo and Anastasiia Vedeneeva, 'Pravitel'stvu podkinuli uglia' [Government left holding the coal], *Kommersant*, 28 November 2018.

80    Vitalii Petlevoi, Artur Toporkov and Ol'ga Adamchuk, 'Bosov prosit u Putina prioritet k BAMu i Transsibu' [Bosov asks Putin for priority access to BAM and Transsib], *Vedomosti*, 25 March 2019.

81    Natal'ia Skorlygina, 'Po zheleznym dorogam rasstaviat prioritety' [Priorities on the railways to be allocated], *Kommersant*, 2 August 2019.

82    Natal'ia Skorlygina and Anatolii Dzhumailo, 'Bilet v tonnel' okazalsia dorog' [Tunnel ticket turns out expensive], *Kommersant*, 26 November 2018; Natal'ia Skorlygina and Anastasiia Vedeneeva, 'Sibantratsit voobrazil sebe tonnel' [Sibantratsit dreamt up a tunnel], Kommersant, 23 April 2019.

Another approach is to use heavier trains, with more powerful locomotives and heavier wagons. In the early debate over the Trans-Siberian/BAM expansion program, the use of more powerful locomotives came to be seen as a way of increasing capacity from the extra 66 mmt/y that work on the line itself could provide to 75 mmt/y. Appropriate funding allocations have been made, although there are difficulties in obtaining locomotives even when funding is available.[83]

Russian Railways has long pursued a program of introducing larger wagons. The standard Russian coal wagon has an axle weight of 23.5 metric tons (the US moved some time ago to 32.4 metric tons; Australia's standard is 37.5 metric tons, with 45 metric tons wagons used on some lines). Twenty-five metric ton wagons were introduced in 2013 and in early 2018 there were 100,000 of them (of a total park of over half a million gondola wagons). There was also talk of moving to 27 metric tons wagons; however, it was recognised that that would require massive upgrades to lines and bridges, and it was decided not to proceed (beyond the short dedicated line from the Urgalugol' mine to Vanino).[84] Even the 25 metric ton wagons can be received only at Nakhodka and Vanino ports. Nevertheless, in 2017 Russian Railways ran 5,800 trains over 8,000 metric tons, up from 800 in 2016. It is claimed that that added 1 mmt to the capacity of the Trans-Siberian in that year (the 25 metric ton wagons operate only on the Trans-Siberian).[85] That is hardly a game-breaking improvement.

The Sakhalin bridge has already been mentioned. It would remove some coal—the figure 46.9 mmt/y is given—from the eastern extremities of BAM, at Selikhin station near Komsomol'sk-na-Amure.[86] But this would be useful only if the proposed deepwater port were built at Il'inskoe, 430 km south of the bridge. A 452 km line from Selikhin to the bridge, and another of 127 km from the bridge to the existing line at Nysh would also be required. While the bridge is of no value to Sakhalin coalminers,

83    Natal'ia Skorlygina, 'BAMu povyshaet lokomotovizatsii' [More locomotivisation for BAM], *Kommersant*, 3 September 2019.
84    Vladimir Shtanov, 'U nas beskonechnye zapasy uglia i vysokii spros za predelami Rossii' [We have limitless coal reserves and high levels of demand beyond Russia's borders], *Vedomosti*, 20 March 2018.
85    'Vagony novogo pokoleniia poddeerzhivaiut rossiiskoi eksport uglia' [New-generation wagons supporting Russia's coal exports], *Ugol'* 5 (2018): 94–95.
86    Natal'ia Skorlygina and Anastasiia Vedeneeva, 'Poluostrov Sakhalin' [Peninsula Sakhalin], *Kommersant*, 16 May 2018.

the port would certainly improve their access to APR markets. Yet, at a cost of ₽253 billion for the bridge and ₽540 billion for the rail lines (US$4 and US$8.6 billion, respectively), it appears that after a burst of interest the bridge will not be built.[87]

## Is it a Good Deal?

Over the last five or so years, Russia has become a significant exporter of coal to the APR and, in doing so, has surpassed even its own expectations. That has encouraged it to set more ambitious targets for the future. Setting aside demand issues, whether those targets will be met depends, on the output side, on whether Kuzbass coal output will continue to grow to make up for shortfalls in forecast supply from new mines in East Siberia and the RFE, assuming those shortfalls are more than temporary startup problems. On the delivery side, questions remain about whether the rail network and ports can cope. Kuzbass coal is like West Siberian oil—one heeds predictions of its imminent demise at one's peril. Ports can probably be expanded as needed; the rail network issues appear less susceptible to blind optimism.

Nevertheless, we can expect significant and increasing amounts of coal to pass through RFE ports. Is it a good deal for Russia? Will the industry make a profit? Will the state get a return on its investment?

The coal industry is totally private, and its private owners are prepared to invest. It is claimed that, from 2010 to 2016, ₽550 billion was invested, 70–80 per cent of which was their own funds, with the expectation

---

87   Andrei Zlobin, 'Stroika i geopolitika. Most na Sakhalin oboidetsia v 3,5 raza dorozhe Krymskogo' [Construction and geopolitics. The bridge to Sakhalin will cost 3.5 times more than the Crimean one], Forbes.ru, 16 May 2018, forbes.ru/biznes/361475-stroyka-i-geopolitika-most-na-sahalin-oboydetsya-v-35-raza-dorozhe-krymskogo. Brief mention is made here of another outlet for Russian coal to the APR, through North Korea. There is a rail line from Khasan on the Russian side of the border to the North Korean port of Rason. At the end of 2013 it was rebuilt at a cost of US$250 million. Depending on the political/diplomatic situation, including the willingness of the Chinese to take coal from North Korea, small shipments are carried on the line—2.5 mmt in 2017. The Russian supplier of that coal has not been identified, but it is said that the unprofitable shipment was made because of pressure from above. See, Natal'ia Skorlygina and Anatolii Dzhumailo, 'Kitai otkryl dorogu ugliu iz Rossii' [China has opened a road for coal from Russia], Kommersant, 6 September 2018.

that they would need to spend two to three times more in the future.[88] Novak said in August 2018 that ₽1 trillion of private investment would be needed to reach output of 560 mmt/y.[89] The coal companies were expected to provide the great bulk of the investment in the 2030 Program, ₽5,014.57 billion, with the federal budget providing ₽281.81 billion (US$133 billion and US$7.5 billion at the mid-2014 exchange rate). The willingness to invest such sums of private capital represents a serious vote of confidence in the APR export strategy, although it is noteworthy that there is very little investment from outside, including from China and the rest of the APR.

While the sector shows dynamism and ambition, there are signs of stress. Sibuglemet went bankrupt and is being managed by the state investment bank VEB.[90] Mechel very nearly followed, with Gazprombank taking half the company's shares in return for restructuring its debts. The company still struggles.[91] There are high levels of indebtedness throughout the sector,[92] and the most dynamic people in the industry, such as Dmitrii Bosov, come across more as adventurers than the builders of businesses.[93]

While government budgetary funding is low compared to the level of private investment, the pressure for increased infrastructure spending is relentless, with spur lines increasingly being accepted as an infrastructure cost for which the state will accept responsibility. One strongly suspects that the bulk of the companies' indebtedness is to state banks, although Mechel's experience reminds us that, while ultimately soft, the loans are not without cost. As a more direct cost to the state, the companies are increasingly offered significant tax concessions, with RFE ports and East Siberian and RFE mines being included in 'Vladivostok free port' and Territories for Accelerated Development (the latter were originally

---

88    O. I. Glinina, 'Ugol'naia promyshlennost' v Rossii: 295 let istorii i vozmozhnosti' [The coal industry in Russia: 295 years of history and new opportunities], *Ugol'* 10 (2017): 4–10, 6, doi.org/10.18796/0041-5790-2017-10-4-10.

89    'Meeting of the Commission on the Development Strategy of the Fuel and Energy Complex and Environmental Safety'.

90    'Bankruptcy Is Not Death Forever, it's Just a Change of Ownership', 1Prime.Ru, 14 June 2019, 1prime.ru/finance/20190614/830071557.html.

91    Petlevoi, 'Gazprombank nashel pokupatelia na 49 %'.

92    'On the State and Prospects of Development of the Coal Industry', Russian Government, 4 April 2016, government.ru/news/22437/, see comments by Sokolov.

93    On Bosov's debts and the lack of profitability of his company, Petlevoi, Toporkov and Adamchuk, 'Bosov prosit u Putina prioritet k BAMu i Transsibu'.

devised explicitly to encourage investment in non-resource projects).[94] In August 2019, there were calls for cuts in the resources tax, despite coal companies' resources tax payments already being very small.[95]

Costs are high because of the standard Russian factors of climate, distance and geology. Russian coal deposits are almost invariably described as 'difficult' and high levels of enrichment are required.[96] Ice acts as a constraint on both mining and transport. Rail wagons and ports have to be equipped to handle frozen coal: in January 2018, all shipments of coal were halted when it was too cold to dig and transport it.[97] Topographically, roads and railway lines have to be laid and power delivered in extremely challenging terrain. But, above all, coal has to be shipped, usually by rail, over extremely long distances. This applies particularly to coal coming from Kuzbass to APR destinations.

Costs are high both for capital investment and operations. The Trans-Siberian/BAM upgrade is more expensive than Russian Railways projects in other parts of the country; the second stage—in nominal terms at least—is more expensive than the first and, arguably, it is all less cost-effective than equivalent infrastructure expansions elsewhere.[98] The El'ga and Elegest spur lines, at around US$2 and US$3.3 billion for 316 and 410 km, respectively, are more expensive than the 388 km rail line originally planned for the controversial Adani mine in Queensland at A$2.3 billion.[99]

By their nature, the benefits of infrastructure investment can be slow in coming. The Australian coal sector experienced a big surge in transport costs because of high capital expenditure, peaking in 2012, followed by a steady decline at a time when output was rising.[100] Russia might

---

94   'On Decisions Following the Meeting on the State and Prospects of Development of the Coal Industry', Russian Government, 12 April 2016, government.ru/orders/22567/. See also Fortescue, 'Russia's "Turn to the East": A Study in Policy Making'.

95   Evgenii Zainullin, 'Ugliu mogut snizit' nalogi' [They might reduce taxes for coal], *Kommersant*, 26 August 2019.

96   For levels of enrichment, see Tarazanov, 'Itogi raboty ugol'noi promyshlennosti', 71.

97   'Coal Did Not Go: Its Loading on the Railways Falls for the First Time in a Year and a Half', *Kommersant*, 2 February 2018, kommersant.ru/doc/3536013.

98   Fortescue, 'Russia's "Turn to the East": A Study in Policy Making', Table 1.

99   Samantha Hepburn, 'Adani's New Mini Version of its Mega Mine Still Faces Some Big Hurdles', *Conversation*, 3 December 2018, theconversation.com/adanis-new-mini-version-of-its-mega-mine-still-faces-some-big-hurdles-108038. As Tsivileva notes, greenfield Australian projects—Adani for example—are further inland, eroding the Australian transport cost advantage, but the rail distances are still nothing like Russia's. See, Tsivileva, 'Osnovnoi benefitsiar 'Kolmar grup'.

100  NERA, *Coal Industry Competitiveness Assessment*, Figure 16.

experience the same, although land distances are always going to be great and so operational transport costs will always be high. This is even when freight rates are no better than break-even for Russian Railways and considerably lower than for other bulk shippers.[101] One notes that in 2018 Evraz's costs went up 23.2 per cent, because it increased the share of its output that went to exports, even when the biggest increase was in relatively cheap shipments to Europe.[102] This suggests that the export price premium has to be considerable for transport costs not to erode profitability.

A National Energy Resources Australia (NERA) report compared Australian coal competitiveness with that of nine peers, of which Russia was one.[103] Competitiveness was measured for four stages: exploration and development, extraction and production, transportation, and closure and rehabilitation. Overall, Russia ranked fifth, behind China, South Africa, Australia and the United States. Unfortunately, the report revealed Russia's score for only one stage—extraction and production— for which it ranked number one (Russia 6.7, average 5.3, Australia 5). That Australia did poorly in that category is not surprising; that Russia did so well is somewhat so. The data underlying the NERA rankings are not provided or accessible. We know that Russian labour costs are low, but so is productivity—according to Voskoboinik and Rozhkov, five to nine times below that of developed countries, including 3.9 times below Australia.[104] Reductions in labour force appear to be at an end and wages keep rising.[105] One would also expect the climate, location and geology issues already described to negatively affect production competitiveness.[106] Russia's transportation score is not provided, but one would expect it to be in that area that it loses any advantages it might have in extraction and production.

101  Farid Khusainov, 'Tarifnye uspekhi ugol'shchikov' [Coalminers' freight rate successes], *Vedomosti*, 16 October 2018.

102  Evraz, *Annual Report & Accounts*, 2018, 59–60, www.evraz.com/en/investors/reports-and-results/annual-reports/.

103  NERA, *Coal Industry Competitiveness Assessment*.

104  Mikhail Voskoboinikov and Anatolii Rozhkov, 'Retrospektivnaia i prognoznaia otsenki effektivnosti tekhnoligicheskogo razvitiia ugol'noi promyshlennosti Rossii' [Retrospective and predictive measures of the efficiency of the technological development of the Russian coal industry], *Ugol'* 2 (2018): 48–53, 48.

105  Tarazanov, 'Itogi raboty ugol'noi promyshlennosti', 71.

106  Tsivileva, while noting that topographically Russia is very difficult and that their operations are closed one month a year because of the cold, considers that Russia has an advantage over Australia in that the climate is stable compared to Australia's cyclones, floods, etc. She also believes that Russia's reputation for poor reliability is undeserved and at least partly the result of Australian propaganda. See, Tsivileva, 'Osnovnoi benefitsiar 'Kolmar grup'.

Australia, even with some weaknesses in competitiveness, has traditionally been able to cover for low margins when prices are low by ramping up volume. That option is not available to Russia, or certainly not on the same scale as Australia. To the extent that it is able to do so, it is with volume from Kuzbass. Kuzbass coal has a transport competitive disadvantage and is lower-margin thermal coal. While Russia has a significant domestic market to fall back on, it is not big enough to cover any significant drop-off in exports.

To conclude that Russia's APR export strategy is a risky one is not to deny that the revival of the Russian coal industry and the move into APR markets have been impressive. While falling demand and prices could leave producers with large unserviceable debts and the state with underutilised infrastructure, the state would likely subsidise producers more heavily—a threatening situation for Russia's budget and its competitors.

# Part 4:
# Russian Energy
# Strategy and the
# Future Ahead

# 8

# Sanctions and Moscow's Adaptation Strategy

Maria Shagina

Following Russia's annexation of Crimea in 2014 and its hybrid war in Eastern Ukraine, the US and EU imposed several waves of sanctions on Russia. This chapter delves into how these sanctions, primarily those imposed on the energy sector, have impacted and shaped Russia's foreign energy strategy. By design, Western sanctions did not aim to limit the current supply of energy exported from Russia, but intended to raise the cost of developing Russia's long-term and technologically challenging projects. This chapter examines Moscow's adaptation strategy and assesses how sanctions have altered (and bolstered) Russia's reliance and strategy in the Asia-Pacific energy market.

The sanctions came in three 'waves'. The first two batches included diplomatic sanctions, visa bans and asset freezes. The third wave—'smart' sectoral sanctions—pinpointed only certain activities of particular Russian energy, defence and financial entities. Within the energy sector, a combination of financial and technological restrictions have been in place since September 2014. The US has prohibited new debt financing with a maturity period exceeding 90 days for Gazpromneft, Rosneft, Novatek, Transneft and their subsidiaries.[1] A ban on technology transfer was designated for Gazprom, Gazpromneft, Lukoil, Rosneft, Surgutneftegas

---

1   Office of Foreign Assets Control, 'Directive 2 (as Amended) Under Executive Order 13662', US Department of the Treasury, 12 September 2014, www.treasury.gov/resource-center/sanctions/Programs/Documents/eo13662_directive2.pdf.

and their subsidiaries. The provision, export and re-export of goods, services or technology for the exploration and production of deepwater, Arctic offshore and shale oil projects in Russia was also restricted.

Following the US, the EU imposed similar financial and technological sanctions that varied in certain aspects. As the EU's energy dependency on Russia has been substantially higher than that of the US, the EU excluded Gazprom and Novatek from their restrictions and spared the gas industry altogether. In addition, the EU's sanctions included a so-called 'grandfathering' clause that validated pre-existing contracts, allowing European companies to do business with sanctioned entities. In contrast to the US, the EU abstained from sanctioning CEOs of Russian energy majors associated with the Kremlin, and limited its sanctions listings to political entities rather than business organisations.[2]

With the US's *Countering America's Adversaries through Sanctions Act* (CAATSA), the once well-coordinated transatlantic sanctions started to diverge. Signed by then US President Donald Trump in August 2017, CAATSA stiffened conditions for Russia's energy sector, while the EU's sanctions continued maintaining the status quo. CAATSA's provisions revised down new debt borrowing for Russian energy companies by limiting it to a 60-day maturity. The scope of technological sanctions was expanded: for example, the technology transfer to Russia's deepwater, Arctic offshore and shale oil projects worldwide (not just in Russia) was prohibited. More importantly, the new regulation introduced secondary sanctions on third parties. Non-US individuals and entities were banned from making significant investments in the construction, modernisation or repair of Russian energy export pipelines with a fair market price of more than US$1 million. Such a provision made the construction of Nord Stream 2 a clear victim of the legislation and aimed to target European companies involved. After the EU's outrage, the legislation was revised, altering the threshold to a 33 per cent or greater ownership and introducing a grandfathering clause, thus leaving Nord Stream 2 out of the legal brackets. In the spirit of transatlantic solidarity, secondary sanctions on Russian export energy pipelines would only be applied in coordination with allies. However, no particular mechanism was specified

---

2    Daniel P. Ahn and Rodney Ludema, 'Measuring Smartness: Understanding the Economic Impact of Targeted Sanctions', US Department of State, Working Paper, January 2017, 30.

in the provision.[3] Since July 2020, the US Department of State has lifted the grandfathering clause, exposing Nord Stream 2 to US extraterritorial sanctions and aggravating tensions with EU allies and Germany in particular.

Other Western allies such as Canada and Australia followed suit and imposed similar financial and technological sanctions, while Norway introduced export controls for goods, services and technology for unconventional projects. Japan and New Zealand imposed only symbolic sanctions and abstained from targeting Russia's energy sector. China, India, South Korea, Singapore and Vietnam did not impose any sanctions on Russia at all.

# Impact of Sanctions on Russia's Energy Sector

The sanctions were exclusively limited to the oil industry, targeting the upstream sector (i.e. exploration and development). As a result, the short-term effects of the sanctions have been modest at best, while Russia's oil and gas production has continued to climb. Throughout 2016 and 2018, Russian oil output growth was at its highest in a decade, and Russian gas exports to Europe hit record levels.[4] Russia's output growth was maintained by the increase of production drilling—58 per cent of which was performed in Western Siberia's brownfields.[5] A steep decline in production and exploration was avoided due to currency devaluation, lavish investments and generous tax breaks. The depreciation of the rouble proved to be beneficial for Russian energy producers. It decreased costs for Russian energy companies, as the drop in roubles discouraged imports and lowered prices for Russian manufacturers.[6] Low mineral extraction tax and export duties kept projects profitable even amid plunging oil

---

3    US Department of the Treasury, *Countering America Adversaries through Sanctions Act*, Public Law, 115–44, 2 August 2017, www.govinfo.gov/content/pkg/BILLS-115hr3364enr/html/BILLS-115hr3364enr.htm.

4    Deloitte, *Obzor neftegazovogo rynka v Rossii—2019* [Overview of the Russian oilfied services market—2019], 10, www2.deloitte.com/content/dam/Deloitte/ru/Documents/energy-resources/oil-gas-survey-2019-en.pdf.

5    Deloitte, *Obzor neftegazovogo rynka v Rossii—2019*, 11.

6    Bud Coote, 'Impact of Sanctions on Russia's Energy Sector', Atlantic Council, 1 March 2018, 3, www.atlanticcouncil.org/in-depth-research-reports/report/impact-of-sanctions-on-russia-s-energy-sector/.

prices. Large financial reserves helped energy companies to offset their debt. Altogether, it cushioned the impact of the sanctions and kept Russian energy companies afloat.[7] In the short term, the uncertainty of the political environment and economic volatility had a more immediate effect on the market rather than the sanctions per se. The drop in oil prices affected investment plans and forced the Russian Ministry of Energy to revise its output forecasts by adjusting the baseline oil price from US$110 to US$42.5 per barrel.

Although these short-term effects are seemingly insignificant, in the long term they are set to have a compounding influence with irreversible negative consequences. The combination of financial and technological sanctions will affect Russia's ability to sustain production volumes in the future. In Western Siberia, the brownfields are gradually depleting, making access to enhanced oil recovery technology crucial. Yet, it is currently denied by the sanctions. Even prior to sanctions, the resource deposits had been depreciating, requiring significant capital investments and state-of-the-art extraction technology. Over the last few years, the effectiveness of drilling has continued to drop, requiring more capital investment in the repair of drilling wells.[8] Currently, Russian firms recover oil at a rate of 25 per cent—a strikingly low figure in comparison with the world's technological leaders whose oil recovery rates lie at 50 per cent.[9] Hydraulic fracturing will remain the key technology to sustain future production levels and will require special software to improve economic optimisation and monitoring performance.[10] In Eastern Siberia, both financial restrictions and technology-related sanctions will be critical for the development of new fields. As the majority of Eastern Siberian fields are underdeveloped, larger investments and advanced technology will be necessary for the exploration and development of resource deposits. Currently, only 9 per cent of oil extraction takes place in Eastern Siberia.[11]

---

7    Tatiana Mitrova, Ekaterina Grushevenko and Artyom Milov, 'The Future of Oil Production in Russia: Life Under Sanctions', Skolkovo Energy Center, Moscow School of Management, March 2019, 4; Deloitte, *2015 Russian Oilfield Service Market: Current State and Trends*, October 2015, 3, www2.deloitte.com/content/dam/Deloitte/ru/Documents/energy-resources/2015-russian-oilfield-service-market-current-trends.pdf.

8    Deloitte, *Obzor neftegazovogo rynka v Rossii—2019*, 8.

9    'Rossiia ostalas' bez sovremennyh tekhnologiy dobychi nefti' [Russia is left without modern technology for oil extraction], Finanz.ru, 3 August 2018, www.finanz.ru/novosti/birzhevyye-tovary/rossiya-ostalas-bez-sovremennykh-tekhnologiy-dobychi-nefti-1027429571.

10    Mitrova, Grushevenko and Milov, 'The Future of Oil Production in Russia', 5.

11    Deloitte, *Obzor neftegazovogo rynka v Rossii—2019*, 11.

For now, Western sanctions have mainly negatively affected Russia's long-term capital-intensive offshore and shale projects. A series of projects were suspended due to the sanctions: a joint project between Lukoil and Total for tight oil exploration on the Bazhenov formation; nine projects between Rosneft and ExxonMobil for tight oil production in West Siberia, geological research in the Black Sea, an offshore oil project in the Okhotsk Sea and test-drilling in the Kara Sea; and a joint project between Gazprom and Royal Dutch Shell for oil and gas production in the Okhotsk Sea.[12] The lack of advanced technology together with low oil prices disincentivised Russian energy majors to invest in unconventional projects. Between 2014 and 2015, spending on offshore Arctic exploration plunged from US$1.8 billion to US$170 million.[13] As a result, no major fields have been discovered since the introduction of sanctions. Given financial and technological constraints, Arctic offshore projects look too risky and potentially unprofitable.[14] Against this background, Gazprom, Rosneft and Novatek officially postponed their Arctic offshore and shale projects until 2030 and asked the government to extend their licence terms due to unexpected delays.[15]

Western sanctions affected Russian energy majors disproportionally. Among Russian energy majors, Rosneft and Gazpromneft were hit the hardest.[16] In particular, Rosneft was impacted by financial sanctions due to its high indebtedness—in 2013 the company's net debt amounted to a staggering US$70.5 billion. Technologically, it was more challenging for Rosneft to pursue its ambitious plans in the Arctic. In contrast with Gazprom, Rosneft's fields are generally further away from the coast, in the deepwaters of the Barents, Pechora and Kara seas and thus require more high-quality technologies such as telemetric, drilling and marine equipment as well as coastal infrastructure.[17]

---

12    Maria Shagina, 'Russia's Energy Sector. Evaluating Progress on Import Substitution and Technological Sovereignty', GRI Special Report, Global Risk Insights, April 2018, 6.

13    Sberbank CIB Investment Research, 'What Happened to the Russian Arctic?', October 2017, 45.

14    In contrast with the Arctic offshore, the development of Arctic onshore is not covered by sanctions and is less costly.

15    Adnan Vatansever, 'Energy Sanctions and Russia: What Comes Next?', Atlantic Council, 5, www.atlanticcouncil.org/in-depth-research-reports/issue-brief/energy-sanctions-and-russia-what-comes-next/.

16    Vatansever, 'Energy Sanctions and Russia', 5.

17    Shagina, 'Russia's Energy Sector', 6.

# Dependency on Western Technology and Financial Markets

Russia's resource-dependent, export-oriented economy hinges on its ability to sustain energy output and exports. As the energy sector accounts for 70 per cent of total export revenue and represents about 50 per cent of Russia's federal budget, Western 'smart sanctions' targeted the sector's key vulnerability—high dependency on foreign imports and services.[18] The latter is an example of weaponised interdependence, whereby advanced states possess technological statecraft and control supply value chains in asymmetrically globalised networks, allowing them to maintain leverage over others.[19] Prior to sanctions, Western oilfield service companies such as Schlumberger, Baker Hughes and Halliburton provided over 50 per cent of technologies for Russia's technically advanced projects.[20] The overall dependency on Western technology in the sector constituted 70 per cent. While the reliance on imported goods in conventional projects was low, the share of foreign equipment in unconventional projects such as offshore, shale and liquefied natural gas (LNG) was up to 80 per cent. The dependency on foreign software programming was particularly high—more than 90 per cent. The domestic analogues of advanced equipment, such as offshore platforms, subsea processing equipment, drilling rigs, catalysts for oil processing, high-pressure pumps and others were largely absent.[21]

Financial sanctions exacerbated Russian energy companies' reliance on Western financing. Prior to sanctions, the Russian financial system was closely intertwined with European and American financial markets. Due to the high reliance on hydrocarbons exports, more than 80 per cent of all currency payments were done in US dollars via the Brussels-based Society for Worldwide Interbank Financial Telecommunication (SWIFT).[22] Russian firms were among the largest borrowers from European institutions, as Western markets offered the most cost-effective loans with

---

18  Tatiana Mitrova, 'Shifting Political Economy of Russian Oil and Gas', Center for Strategic & International Studies, 23 March 2016, 2, www.csis.org/analysis/shifting-political-economy-russian-oil-and-gas-0.

19  Henry Farrell and Abraham Newman, 'America's Misuse of its Financial Infrastructure', *National Interest*, 15 April 2019, nationalinterest.org/feature/america's-misuse-its-financial-infrastructure-52707.

20  'Negative Outlook for Russian Economy as Sanctions Bite', *Strategic Comments* 21, no. 5 (March 2015), doi.org/10.1080/13567888.2015.1029240.

21  Shagina, 'Russia's Energy Sector', 6.

22  Henry Foy, 'Can Russia Stop Using the US Dollar?', *Financial Times*, 3 October 2018.

low interest rates. In particular, by 2014, Rosneft accrued US$26.2 billion in debt, which had to be repaid by the end of 2015. The majority of the debt was owned by the US, EU and Japanese firms, making Rosneft especially vulnerable to financial restrictions.[23] The prohibition on long-term debt financing undercut the company's development plans for capital-intensive unconventional projects.

## Russia's Response to Sanctions

Accelerated by Western sanctions, Russia's import substitution aimed to mitigate the country's economic and technological vulnerabilities. Although the idea of import substitution was floated well before the geopolitical rift between Russia and the West, it is Western sanctions that have mobilised the launch of an institutionalised and well-funded program. Originally designed as a strategy for spurring economic growth and stimulating competitiveness, import substitution became a strategy for the securitisation of the economy after sanctions were introduced.[24] With the mounting geopolitical tensions between Russia and the West, the import substitution strategy was viewed through the lens of security concerns. Both national security strategy and economic security strategy called for building domestic capabilities in order to reduce the country's vulnerability and to enhance its economic sovereignty.[25] Import substitution was perceived as a way for Russia to shield itself from external threats, including the 'discriminatory measures' used by hostile foreign powers.[26]

Launched in 2015, the Russian Government Commission on Import Substitution created an institutional framework for the replacement of over 2,000 products and technologies across 19 branches of the economy. Within the energy sector, the Ministry of Energy elaborated

---

23  'Russia Armors Rosneft Against EU Sanctions', *Stratfor*, 8 September 2014.
24  Richard Connolly, *Russia's Response to Sanctions: How Western Economic Statecraft Is Reshaping Political Economy in Russia* (Cambridge: Cambridge University Press, 2018), 69, doi.org/10.1017/9781108227346.
25  Richard Connolly and Philip Hanson, 'Import Substitution and Economic Sovereignty in Russia', Chatham House, 9 June 2016, 3, www.chathamhouse.org/publication/import-substitution-and-economic-sovereignty-russia.
26  'Decree of the President of the Russian Federation of December 31, 2015 No. 683', President of Russia, accessed 27 August 2020, kremlin.ru/acts/bank/40391; Ministry of Energy of the Russian Federation, 'Energeticheskaia strategia Rossii na period do 2035 goda' [Energy security of the Russian Federation until 2035], 2014, ac.gov.ru/files/content/1578/11-02-14-energostrategy-2035-pdf.pdf.

its own plan with 45 import substitution sections. It was projected that the program would help reduce dependence on imports from 70–90 per cent to 40–50 per cent by 2020. In the short term (by 2016), hydraulic fracturing and directional drilling technologies were planned to be replaced. In the mid-term (by 2018), software for the drilling and exploration of hydrocarbons, high-powered gas turbines, catalysts for oil processing and petrochemicals were scheduled to be substituted among other technologies. In the long term (by 2030), technologies for offshore projects were slated to be domestically produced. By 2035, it was expected to fully substitute foreign technology in the LNG sector.[27]

To stimulate the import substitution program, the Russian Government provided generous support to meet its lofty ambitions. Nearly ₽375 billion were allocated to the program, including some ₽105 billion of government support from the federal budget and the Industrial Development Fund (IDF). The government offered comprehensive support, ranging from tax breaks, state-subsidised credit lines and special investment contracts to favourable procurement regulations. The Ministry of Energy announced that it would compensate 50 per cent of the cost for pilot industrial studies and subsidise 10 per cent of the cost for the heavy industry sector.

To enhance the process of import substitution and ensure its effectiveness, various coordination centres were launched. In 2015, the Scientific and Technical Council for the Development of Oil and Gas Equipment was created, which includes 14 expert groups in key areas such as Equipment for Offshore Projects, Subsea Production Complexes, Gas Transportation Technologies and Equipment, and Natural Gas Liquefaction Technologies. Additionally, the Information Centre, Centre of Reverse Engineering, and Single Centre for Oil and Gas Substitution were created to stimulate the program. These aimed to foster communication across energy companies, synchronise investment projects and explore the potential of national manufacturers in order to avoid unnecessary parallel substitution.[28]

---

27    Ministry of Energy of the Russian Federation, 'Energeticheskaia strategia Rossii na period do 2035 goda'.
28    Shagina, 'Russia's Energy Sector', 10.

# Outcomes of Russia's Import Substitution

Outlined in a Soviet style, the program's timeline was overly optimistic, leading to many unfulfilled or postponed targets. The progress on import substitution has been a partial success, as Russian energy majors managed to supplant certain foreign equipment and technology with homegrown analogues. Gazpromneft developed full-cycle technology for shale oil fracking, Gazprom localised key aspects of LNG storage manufacturing with Russian producers and Lukoil developed drilling platforms for the Caspian Sea. However, the abovementioned examples are single cases and do not represent a widespread trend across the sector. The majority of the substituted items are low-tech imports that do not require significant investments in research and development. In those cases where advanced technology was successfully supplanted, as a rule, it involved foreign suppliers. For example, Lukoil is the first Russian company to successfully implement multistage hydraulic fracturing in Western Siberia. This technology of enhanced oil recovery was, however, acquired from Schlumberger, a leading US oilfield service provider. Gazpromneft's 'Prirazlomnaya' offshore platform is branded as the only Russian platform involved in oil extraction in the Arctic. However, 90 per cent of the platform's components were imported, including a wellhead from Norway. To process and interpret seismic data, Gazpromneft developed Russia's first integral data platform 'Prime'. Nevertheless, Russian state-owned companies, including Rosneft, Roscosmos, Rosnano, Rostec, Rosatom, Russian Railways and VTB Bank preferred foreign products. They welcomed the localisation of foreign software with SAP, Oracle and other IT leaders as the domestic analogues of software programs were of low quality.[29]

As Russian analogues often did not fully match companies' technological requirements or could not compete with market prices, many projects were delayed or required adjustments. For example, Novatek limited the operational capacity of its third LNG plant due to the company's goal to employ Russian technology exclusively. Compared to Novatek's Arctic LNG 2, which has the capacity to produce 6.6 mmt per train, the capacity of the third LNG plant will be limited to 1.6 mmt, as the substitution of high-powered gas turbines is still unsuccessful. The Zvezda Shipyard,

---

29 'Inostrannyi soft vozmut v gruppu' [Foreign software will be included into a group], *Kommersant*, 4 July 2019, www.kommersant.ru/amp/4019584.

Rosneft's flagship project of import substitution required lavish financial support from the government and foreign partners for technology transfer in shipbuilding. The shipyard was granted over 40 orders for the construction of vessels, including 17 LNG ice tankers for Novatek's Arctic LNG 2, but lacked domestic capabilities and expertise. The estimated costs for homegrown substitutes ballooned and were reportedly one and a half times higher than vessels ordered abroad. The government pledged to cover the cost difference to ensure that domestic production withstands competition on the market.[30] To compensate the lack of technological expertise, the Zvezda Shipyard signed agreements with Hyundai Heavy Industries and Samsung Heavy Industries, the two leading South Korean companies in shipbuilding.

The homegrown production failed due to a variety of factors, ranging from the decade-long negligence of research and development departments, poor inter-sectoral coordination and cooperation as well as rent-seeking. For years, Russia's scientific-technological base remained chronically underfunded, leading to a glaring technological lag in innovative development between Russian research and development and its foreign counterparts. Yet, restrictions on technology transfer did not encourage Russian companies to invest in research and development— in 2015, only 9 per cent of Russian energy companies were prepared to do so.[31] In a vicious circle, the companies were disincentivised to invest in technological advancements that would ensure high quality and market profitability due to Russia's adverse business climate and high domestic production costs.

Poor coordination of the program of import substitution often led to cost inefficiency. In many cases, it resulted in double production of the same item, leaving out other categories of items that did not have analogues in Russia. Those firms designated by the Russian Government enjoyed privileged access to state resources and were awarded a lion's share of state contracts, while small and middle-sized companies were effectively sidelined. As the case of catalyst substitution aptly demonstrated, Gazpromneft's project 'Catalytic Systems' was granted a national status, receiving generous preferences and funding from the state. At the same

---

30   'Zvezdu podtianut v rynku subsidiiami' [The Zvezda shipyard will be brought into the market with subsidies], *Kommersant*, 31 January 2019, www.kommersant.ru/doc/3868358.
31   'Opros rukovoditelei i spezialistov neftegazovogo sektora' [Expert survey in the oil and gas sector], Deloitte, 2016.

time, other private actors such as KNT Group, which by 2017 had successfully managed to replace the US Grace and German BASF on the Russian catalyst market, remained neglected and unsupported by the government.[32]

The Russian energy majors also showed no willingness to cooperate and exchange their in-house know-how. Rosneft and Novatek refused to join a single engineering centre for LNG projects initiated by Gazprom. The initiative would become a single EPC (engineering, procurement and construction) centre, encompassing the whole production cycle. Facing fierce domestic competition, the Russian energy majors were reluctant to share their technology and expertise with each other. Instead, Novatek announced that it would independently develop its own engineering capacities, together with French Technip, while Rosneft supported the idea of a single competence centre, but on a voluntary basis.

Finally, the generously funded program of import substitution created a negative stimulus for both state and private actors. Lacking monitoring control over implementation, the program suffered from Russia's inherent problems—rent-seeking and rampant corruption. Between 2014 and 2018, domestic producers intentionally inflated costs for locally manufactured items or failed to meet targets on time to obtain more state-subsidised funding. As a result, the public resources allocated for IDF ballooned to more than 12 times the original amount, totalling ₽87.9 billion.[33] Government authorities and strategic firms prioritised their personal gains and were ready to exploit state resources, despite the government's calls to safeguard economic security.

The protracted progress on import substitution forced the Russian Government to adjust its strategy. On the one hand, the reorientation to non-Western markets was no longer viewed as a short-term plan and the pivot to Asia remained crucial. Conversely, localisation of foreign imports and technology became a quintessential solution to the lingering import substitution. Localisation proved to be an excellent opportunity to supplant advanced equipment while preserving high quality. As Russian subsidiaries of foreign companies were exempted from sanctions, both Western and Asian companies were eager to partake

---

32  'Importozameshchenie v neftegazovoi promyshlennosti' [Import substitution in the oil and gas sector], Neftegaz, 2018, 11, 13.
33  'Importozameshchenie s samonavedeniem' [Import substitution with self-correction], *Kommersant*, 26 June 2019, www.kommersant.ru/amp/4012894.

to maintain their market shares in Russia. Gradually, the protectionist requirements for localisation were relaxed: for example, being unable to produce homegrown high-powered gas turbines, Power Machines lobbied for laxer requirements for localisation to guarantee the technology transfer from Western producers.[34]

In the financial sector, the Russian Government took several measures to alleviate the impact of sanctions and to decrease dependency on Western financial markets. In the aftermath of sanctions, state-directed financing became crucial for Russian energy companies. The Russian state effectively shielded strategic companies, including energy majors, from the impact of sanctions to ensure their survival in adverse market conditions.[35] The growth of the state in the Russian economy accelerated, acting effectively as a lender of last resort. Between 2016 and 2018, government funding of the banking sector more than doubled, increasing from US$3.55 billion to US$8.44 billion.[36]

To reduce its dependence on Western financial institutions and the US dollar, the Russian Government made necessary steps for the de-dollarisation of the Russian economy. The share of dollar-denominated external debt decreased, while the shares of euro, yuan and gold rose substantially in the Russian sovereign reserves.[37] In the aftermath of the Ukraine crisis, foreign suppliers of goods and services were forced to accept payments in roubles.[38] The so-called 'sanctions clauses' became more widespread: they stipulated that if a Russian entity was prohibited from paying in US dollars, it could do so in Swiss francs, British pounds or euros.[39] Gradually, the euro was chosen as a safe alternative to reduce exposure to the US nexus. Following the trend, the share of dollars in Sino-Russian bilateral trade fell below 50 per cent in 2019, while the euro gained traction as the payment currency, increasing from 7.3 per cent in

---

34 'Turbiny perekinuli cherez blok' [Turbines were thrown over the bloc], *Kommersant*, 4 July 2019, www.kommersant.ru/amp/4019612.
35 'Negative Outlook for Russian Economy as Sanctions Bite'.
36 Thomas Grove and Alan Cullison, 'US Sanctions Tighten Putin's Circle, Extend Kremlin's Reach', *Wall Street Journal*, 11 September 2019.
37 Maximilian Hess, 'Geopolitics, Sanctions and Russian Sovereign Debt Since the Annexation of Crimea', Foreign Policy Research Institute, 25 June 2019, 8, www.fpri.org/article/2019/06/geopolitics-sanctions-and-russian-sovereign-debt-since-the-annexation-of-crimea/.
38 'Russia, Wary of Sanctions, Wants Exporters to Be Paid in Roubles', *Reuters*, 14 May 2014, www.reuters.com/article/russia-exports-rouble/update-2-russia-wary-of-sanctions-wants-exporters-to-be-paid-in-roubles-idUSL6N0O01RI20140514.
39 Hess, 'Geopolitics, Sanctions and Russian Sovereign Debt'. 11.

2018 to 21.9 per cent in 2019. As neither Russian nor Chinese banks had experience dealing with yuan and roubles, the euro was preferred as the most reliable option.[40] Although the vast majority of hydrocarbons have traditionally been traded in US dollars, Russian energy majors started to use the euro as the default payment for its oil and products sales.[41] The transatlantic rift between the US and EU encouraged Brussels to reduce its reliance on US-centred financial systems. The EU declared its intention to create a euro-denominated price benchmark for crude oil to increase the share of the euro in oil trading.[42] Similarly, disagreeing with the US's reimposition of sanctions on Iran, the EU initiated special purpose vehicles as an alternative to SWIFT. Both EU initiatives could become a convenient and legitimate way for Russia to avoid the US nexus in the future.

## Russia's Pivot to Asia

Russia's pivot to Asia has been touted for a long time, but it was only after the Ukraine crisis that the turn to the East became more urgent and pronounced. As none of the Asian states imposed energy sanctions, China, South Korea, Japan, India and Singapore proved instrumental in alleviating the sanctions' burden and providing additional time for Russia to adjust to external pressures. The Asia-Pacific has become a crucial alternative to the European energy market and Western technology, equipment and capital. To offset its former dependence on European energy demand, Russia announced an energy shift towards burgeoning Asian and Chinese markets. Despite being a latecomer, Russia has managed to gain a foothold in the Asia-Pacific energy market. In 2016–17, it became China's largest supplier of crude oil on an annual basis, surpassing Saudi Arabia. Russia is also poised to become a major supplier of natural gas to China within the next decade. With the start of the Power of Siberia in late 2019 and other potential projects, Russia will ramp up its gas export to full capacity.

---

40 'Dolya dollara v oplate eksporta iz Rossii v Kitai vpervye upala nizhe 50%' [The Share of US dollar in payments for Russia's export to China fell below 50% for the first time], *RBC*, 26 July 2019, www.rbc.ru/economics/26/07/2019/5d39ad439a79477f145b23b0.
41 'Sanctions-Hit Rosneft Requests Payment in Euros in Naphtha Tender', *Reuters*, 15 August 2019, www.reuters.com/article/us-russia-rosneft-tenders-euro/sanctions-hit-rosneft-requests-payment-in-euros-in-naphtha-tender-idUSKCN1V41QS.
42 Yusho Cho and Takeshi Kumon, 'China, Russia and EU Edge Away from Petrodollar', *Nikkei Asian Review*, 7 January 2019, asia.nikkei.com/Economy/China-Russia-and-EU-edge-away-from-petrodollar.

It envisages increasing hydrocarbons exports to Asia to 20–25 per cent by 2035, while the 2040 energy forecast projects a further rise to 32–36 per cent.[43] As an illustration of Russia's substantial pivot to the East, Novatek plans to ship 80–85 per cent from its Arctic LNG 2 to the region.[44]

By providing equipment and services, Asian countries have not only cushioned the effects of the sanctions but also enabled the continuous operation of Russia's energy projects. Chinese oilfield services replaced Western companies and became a notable alternative supplier of drilling rigs; for example, the share of Yantai Jereh Oilfield Services Group rose to 45 per cent on the Russian market. Although the quality of Chinese equipment did not necessarily meet requirements for drilling in the Russian Arctic and Eastern Siberia, with time, Beijing's technology has significantly improved and is now used for the development of subsea and hard-to-extract resources. China Offshore Oil Engineering Company mastered its ocean engineering technology while participating in Yamal LNG,[45] and two of Russia's largest offshore fields over the last decade were discovered using the Chinese semisubmersible drilling rig 'Nan Hai 8'.[46] Another drilling rig that operates in the Arctic—Gazprom's 'Arkticheskaya'—underwent repair work in Singapore. South Korean shipbuilding companies provided the world's most cutting-edge shipbuilding technologies for the construction of eco-friendly gas-powered tankers for Russia's Arctic projects. Novatek's 15 LNG vessels for Yamal LNG were built by Daewoo Shipbuilding & Marine Engineering (DSME), while Hyundai Heavy Industries and Samsung Heavy Industries signed an agreement with Rosneft's Zvezda Shipyard to transfer technology used in the construction of 17 LNG carriers for Arctic LNG 2. Japanese

---

43   Ministry of Energy of the Russian Federation, 'Energeticheskaia strategia Rossii na period do 2035 goda'; A. A. Makarov, T. A. Mitrova, V. A. Kulagin, eds, *Global and Russian Energy Outlook 2019* (Moscow: ERI RAS – Moscow School of Management SKOLKOVO, 2019), 134.

44   'Novatek Plans to Send 80% of Future Arctic LNG Output to Asia: CEO', S&P Global Platts, 7 June 2019, www.spglobal.com/platts/en/market-insights/latest-news/natural-gas/060719-novatek-plans-to-send-80-of-future-arctic-lng-2-output-to-asia-ceo.

45   Erica Downs, 'China-Russia Energy Relations: Better Than Ever', in *The Emerging Russia-Asia Energy Nexus*, ed. Erica Downs et al., *NBR Special Report* 74 (December 2018): 25.

46   Atle Staalesen, 'Chinese Rig Makes Second Large Discovery in Russian Arctic Waters', *Barents Observer*, 20 May 2019, thebarentsobserver.com/en/industry-and-energy/2019/05/chinese-rig-makes-second-large-discovery-russian-arctic-waters.

partners provided expertise for the building of LNG modular plants. JGC Corporation and Chiyoda Corporation won an EPC tender, covering the engineering, procurement and construction of Novatek's Yamal LNG.[47]

Strapped for cash, Russian banking institutions and energy companies also turned to the East. The Asian credit organisations linked to governments became the main financial vehicle for the provision of financial support. Decoupled from Western financial systems, China Development Bank (CDB), Silk Road Fund, Export–Import Bank of China, Japan Bank for International Cooperation (JBIC) and Export–Import Bank of Korea mitigated the sanctions' risks and signalled to the private sector that the state would guarantee support. For example, CDB, Export–Import Bank of China and Silk Road Fund agreed to provide loans to US-sanctioned Novatek, covering the necessary amount of external funding. Support from China's government-backed institutions ensured that Yamal LNG's launch was on time and on budget.[48] Similarly, the government-backed JBIC provided several loans to Novatek, Sberbank and Transneft—all of which are sanctioned by the US.[49] In contrast, Asian private banks and financial institutions were reluctant to lend unless their respective governments provided assurances for mitigating the sanctions' risks. Fearing penalties from the US, Chinese, Japanese and South Korean private businesses were wary of lending to Russia's sanctioned entities and often over-complied with Western restrictions. For instance, Japanese companies refused Rosneft's offer to buy a share in the Far East LNG, the Eastern Petrochemical Company and the Zvezda Shipbuilding Complex, while both Japanese and Korean energy majors hesitated over whether to acquire equities in Arctic LNG 2. It was only after the Japan Oil, Gas and Metals National Corporation (JOGMEC), a government agency, covered 75 per cent of investments that Mitsui & Co., a private Japanese trading house, agreed to participate in Novatek's second LNG project.[50]

The Russian Government was compelled to open the door to Asian equity participation in the energy sector due to Western sanctions. As a consequence, the Asian presence in Russian energy projects has strengthened remarkably: China's National Petroleum Corporation and

47   Maria Shagina, 'Under Pressure: Russian Energy Cooperation with Japan and South Korea since Western Sanctions', *Russia Political Economy Project*, 7 February 2019, 5, 8.
48   Downs, 'China-Russia Energy Relations: Better Than Ever', 25.
49   Shagina, 'Under Pressure', 5–6.
50   'Signing of Share Purchase Agreement for Equity Participation into Arctic LNG 2 Project in Russia', press release, Mitsui & Co., 29 June 2019, www.mitsui.com/jp/en/release/2019/1228966_11219.html.

Silk Road Fund acquired stakes in Novatek's Yamal LNG and Arctic LNG 2; Beijing Gas bought 20 per cent of Rosneft's Verkhnechonskneftegaz; China's Siponec took stakes in SIBUR, Russia's top petrochemical company; India's ONGC Videsh acquired stakes in Rosneft's Vankorneft; and Japan's Mitsui & Co. and JOGMEC acquired a 10 per cent stake in Arctic LNG 2.

Mutually established intergovernmental investment funds and alternative financial arrangements became another way of reducing exposure to the US and securing financial operations. Despite being under US sanctions, the Russian Direct Investment Fund (RDIF) reportedly attracted over US$40 billion in joint funds through long-term strategic partnerships with China, South Korea, India, Japan, Thailand and Vietnam among other countries.[51] For example, RDIF and JBIC established a US$1 billion investment fund for projects in energy, Far East industry and technology development. Due to financial restrictions, Rosneft used pre-payment arrangements with oil traders and Chinese firms against future oil deliveries.[52] In a bid to alleviate Russia's dependence on US dollars, the de-dollarisation of the economy was promoted. Although the use of local currencies such as the yuan and the rouble was not widespread, the share of euros increased considerably, gradually replacing the greenback. Currency swaps between Russia and China were launched and yuan clearing services with Chinese financial institutions were started.[53] Additionally, Russia and China have been looking into developing alternatives to SWIFT. Moscow's newly launched System for Transfer of Financial Messages allegedly covers 18 per cent of all Russian money transfers, while gradually expanding its network to other countries. Russia has been looking at coordinating its system with China International Payments System and potentially expanding it to Turkey and Iran.[54]

---

51 'RDIF Partnerships', Russian Direct Investment Fund, accessed 27 August 2020, rdif.ru/Eng_Partnership/.

52 Connolly, *Russia's Response to Sanctions*, 107.

53 'China's ICBC Starts Renminbi Clearing Services in Russia', *Xinhua*, 22 March 2017, news.xinhua net.com/english/2017-03/22/c_136149394.htm.

54 'Trash Discovery Shows Turkey Eyes Putin's Anti-Sanctions Network', *Moscow Times*, 21 August 2019, www.themoscowtimes.com/2019/08/21/trash-discovery-shows-turkey-eyes-putins-anti-sanctions-network-a66965; 'Russian & Chinese Alternatives For SWIFT Global Banking Network Coming Online', *Russia Briefing*, 17 June 2019, www.russia-briefing.com/news/russian-chinese-alternatives-swift-global-banking-network-coming-online.html/.

Accelerated by Western sanctions, import substitution was launched to safeguard Russia's economic and technological sovereignty. Originally designed as a way to stimulate economic growth and competitiveness, import substitution incrementally descended into selective protectionism with political undertones, directed at shielding strategic firms in revenue-generating sectors. Striving to securitise the economy, the Russian state has become a lender of last resort, significantly increasing its encroachment into the economy and limiting information access on sanctioned entities.

Over the last four years, the policy of import substitution has failed to achieve tangible results. While there are some successful examples of homegrown equipment, they either originate from low-tech categories or were produced with the help of foreign suppliers. Up until now, targets on key advanced equipment and technology have not been met. Due to the lack of domestic capabilities, poor inter-sectoral coordination and rent-seeking, the progress on substitution has been protracted and weighed down by uncompetitive prices and low quality. As a result, import diversification to non-Western markets and localisation of foreign products and technology has gradually replaced Russian-made import substitution. Russian energy majors have become increasingly dependent on Chinese funding, equipment and services. The failure to develop its own equipment will be detrimental to Russia's local manufacturing and technological development in the future. As Chinese financial support often comes with a binding condition on the use of Chinese technology and services, Beijing will have considerable leverage over the development of Russia's energy projects and their price policy.

While Russia's pivot to Asia has proved crucial in terms of alleviating the burden of Western sanctions, this is largely contingent on backing from Asian governments. The Asian private sector has largely remained wary of engaging with sanctioned Russian individuals and entities. With US sanctions expanding, Asian governments' backing will be crucial for the mitigation of reputational risks and avoidance of penalties in the future.

# 9

# The 2019 Energy Security Doctrine and Debates around It in Russia

Tatiana Romanova

On 13 May 2019, the President of Russia approved a new energy security doctrine (ESD). This is the first such doctrine that Moscow has published (the previous two were either released as drafts or only summarised by their authors and by the Ministry of Energy). The publication of the doctrine is the result of dramatic changes in the international arena, which Russian neo-revisionist politics have provoked since 2014. To quote the secretary of Russia's Security Council Nikolay Patruchev, 'serious changes have occurred both in the world and in our country, new challenges and threats have emerged, and we could not but react to them'.[1] These changes increased the West's concern about dependence on Russian hydrocarbons and led to sanctions against Russia that included restrictions on the supply of technologies for oil exploration and access to long-term finance, which in turn have affected long-term prospects for the development of Russian oil.

---

1    N. Patrushev, 'Patrushev: Odobrena novaya doktrina energeticheskoi bezopasnosti' [Patrushev: A new energy security doctrine is approved], *Rossiiskaya gazeta*, 29 November 2018.

Visionary documents (i.e. concepts, strategies and doctrines) abound in Russia, although their legal status remains uncertain.[2] Such documents tend to pursue at least three goals. First, they set policy priorities. In this case, the very preparation of the text and accompanying debates are of crucial importance. Second, they outline a program of actions in a particular field. These two types of documents can remain confidential, as they represent the steps that policymakers and bureaucracies might follow. The third goal of visionary documents is to outline the position for partners and outsiders. This is when publication of the final text becomes important, as demonstrated in the case of the 2019 ESD.

Preparation of the 2019 ESD was fairly secretive. Prior to its publication, the only official mention of it came from the Security Council in December 2017 (when the need to adopt a new doctrine was recognised) and in November 2018 (when the draft was approved). Predictably, the Security Council was central to its preparation. Any debate about the preparation of the 2019 ESD (if it took place) was not made public. Yet, we can discern a number of controversial or debate-worthy issues in the ESD from the documents to which it refers (or does not refer), from general discussion about points covered in the ESD and from reaction to the ESD. Three groups of issues can be identified: geopolitical/market paradigms, energy mix, and geography and diversification. After describing the historical context relevant to the ESD, I examine these issues, focusing on the nature of changes, their novelty and relevant debates among key stakeholders—the state, companies and experts.

# Historical Perspective on Russia's Energy Security Doctrines

Russia's three ESDs were prepared by the Ministry of Energy and approved by the Security Council before being put in the form of a presidential decree. However, as mentioned above, neither the first nor the second

---

2    D. V. Iroshnichenko and S. V. Nesterov, 'Ponyatie i klassifikatsiya konteptualnyh i doktrinalnyh dokumentov Rossiiskoi Federatsii' [Concept and classification of conceptual and doctrinal documents of the Russian Federation], *Pravovaya initsiativa* 7 (2013), 49e.ru/ru/2013/7/7; M. A. Mushinsky, 'Strategii, kontsepsii, doctriny v pravovoi sisteme Rossiiskoi Federatsii: problemy statusa, uridicheskoi tehniki i sootnosheniya drug s drugom' [Strategies, concepts, doctrines in the legal system of the Russian federation: problems of status, legal techniques and correlation], *Uridicheskie tehniki* 9 (2015): 488–99.

were published. Yet, their drafts were presented and both documents were explained by experts that took part in their elaboration and by the Ministry of Energy.

The first Russian ESD was prepared in December 1997 after nearly two years of debates among experts.[3] A relatively short document, it defined energy security as a state that had to be achieved in the context of both external and internal threats. It emphasised economic and sociopolitical threats and paid little attention to external challenges. This approach seems logical given the overall political and international climate of the 1990s when Russia did its best to become a good (but also key) member of the international community and mostly concentrated on domestic reforms. This approach also mirrors the first (1992) Russian foreign policy concept.

The second ESD was adopted in November 2012 after two years of intense debate by experts. It was even more concise than the 1997 document.[4] In defining 'energy security', it emphasised both the supply and demand of 'citizens, society, state, economy', thereby reflecting the importance of production and consumption. Building on advanced studies, it stressed resource availability, economic affordability, environmental sensitivity and technological achievability.[5] Its definition of 'global energy security' underlined Russia's international ambition to be a 'global energy superpower'—a goal frequently attributed to Russian President Vladimir Putin.

Compared to the earlier document, the 2012 ESD included a more elaborate catalogue of threats. It started with internal economic threats (e.g. quality of energy reserves, quality of exploration and production equipment, and low level of investments) and sociopolitical threats (e.g. labour conflicts and terrorist attacks), but it also added technological (i.e. man-made) and natural threats. Finally, it reflected on external economic and political threats, which included insufficient geographical diversification (i.e. high share of European market in the export of Russian hydrocarbons), high politicisation of energy relations, instability

---

3    'Proekt doctrine energeticheskoi bezopasnosti' [A draft of energy security doctrine], *Energeticheskaya politika* 2 (1996): 2–7.

4    S. M. Senderov, 'Strategy obespecheniya energeticheskoi bezopasnosti Rossii' [Strategy for securing energy security for Russia], Proatom, 23 May 2013, www.proatom.ru/modules.php?name=News&file=article&sid=4532.

5    V. V. Bushuev, N. I Voropay, S. M. Senderov and V. V. Saenko, 'O doctrine energeticheskoi bezopasnosti Rossii' [On Russia's energy security doctrine], *Ekonomika regiona* 2 (2012): 40–50; B. K. Sovacool and I. Mukherjee, 'Conceptualizing and Measuring Energy Security: A Synthesized Approach', *Energy* 36 (2011) 5343–55, doi.org/10.1016/j.energy.2011.06.043.

of global energy and financial markets, vulnerability of transit and limits on Russian companies' access to exploration worldwide. The 2012 ESD also introduced a system of regular monitoring for the purpose of energy security, which again mostly emphasised internal economic, technological and sociopolitical threats, thus fixing their primacy.

The 2012 ESD revealed an ambiguous attitude to energy saving and climate change. On the one hand, it stressed the importance of energy saving. Yet, on the other, it emphasised the negative influence of the climate on energy production and transportation (rather than the other way around) and pointed out that Russia might be forced to purchase unnecessary energy technologies under the cover of energy efficiency and the fight against climate change.

Like the first ESD, the 2012 doctrine reflected the mood at the time of its approval. By then, Russia had become more assertive and was seeking to use its abundant natural resources to achieve a more important role in the international arena. The document suggested that Russia might hold a different attitude on pertinent global issues and, in that sense, was similar to the foreign policy concept of 2013.

The ESD released in 2019 is different from its 2012 predecessor in many respects.[6] It makes early reference to the 2015 National Security Strategy and 2017 Economic Security Strategy, emphasising import substitution, but does not refer to the 2009 Energy Strategy[7] until the end, thereby establishing its conceptual primacy. It contains fewer definitions than earlier iterations and notably omits a definition of global energy security, reflecting Russia's moderated international ambition. While a definition is provided for 'energy security', 'population' is offered as a substitute for 'citizens and society', reflecting a particularly Russian style of relations between the state and society.

The 2019 document contains a detailed section (8 out of 18 pages) on challenges, risks and threats. These are described in terms of a hierarchy, whereby challenges create stimuli and potential problems, risks exacerbate potentially dangerous issues and threats to energy security are the phenomena that have to be countered. Challenges, risks and threats are divided into three thematic subcategories: external economic, political and military;

---

6    President of Russia, *Doktrina energeticheskoi bezopasnosti* [Energy security doctrine], no. 216, 13 May 2019.
7    Pravitelstvo Rossiiskoi Federatsii, *Energeticheskaya strategiya Rossii na period do 2030 goda* [Energy strategy of the Russian Federation to 2030], no. 1715-p 13 November 2009.

internal economic; and cross-border (terrorist, environmental) groups. In sharp contrast to the previous doctrines, this catalogue demonstrates the primacy of external factors over internal ones. Importantly, the interpretation of internal factors is different: while outdated equipment, insufficient exploration and the poor quality of labour resources are mentioned, incoherent development of the sector, excessive environmental demands and criminal activity in the energy sector are prioritised. This clear change in focus predetermines a bigger state involvement.

Like its predecessors, the 2019 ESD is a child of its time. It reflects Russia's decision in 2012 to concentrate on external policy rather than domestic reforms and the situation the country found itself in following the 2014 crisis in Ukraine and imposition of Western sanctions. To better understand these changes and the plurality of options that are currently available, the next sections dwell in more detail on the three groups of issues identified above: market economics vs geopolitics, energy mix and geographical diversification.

# Geopolitics Beats Market?

The approach to energy relations referred to as 'geopolitics' is rooted in the neorealist tradition of international relations, which concentrates on power politics and the fight for survival with little regard for transnational relations. It is linked to traditional, statist forms of organisation. This paradigm views energy as a strategic commodity rather than an average good and is based on state involvement in the management and transportation of resources and all major energy deals. As there is substantial obscurity in state decision-making about the management of the sector, a particular approach is required.[8] The geopolitical approach presupposes centralised, top-down decision-making, as well as a negative understanding of external dependence and the need to manage this dependence.[9]

---

8    A. Correljé and C. van der Linde, 'Energy Supply Security and Geopolitics: A European Perspective', *Energy Policy* 34 (2006): 532–43, doi.org/10.1016/j.enpol.2005.11.008; D. Finon and C. Locatelli, 'Russian and European Gas Interdependence: Could Contractual Trade Channel Geopolitics?', *Energy Policy* 36 (2008): 423–42, doi.org/10.1016/j.enpol.2007.08.038; S. Peters and K. Westphal, 'Global Energy Supply: Scale, Perception and the Return to Geopolitics', in *International Handbook of Energy Security*, ed. H. Dyer and M. J. Trombetta (Edward Elgar Publishing, 2013), 92–113, doi.org/10.433 7/9781781007907.00014; E. Stoddard, 'Reconsidering the Ontological Foundations of International Energy Affairs: Realist Geopolitics, Market Liberalism and a Politico-Economic Alternative', *European Security* 22, no. 4 (2013): 437–63, doi.org/10.1080/09662839.2013.775122.

9    T. Casier, 'The Rise of Energy to the Top of the EU-Russia Agenda: From Interdependence to Dependence?' *Geopolitics* 16, no. 3 (2011): 536–52, doi.org/10.1080/14650045.2011.520862.

Conversely, a market approach to energy policy is based on a neoliberal vision of international relations—positive interdependence—and a neoclassical vision of markets, which can resolve all problems with supply and demand.[10] This approach starts with the premise that energy is just a commodity like any other. Hence, markets are the most appropriate vehicle to manage it. In this approach, states are rule providers, insofar as they ensure transparent, universal rules and the work of legal instruments.[11] This approach, which presupposes long-term cooperation rather than competition, is not territory-based, involves various transnational actors (e.g. companies and consumers) and leaves most of the solutions to the market.

Conventionally, Russia is depicted as being geared towards a geopolitical approach. However, some studies have challenged this assumption, identifying important market trends in Russian energy thinking.[12]

The 2009 Energy Strategy is ambiguous on the subject of markets.[13] The creation of a market environment is one of its 'main vectors'; however, it also emphasises market mechanisms, institutions of open trade in energy resources, infrastructure for transportation of these resources and increases in domestic gas prices. At the same time, it prioritises budgetary efficiency of the sector—being the difference between what the state invests in the sector and its return in the form of taxes and revenues—as well as modernisation and stable institutional structures. The danger of reliance on imported technologies is also stressed. A new energy strategy drafted in 2017 preserved this emphasis on market principles and advocated the need to 'change the correlation between state regulation and market competition in favour of the later (liberalisation)'.[14]

---

10   Casier, 'The Rise of Energy to the Top'; Correljé and van der Linde, 'Energy Supply Security and Geopolitics'; Stoddard, 'Reconsidering the Ontological Foundations'.

11   J. Bielecki, 'Energy Security: Is the Wolf at the Door?', *Quarterly Review of Economics and Finance* 42, no. 2 (2002): 235–50, doi.org/10.1016/S1062-9769(02)00137-0; A. Goldthau and N. Sitter, 'A liberal Actor in a Realist World? The Commission and the External Dimension of the Single Market for Energy', *Journal of European Public Policy* 21, no. 10 (2014): 145–72, doi.org/10.1080/13501763.2014.912251; A. Goldthau and J. M. Witte, *Global Energy Governance: The New Rules of the Game* (Washington, DC: Brookings Press, 2010).

12   T. Romanova, 'Is Russian Energy Policy towards the EU Only about Geopolitics? The Case of the Third Liberalisation Package', *Geopolitics* 21, no. 4 (2016): 857–79, doi.org/10.1080/14650045. 2016.1155049; M. Siddi 'The Role of Power in EU–Russia Energy Relations: The Interplay between Markets and Geopolitics', *Europe-Asia Studies* 70, no. 10 (2018): 1552–71, doi.org/10.1080/096681 36.2018.1536925.

13   Pravitelstvo Rossiiskoi Federatsii, *Energeticheskaya strategiya Rossii na period do 2030 goda.*

14   Ministry of Energy, *Proekt enoergostrategii Rossiiskoi Federatsii na period do 2035 goda* [Draft energy strategy of the Russian Federation to 2035], 2017, accessed 14 August 2019, www.energystrategy.ru/ab_ins/source/ES-2035_09_2015.pdf.

The 2019 ESD does not openly reject market logics, though it significantly moderates previous timid attempts to apply market principles in Russia. It does this by emphasising the danger of incoherent development without active state interference. Rather than creating the conditions for businesses to act in this field, it stresses the state's need to perfect territorial energy structures and regulate energy prices in Russia. The need for greater state involvement stems from a set of newly identified threats: criminal activities, ranging from inappropriate use of budgetary sources and counterfeiting to corruption and shadow economy; and the activities of security services and other institutions of foreign states. The threat posed by criminal activities was flagged in the lead-up to the release of the 2019 ESD, so it was not unexpected.[15] Nevertheless, it lays ground for an active state involvement, which is the essence of the geopolitical approach to energy.

The 2019 ESD bluntly underlines the need to:

> Develop competition … in the [Russian] internal market and to eliminate competition, which does not respond to the economic interests of Russia, among different types of Russian energy resources exported to the global energy markets.[16]

This is in relation to competition between Russian pipeline gas and liquefied natural gas (LNG). Further moderating the application of market principles, the 2019 ESD highlights the need for import substitution for various technologies and equipment as a consequence of Western sanctions, which have also contributed to an increased role of the state. The doctrine emphasises that the state has to create conditions to 'ensure technological independence of Russia's energy sector and its competitiveness'.[17] While concerns about imported technologies were present in the 2012 ESD and 2009 Energy Strategy, they have become more salient because of sanctions. In 2017, the new energy strategy draft observed:

---

15 'Today, Astrakhan Hosted a Visiting Meeting of the Secretary of the Security Council of the Russian Federation in the Southern Federal District', Security Council of the Russian Federation, 5 May 2019, www.scrf.gov.ru/news/allnews/1074/. See also V. Putin, *Zasedanie Soveta Bezopasnosti Rossiiskoi Federatsii*, [Meeting of the security council of the Russian Federation] 29 November 2018, kremlin.ru/events/president/news/59262.

16 President of Russia, *Doktrina energeticheskoi bezopasnosti*.

17 President of Russia, *Doktrina energeticheskoi bezopasnosti*.

> [The] dependence of [the] Russian energy sector on foreign
> technologies, equipment, machinery and materials reached
> a critical level in some fields and thus created a threat to the energy
> security of Russia.[18]

This is understandable, given that Russia is as much as 60 per cent
dependent on foreign technologies, according to some assessments.[19]
Therefore, the state has pledged to contribute to import substitution and
to develop Russian industrial and scientific potential, not just to enhance
its energy superpower status, but also, and more importantly, to guarantee
its very energy security—that is, the stability of supply both internally
and externally.

Despite those tendencies that clearly strengthen Russia's traditional
geopolitical approach, market rhetoric is still very present in the 2019
ESD. According to the doctrine, the state has to regulate to ensure
'competitiveness' of the Russian energy sector. Sanctions are framed as
a means of unfair competition rather than as a political instrument meant
to signal disagreement with Russia's behaviour in the international arena
(this is true of Russian political discourse at large).[20] Hence, there is a clear
interest to preserve the market agenda, not only as a cover but also as an
acceptable explanation of the West's behaviour.

Debates around market vs geopolitics have not been that ardent in
Russia. Some experts praised the document while others stated that it was
unnecessary and that market competition should be promoted instead.[21]
Others claimed that the goal of market promotion was too declaratory and
did not reflect the real situation.[22] For their part, companies concentrated
on the need to decrease tax burdens and to allow for more flexible prices
internally. LNG producers challenged the need to have a coherent line

---

18    Ministry of Energy, *Proekt enoergostrategii Rossiiskoi Federatsii na period do 2035 goda.*
19    Novak cf. G. Starinskaya, 'Chto izmenilos v rossiiskom TEKe za vremya sanktsii' [What has
changed in the Russian fuel and energy complex during the sanctions], *Vedomosti*, 19 December
2017, www.vedomosti.ru/business/articles/2017/12/19/745720-rossiiskom-teke.
20    See, for example, V. Putin, *Zasedanie Soveta Bezopasnosti Rossiiskoi Federatsii,* 29 November 2018.
21    Grivach, A. 'Expert otsenil doktrinu energeticheskoi bezopasnosti Rossii' [The expert assessed
the doctrine of Russia's energy security], IZ, 14 May 2019, iz.ru/877856/2019-05-14/ekspert-
otcenil-doktrinu-energeticheskoi-bezopasnosti-rossii. See also D. Chugunoff, 'Rossiiskii Neftegaz',
Facebook Group, 16 May 2019, www.facebook.com/groups/437496816287290/?ref=bookmarks.
22    Marinchenko cf. E. Kravchenko, 'Putin podpisal novuu doktrinu energobezopasnosti' [Putin
signed a new energy security doctrine. What is he preparing Russia for?], Forbes.ru, 14 May 2019, www.
forbes.ru/biznes/376041-putin-podpisal-novuyu-doktrinu-energobezopasnosti-k-chemu-ona-gotovit-
rossiyu?fbclid=IwAR27NP0YlEowBy4Z5GqhZ-c6xHU4C7AKxne9d5QTSzdBWvJBUe5xAGr7Ftw.

on the export of Russian resources, which would ultimately preserve the interests of Gazprom.[23] Others complained that the 2019 ESD does not provide guidance on how companies should align their export interests.[24]

Reflecting ambiguity in the government's approach, the most controversial issue is probably import substitution. For example, Russia's minister of energy, although admitting the need to foster the development of Russian technologies, stressed that this did not detract from market principles. However, experts warn that this will likely mean an increase in price and duplication of existing technologies, in many cases, to a lower standard. In the meantime, industrialists are optimistic about their ability to reach a target of 70 per cent independence in technologies, and an import substitution lobby has emerged to compete for state resources.[25]

In sum, the 2019 ESD tipped the balance between markets and geopolitics in favour of the latter. While some experts challenge the prudence of this step, companies mostly agree with it. Some disagreement exists in the area of export coherence, but the most debated topic is import substitution. These trends are not new; instead, they reinforce existing and historical tendencies, such as Russia's unwillingness to introduce competition and its concern about technological dependence. However, the justification for a geopolitical approach is new in some respects (e.g. criminal activities in the field of energy, danger of import dependence and sanctions). Russia's framing of Western measures in economic rather than political terms is also noteworthy.

## Energy Mix

The roots of present debates about energy mix lie in the concept of energy transition, which describes how the structure of primary energy resources changes over time.[26] The current stage is linked to the increased

23    See, for example, Mihelson in V. Putin, *Zasedanie Soveta Bezopasnosti Rossiiskoi Federatsii*, 29 November 2018; 'NOVATEK ran across Europe to Gazprom', *Kommersant*, 5 August 2019, www.kommersant.ru/doc/4052442?utm_source=newspaper&utm_medium=email&utm_campaign =newsletter.
24    Ushkov cf. Kravchenko, 'Putin podpisal novuu doktrinu energobezopasnosti'.
25    G. Shmal, 'Ot importozamescheniya k importonezavisimosti' [From import-substitution to import-independence], *Sfera nefi i gaz* 2, no. 70 (2019): 18–21.
26    V. Smil, *Energy Transitions: History, Requirements, Prospects* (Santa Barbara: Praeger, 2010); V. Smil, *Energy and Civilization: A History* (MIT Press, 2018); B. K. Sovacool, 'How Long Will It Take? Conceptualizing the Temporal Dynamics of Energy Transitions', *Energy Research & Social Science* 13 (2016): 202–03, doi.org/10.1016/j.erss.2015.12.020.

role of renewables; electricity and energy efficiency; the phasing out of nuclear energy and oil; and decentralised electricity systems, both in terms of generation and consumption.[27] Energy transition is driven by technological developments and policy choices (e.g. climate agenda), and by the will of importing countries to increase their energy security through domestic actions, both in terms of supply and demand.[28] Energy transition is important for Russia in two ways: in relation to the supply of internal market and the affect it has on exports. While both points are present in current debates, the second has been much more significant in the discussion that accompanied the 2019 ESD.

The 2009 Energy Strategy paid considerable attention to the structure of the Russian energy mix, concentrating on the need to enhance the use of coal (including clean technologies), reduce the internal consumption of gas, improve the structure of exports through the use of processed rather than primary energy goods and support the use of nuclear technologies.[29] Renewable sources of energy were the last to be mentioned and their support was mostly declaratory. The 2017 energy strategy draft also recognises the need to develop renewables, but again mentions them towards the end of the list of priorities.[30] Moreover, it stresses the need to diversify in the areas of oil and gas through the production and export of more processed energy goods and LNG.

There has been a decrease in global energy demand as well as a change in its structure as a result of moves towards energy efficiency, energy saving and new energy sources (including renewables and LNG). The 2019 ESD recognises this as an external economic challenge for Russian energy security.[31] Moreover, the 2019 ESD takes notice of increased competition in global energy markets, which has intensified due to the entry of new suppliers. The doctrine also conceptualises the increased salience of climate

---

27   J. Trüby and H.-W. Schiffer, 'A Review of the German Energy Transition: Taking Stock, Looking Ahead, and Drawing Conclusions for the Middle East And North Africa', *Energy Transitions*, 2 (2018): 1–14, doi.org/10.1007/s41825-018-0010-2; C. Hager and C. H. Stefes, *Germany's Energy Transition: A Comparative Perspective* (New York: Palgrave Macmillan, 2016), doi.org/10.1057/978-1-137-44288-8.

28   A. A. Makarov, T. A. Mitrova and V. A. Kulagin, *Global and Russian Energy Outlook 2019* (Moscow: Institut energeticheskih issledovanii RAN, Skolkovo, 2019).

29   Pravitelstvo Rossiiskoi Federatsii, *Energeticheskaya strategiya Rossii na period do 2030 goda*.

30   Ministry of Energy, *Proekt enoergostrategii Rossiiskoi Federatsii na period do 2035 goda*.

31   'Assistant Secretary of the Security Council of the Russian Federation Alexander Abelin Told Reporters That the New Doctrine of Russia's Energy Security Will Help to Forestall New Threats in This Area', Security Council of the Russian Federation, 16 May 2019, www.scrf.gov.ru/news/allnews/2593/.

policy and transfer to green technologies as an external political challenges to Russia's energy security. According to the 2019 ESD, although Russia 'supports international efforts to prevent climate change', it 'considers [it] unacceptable to analyse climate change issues and environmental protection from a biased point of view and to infringe on the interests of states, producing energy resources'.[32]

The 2019 ESD's characterisation of the green energy agenda as 'a challenge' was ridiculed by experts.[33] Yet, it is worth remembering that a 'challenge' is defined in the document as something that creates both problems and opportunities. This distinguishes the 2019 ESD from the 2012 ESD, which mostly treated the climate agenda as a threat and seemed not to notice renewables. Indeed, some experts claim that the 2019 ESD signifies a paradigmatic shift because renewables are now treated as a challenge.[34] According to the head of Russian Greenpeace's energy program, it is the first official Russian document to take proper notice of changes in the energy sector, and to treat renewables seriously.[35] This groundbreaking change is likely to foster the most debate in coming years.

The distinction between external economic and political challenges is curious when it comes to energy transition. While, for Russia, the former are associated only with increased competition, the latter are about policy decisions imposed globally, which are believed to be artificially disadvantaging Russian resources in the international market.

Surprisingly, the linked topics of energy mix and the external competitiveness of Russia's resources have emerged as most the contentious in the context of the 2019 ESD. The position of state officials and big energy companies has remained predictably sceptical, with Vladimir Putin recently repeating a set of notorious arguments against renewables (i.e. that they lead to the death of birds, the multiplication of worms and make human life uncomfortable due to the installation of large equipment).[36] According to Russian Member of Parliament Pavel Zavalny, the 'availability and low

---

32   President of Russia, *Doktrina energeticheskoi bezopasnosti*.

33   D. Chugunoff, 'Rossiiskii Neftegaz', Facebook Group, 16 May 2019, www.facebook.com/groups/437496816287290/?ref=bookmarks; M. Korchemkin, 'Rossiiskii Neftegaz', Facebook Group, 15 May 2019, www.facebook.com/groups/437496816287290/?ref=bookmarks.

34   Ivanov cf. Kravchenko, 'Putin podpisal novuu doktrinu energobezopasnosti'.

35   cf. A. Komrakov, 'Doktrina krugovoi energeticheskoi bezopasnosti' [Energy security doctrine], *Nezavisimaya gazeta*, 14 May 2019.

36   E. Vavina, 'Putin Stood up for Birds and Worms Suffering from Renewable Energy', *Vedomosti*, 10 July 2019, www.vedomosti.ru/business/articles/2019/07/09/806215-putin-vstupilsya-za-ptits.

prices for hydrocarbons as well as [the] geography of renewables make the development of the latter economically non-profitable'; their use, he argues, should be limited to that of supporting traditional means of energy, especially in remote regions.[37]

For the most part, big companies do not notice renewables. Igor Sechin, CEO of Rosneft, declared recently that reports 'of the oil death [are] an exaggeration', and that 'oil will remain the basis of global energy for 20–30 years to come'.[38] In his view, sanctions and other decisions of regulators only distort the free market. To the extent that the state and companies have shown increased interest in LNG, this has been about generating more flexibility in global markets, including Russia's diversification from traditional European markets to Asian ones (see below).

Generally speaking, energy experts have engaged in a more intensive exchange of views than state officials or big companies over the 2019 ESD. While many support the official position, their arguments vary greatly. Some insist that Russia should concentrate on economic development, for while support for clean energy is 'noble and fashionable', it is not profitable.[39] Others describe hydrocarbons as the cheapest means of energy, and renewables as nothing but a political story, subsidised by traditional energy.[40] Proponents of green energy argue that renewables and energy efficiency fail to get proper attention in Russia. Part of the problem is that the 2019 ESD sees items that might ensure progress in the global energy market as threats to Russian exports, and fails to see that Russia is drowning in outdated energy production.[41] Others stress that the ESD is based on the idea that all new things are invented to harm Russia.[42] Tatiana Mitrova, while not referring directly to the ESD, argues that Russia does not pay sufficient attention to climate change, and that this reduces the possibility of new technological development.

---

37    'Pavel Zavalny Commented on Anatoly Chubais's Idea of Introducing a Carbon Tax', Duma, 13 June 2019, duma.gov.ru/news/45281/.

38    'Igor Sechin Made a Keynote Speech at the X Eurasian Economic Forum in Verona', Rosneft, 19 October 2017, www.rosneft.ru/press/news/item/188133/.

39    Bykov cf. Komrakov, 'Doktrina krugovoi energeticheskoi bezopasnosti'.

40    K. Simonov, 'Voprosy k ispolnitelyam' [Questions to the performers], IZ, 17 May 2019, iz.ru/878846/konstantin-simonov/voprosy-k-ispolniteliam.

41    Chugunoff, 'Rossiiskii Neftegaz'.

42    M. Korchemkin, 'Rossiiskii Neftegaz', Facebook Group, 15 May 2019.

This attitude cannot and will not change global developments; instead, Russian budget receipts from the export of energy resources will most likely decrease, even though natural gas will preserve its position.[43]

In sum, while Russian policy preferences for traditional resources remains the same, debates around the 2019 ESD demonstrate a gradual shift in attitude towards renewables and clean energy at large. They have become much more central in Russian energy discussions and an increasing number of Russian specialists stress their role in the energy transition, which will have serious implications for Russian exports and budgetary receipts. Yet, the 2019 ESD and most officials treat renewables and clean energy as (unfair) competition and, in some cases, as external political challenges. Internally, debates about the need to promote clean energy choices remain modest.

# Geographical Diversification

The third group of issues that are important in the 2019 ESD stem from the way it promotes diversification of energy markets. Geographical diversification is not a new topic. Analysts have talked about the EU's and Russia's race towards diversification since at least the turn of the century.[44] The key rationale for diversification is grounded in the EU's liberalisation packages, which upset previous arrangements in EU–Russian trade in gas. Curiously, the EU's policy choices, which are rooted in market thinking, are conceptualised by Russia as political steps to decrease the share of Russian resources.

The need to enlarge the share of the Asian market (to balance the loss of European consumers of Russian oil and natural gas) has been present in Russia for quite some time. For example, the 2009 Energy Strategy stresses the need to diversify channels of transportation of Russian oil and gas to Europe to maintain the share in traditional markets and enhance the security of supply *and* to diversify to Asia. The latter is linked to

---

43   T. Mitrova, Y. Melnikov, D. Chugunoff and A. Glagoleva, *Vodorodnaya ekonomika – put k nizkouglerodnomu razvitiu* (M: Skolkovo, 2019). See also A. Sobko, 'Rossiya prospala energoperehod: chto my poteryaem' [Russia slept through the energy transition: What will we lose], RIA Novosti, 21 July 2019, ria.ru/20190721/1556719899.html; Makarov, Mitrova and Kulagin, *Prognoz razvitiya energetiki mira i Rossii.*
44   A. Monaghan, 'Dilemmy energeticheskoi bezopasnosti' [Dilemmas of energy security], *Pro et Contra*, May–June 2016.

the need to develop oil and gas resources and the economy of Russia's Asian territories.[45] New programs of exploration have been initiated and diversification strengthened through the construction of an oil pipeline—Eastern Siberia – Pacific Ocean (with a projected capacity of up to 80 mtoe)—a gas pipeline—the Power of Siberia (with an intended capacity of up to 38 bcm)—and through plans to build gas storage and cooperate in electricity generation with China.[46]

The 2012 ESD described insufficient geographical diversification of export markets as a threat to Russia's energy security. The 2017 updated energy strategy draft did not mention European markets at all (but underlined the need to preserve traditional markets).[47] Instead, it set a diversified energy resources export structure with a much higher share of the Asia-Pacific region as a goal.

There is considerable continuity in the 2019 ESD in terms of thinking about geographical diversification. However, it puts some emphases differently. First, it frames the reduction of Russia's share in traditional (European) markets, which is due to energy transition and restrictions that affect some Russian exports, as a threat to Russia's energy security (security of supplier). The document does not openly name European markets but clearly refers to the EU's policy choices. Second, the 2019 ESD develops an argument about 'the migration of the centre of global economic growth to the Asia-Pacific region' and treats this as a challenge (providing both opportunities and threats) that the Russian energy sector has to deal with. In itself, this economic argument is not new.[48] Yet, it has become much more salient in the new doctrine.

At the same time, the political aspects of diversification that support Russia's vision of a polycentric world and provide for close cooperation with China to challenge the authority of the West are not mentioned. This absence or silence can be seen as supporting the dominant discourse, whereby Russia is conducting a purely economically grounded energy policy—unlike the West, which uses sanctions to challenge normal economic competition.

---

45    Pravitelstvo Rossiiskoi Federatsii, *Energeticheskaya strategiya Rossii na period do 2030 goda*.

46    'Report by Alexey Miller, Chairman of the Gazprom Management Committee at the Annual General Shareholders Meeting', Gazprom, 30 June 2017, www.gazprom.ru/press/news/miller-journal/2017/340087/.

47    Ministry of Energy, *Proekt enoergostrategii Rossiiskoi Federatsii na period do 2035 goda*.

48    See, for example, 'Igor Sechin Made a Keynote Speech at the 4th Eurasian Forum in Verona', Rosneft, 22 October 2015, www.rosneft.ru/press/today/item/176755/.

Among companies, Rosneft and Gazprom remain the biggest proponents of diversification. They demonstrate their commitment via the construction of pipelines and by increasing their exports to the Asia-Pacific region (APR). Rosneft, in particular, declared in late 2018 that Asian markets were more important than European ones (48 per cent vs 40 per cent).[49] Novatek began supplying LNG to China via the Northern Sea Route in 2018, reducing the duration of delivery from 35 to 19 days and thereby increasing its attractiveness. It is clear that Russian companies support diversification; however, any increase in the supply of Russian LNG, not to mention the construction of gas pipelines, will predictably increase the salience of debates about the inefficiency of coordination of Russian export strategies in hydrocarbons.

Surprisingly, there is consensus among experts about the need for diversification from Europe to Asia. One line of debate is about whether this diversification is real. Some believe that geographical diversification proceeds with normal speed as it should; however, others maintain that it is slow and is more declaratory than real.[50] Some experts point out that, despite official recognition that traditional markets are less and less significant, export infrastructure in that direction is still bolstered (e.g. Nord Stream, South/Turkish Stream) and existing capacities exceed what is needed to meet current obligations (i.e. ground and sea transportation). Consequently, in that sense, the 2019 ESD is seen as offering rhetorical change only.

Another line of expert discussion is about the economic salience of diversification. Observing price dynamics, some experts argue that Asian markets are becoming increasingly attractive compared to European ones. Previous conclusions about the higher profitability of European markets have been challenged on a number of grounds, including competition in European markets as a result of liberalisation, limits on long-term contracts with oil indexation, inflows of LNG, and increased demand in Asian markets.[51] On the last point, studies stress favourable gas price dynamics

---

49  V. Petlevoy, 'Osnovnym exportnym rynkom dlya 'Rosnefti' vmesto Evropy stala Aziya [Asia has become the main export market for Rosneft instead of Europe], *Vedomosti*, 7 November 2018, www.vedomosti.ru/business/articles/2018/11/07/785822-rosnefti-vmesto-evropi-stala-aziya.
50  M. Korchemkin, 'Rossiiskii Neftegaz', Facebook Group, 14 May 2019, www.facebook.com/groups/437496816287290/?ref=bookmarks.
51  Kornilov and Tanurkov cf. Petlevoy, 'Osnovnym exportnym rynkom dlya 'Rosnefti' vmesto Evropy stala Aziya'.

in Asia.[52] Yet, the durability of this remains a contested issue. At the same time, some experts highlight the political rationale of cooperation with Asian countries (in particular China).[53]

In sum, although the 2019 ESD maintains the need to diversify export markets from Europe to Asia, its nuances are different from earlier documents. First, the doctrine does not mention European markets. Second, the economic rationale for diversification towards Asia is not only stressed but also reinforced by experts. While companies continue their penetration into Asian markets, experts debate whether the proclaimed goal of diversification and its implementation is real or merely declaratory.

# Conclusion

Although the 2019 ESD is presented as a response to a radically new global situation and Russia's position in it, the three groups of issues reviewed above show much more continuity than change. The ambiguity between geopolitics and market economics has been maintained, although the shift to geopolitics and closer state involvement has been strengthened. In that sense, Russia has regained its traditional course. Similarly, the diversification of markets from Europe to Asia has been maintained.

Yet, at the same time, subtle differences can also be discerned. Geopolitics is driven by the sense of external threats (including sanctions) and internal dangers. While the influence of the Russian state in the energy sector has increased, the key reason, according to the official discourse, is unfair competition from the West in the form of sanctions. Whereas before 2014, Russia talked about discrimination on political grounds, the present rhetoric stresses economic reasoning. Economic justifications (rather than political ones) are also used to justify diversification to Asia.

The most noticeable change in the 2019 policy debates concerns energy mix. Without fully embracing energy transition, the 2019 ESD recognises green energy, energy efficiency and climate change as challenges.

---

52   A. Sobko, 'Gaz desheveet, potomu chto neft dorozhaet: nachalas novaya epoha' [Gas is getting cheaper because oil is getting more expensive: A new era has begun], RIA, 4 July 2019, ria.ru/2019 0704/1556152605.html.
53   A. A. Makarov, T. A. Mitrova and V. A. Kulagin, *Global and Russian Energy Outlook 2019.*

And, although its policy choices remain unchanged, a certain degree of novelty stems from its very recognition of green energy and its influence on Russia's export of hydrocarbons.

The three groups of issues examined—market economics vs geopolitics, the energy mix and geographical diversification—are interrelated. Whereby, geopolitics constrains the development of clean energy and renewables, which directs the diversification of markets, and geographical diversification results in gains that become more salient as a result of the EU's policy choices on green energy. The issue that causes the most debate in Russia today is energy mix. Here the views are polarised between those that profess the inevitability of the energy transition and the need for Russia to adopt it, and those who still believe that traditional resources will maintain their centrality because renewables (and climate change) are an expensive political choice. Discussion about geopolitics vs market economics are largely missing in such debates. Where they exist, they involve experts who insist on the need for a true market, companies that insist on export competition and others who are happy with the status quo. Debates about geographical diversification tend to focus on whether it is actually happening and the extent to which it is economically justified.

The evolution from political to economic reasoning is noticeable in Russian discourses about energy. It is visible in debates about geopolitics vs market economics, in discussions about energy mix and in questions over the motivation for geographical diversification from Europe to Asia. In sum, Russian debates reveal a wide variety of opinions, which is healthy for policy debates. However, the extent to which this variation affects policymaking is unclear. Noticeably, while some believe that the ESD is a result of experts' deliberation, others insist that policy discussions have not been sufficient and a further set of studies is needed to verify the 2019 ESD's conclusions.[54]

---

54  Simonov, 'Voprosy k ispolnitelyam'. See also Chugunoff, 'Rossiiskii Neftegaz'.

# Conclusion

## Elizabeth Buchanan

This book has illustrated the primacy of the Asia-Pacific region in Russia's developing foreign energy strategy. While not necessarily a 'pivot' to the East, the Kremlin's new-found perception of its energy export potential as flexible and agile enough to move between both Europe and Asia warrants further attention. After all, increased Russian product dilutes the potential market share for others. While some may argue that competition is good for markets, with consumers and end users winning in the energy price 'wars' that result from over-supplied markets, from an energy security perspective, weathering such shifts requires a clear, cohesive national energy strategy—something Australia still lacks.

On the doorstep of vast reserves, the Asia-Pacific will account for the majority of growth in terms of future energy demand. For Moscow, this is a welcome reorientation of economic growth and energy demand. Russia's energy sphere accounts for more than a quarter of its gross domestic product and almost two-thirds of the Russian export market. Moscow is planning for the Far East to account for 40 per cent of Russia's oil and gas exports. Russian liquefied natural gas exports to Asia are expected to rise from 6 per cent to 30 per cent by 2035, which is fitting given the future of global energy demand is also to be found in the Asia-Pacific.

An array of direct and indirect implications for Australia stem from Russian foreign energy strategy in Asia. Of course, the starkest is that Australia is set on a potential collision course when it comes to fuelling the Asia-Pacific. The Australian Government should watch Russia's Northern Sea Route (NSR) development closely, as a key component of Russia's new energy strategy (as outlined by Tatiana Romanova) is the creation of a new global energy corridor for Asia. This has substantial implications for Australia. The Asia-Pacific currently relies on the Malacca Strait corridor to receive goods and most of our energy needs. This corridor is congested, poorly secured and has long lead times—all of which factor into increasing transportation costs. These costs are carried over to the consumer. Russia's NSR, which can currently operate 3–4 months of the year for Asia (and year-round for Europe), offers a viable alternative to fuel the Asian market in terms of liquefied natural gas (LNG). Thanks to climate change, in the coming years the NSR will be passable year-round. This reorientation of global energy corridors provided by the NSR will ultimately make Australia an extremely expensive import and export market.

In both supply and demand terms, Canberra is at the mercy of market shifts and geopolitical developments in the Asia-Pacific (and, in some places, contested, regional sea lines of communication), and is facing increased LNG competition from allies and adversaries alike, not to mention the increased threat posed by cyber-attributed attacks on critical infrastructure internationally. Australian energy security is at risk in numerous ways: for example, targeted attacks on shipping logs, and logistical platforms tracking or calculating fuel at sea on its way to Australia. A tanker's navigation system might be targeted, the energy major's cyber system could be infiltrated and Australian fuel delivery orders doctored. Climate change is evidently eroding Australia's coastal communities, which will no doubt impact the port infrastructure we rely upon to receive fuel supplies.

Australia's mining boom was great while it lasted. But policymakers failed to futureproof Australian energy security during those days, and the window for action during today's LNG advent is closing swiftly. Of course, it is easy to argue that competing states have undermined our energy security position, particularly Russia in the Asia-Pacific LNG sphere. However, the real hurdle is overcoming the national 'she'll be right' mentality that permeates all energy stakeholders—policymakers, energy firms and the private sector as well as the local citizen consumer.

Further areas for research into this complex challenge include questioning the utility of nationalising the Australian energy sector. The state leaves (what little energy security planning we do) to the private sector to manage. Australia is the only member state of the International Energy Agency to consistently fail to uphold its obligation to have adequate emergency fuel stockpiles. In early 2020, Canberra made some moves to rectify this national challenge—by tapping into the US emergency oil stockpile.

Given the vast array of regional stockpile options at hand—India or South Korea, for example—the turn to America clearly demonstrated the influence of politics.

The year 2020 also ushered in another variable to the energy security picture: COVID-19. The pandemic has further underscored the strategic primacy of supply security and sea lines of communication. Conversely, energy demand has contracted to the point that there is a global supply glut, driving down energy prices and eroding Australia's export market demand. This strategic shock has highlighted the need to think long term and in 'new ways' about energy security. Self-sufficiency is back in vogue and Australia is increasingly talking about green energy economies and renewables in our energy mix. Society is also warming to increased discussion around the role of nuclear energy in Australia's energy future.

The Asia-Pacific will account for the majority of growth in terms of future global energy demand. For Moscow, this is a welcome nearby sphere for economic growth and energy demand. Russia's edge remains its cheaper gas product, geographical proximity to Asia's growing market and clear strategic policy for energy exports. Australia could craft a viable energy export policy and seek to develop a cheaper product, but it cannot change geography. Canberra needs to rethink the paradigm.

To ensure energy security for the nation, Australia should be looking to avenues to end its energy import over-reliance. As well as developing an indigenous energy alternative—whether nuclear or using our own LNG exports—Australia needs to reduce its over-dependency on foreign energy supplies. On the export side, Australia must innovate with regards to the Asia-Pacific market. Noting the Pacific Step-Up strategy of the Australian Government, priority could be assigned to developing green energy economies with our nearby Pacific Island neighbours.

Crafting a serious energy security strategy is not an insurmountable task for Australia—anything would be an improvement. That said, there is great opportunity and agility to think outside the box and table a strategy that gets the energy security balance just right—for the long haul. Russia views energy as a strategic commodity; for Australia to have a fighting chance at securing its energy future, Canberra ought to start doing the same.

# Contributors

**Air Vice-Marshal John Blackburn AO (retired)**
**Institute for Integrated Economic Research, Australia**

John Blackburn is a leading Australian strategist. He has most recently been deputy chairman of both the Kokoda and Williams foundations where he has led key efforts to reshape Australian and allied thinking about defence transformation appropriate to the evolving strategic environment. He joined the Royal Australian Air Force in 1975. In 1996 he was promoted and appointed to command No. 41 Wing, which put him in charge of all military air defence radar/C2 and surveillance units and all military air traffic control. His later appointments included director general of policy and plans in Air Force Headquarters, and director general of military strategy in Defence Headquarters. On promotion to air vice-marshal in 2002, he became head of strategic policy for defence. In this latter position, he was responsible for the development of Australian Defence Force (ADF) strategic policy and led the development of the Defence Joint Vision, the Future War Fighting Concept and the Network-Centric Warfare Concept and Roadmap for the ADF.

**Dr Elizabeth Buchanan**
**Deakin University, Canberra**

Elizabeth Buchanan is Lecturer of Strategic Studies with Deakin University for the Defence and Strategic Studies Course (DSSC) at the Australian War College. Elizabeth is a Non-Resident Fellow at the Modern War Institute at West Point Military Academy and is the inaugural Co-Director of the Modern War Institute's Polar Security Research Initiative—*Project 6633*. She holds a PhD in Russian Arctic strategy from The Australian National University. She was the Visiting Maritime Fellow at the NATO Defense

College in Rome focusing on Arctic geopolitics, has been a Visiting Scholar with the Brookings Institution and has work experience in the global oil sector.

## Associate Professor Stephen Fortescue
## University of New South Wales

Stephen Fortescue gained a PhD in Soviet politics from The Australian National University (ANU) in 1977. He worked in Soviet-related business from 1977 to 1981. Later, he held research positions at ANU (1981–84) and the University of Birmingham (1985–86). He took up an academic post at the University of New South Wales (UNSW), Sydney, in 1987, and remained there until his retirement in 2013. He is Honorary Associate Professor, School of Social Sciences, UNSW, and Visiting Fellow, Centre for European Studies, ANU. His current research interests include Russian policymaking processes, policy related to the Russian Far East, and commercial engagement with the Asia-Pacific and Russian industry policy.

## Professor Jakub M. Godzimirski
## Norwegian Institute of International Affairs

Jakub M. Godzimirski has been working on Russian foreign and security policy issues at the Norwegian Institute of International Affairs for more than 20 years, paying special attention to the role of energy resources in Russian grand strategy. In addition, he also has worked on European policy and its impact on developments in Central and Eastern Europe, including relations with Russia.

## Shoichi Itoh
## Institute of Energy Economics, Japan

Shoichi Itoh is a senior analyst and manager at the Institute of Energy Economics, Japan. He has extensive expertise in global energy markets and geopolitics, and is a frequent speaker on energy security around the world. He held visiting fellowships at the Center for Strategic and International Studies in 2010, at the Brookings Institution in 2009 and at the Monterey Institute of International Studies in 2006. He also served at the Consulate General of Japan in Khabarovsk as political and economic attaché in 2000–03. He earned masters degrees at the University of London and the University of Tsukuba. Itoh has spearheaded a variety of policy projects, particularly on the US–Japan alliance, and has published widely on international relations and energy links among Japan, China, Russia and the US.

## Professor Keun-Wook Paik
## Independent Researcher and Consultant

Keun-Wook Paik is an acknowledged authority on Eurasian energy, in particular on Sino-Russian oil and gas cooperation, China's natural gas industry and Democratic People's Republic of Korea's offshore oil exploration. He is the author of *Sino-Russian Oil and Gas Cooperation: The Reality and Implications* (Oxford University Press, 2012). Paik was previously an Associate Fellow of the Energy, Environment and Resources program at Chatham House. He was a senior research fellow at the Oxford Institute for Energy Studies. He is also an Adjunct Professor at Yonsei-Seri EU Centre under the Institute of East and West Studies, Yonsei University, and the University of Jilin. He was an Adjunct Professor at China University of Petroleum (Beijing). During the last two decades, he has been advising energy-related institutions in Russia, China, Korea, Japan and the US, as well as the UN, with regard to the geopolitics of pipeline development in North-East Asia, China's natural gas expansion, and the Democratic Republic of Korea's oil exploration and development issues.

## Associate Professor Tatiana Romanova
## Saint Petersburg State University, Russia

Tatiana Romanova holds a PhD from Saint Petersburg State University and an MA from the College of Europe, Brugge. She is an Associate Professor at Saint Petersburg State University and at Higher School of Economics, Moscow. Director of the Jean Monnet Centre of Excellence, she holds the Jean Monnet Chair. Her research interests include EU–Russian economic, legal and political relations, normative competition, resilience, legal approximation, sanctions, energy markets and security, Russian foreign policy, EU institutions and decision-making.

## Professor Peter Rutland
## Wesleyan University, Connecticut

Peter Rutland works on contemporary Russian politics and political economy, with a side interest in nationalism. Recent articles cover topics such as Russian 'soft power', the structure of the Russian elite, and Russia's performance in science and technology. He blogs about nationalism around the world at Nationalism Watch, and is currently working on the project 'Visualizing the Nation', which explores how political nationalism has expressed itself through visual media—film, television and the internet. He has taught at Wesleyan since 1989. Before that he taught at the University of Texas at Austin, and at the University of York and London University in the UK. He has a BA from Oxford and a DPhil from York. He has also been a visiting professor at Columbia University, and is an associate of the Davis Center for Russian and Eurasian Studies at Harvard University.

## Dr Maria Shagina
## University of Zurich, Switzerland

Maria Shagina is a CEES Postdoctoral Fellow at the Center for Eastern European Studies at the University of Zurich. She is currently affiliated with the Geneva International Sanctions Network. As a political risk analyst for Global Risk Insights, she covered energy politics and sanctions in post-Soviet countries. Previously, she was a JSPS Postdoctoral Fellow at Ritsumeikan University and a Visiting Fellow at the Centre for Russian, European and Eurasian Studies, University of Birmingham. She holds a PhD in Political Science from the University of Lucerne, Switzerland.

## Dr Morena Skalamera
## Leiden University, Netherlands

Morena Skalamera is Assistant Professor of Russian and International Studies at Leiden University. She teaches courses in international political economy, with a regional focus on Russia and Eurasia. Her research interests include Eurasian, Russian and post-Soviet politics, and the geopolitics of energy in Eurasia. She has conducted extensive field research in post-Soviet Eurasia, especially in Russia, Central Asia and Turkey. Her current writings focus on issues of identity politics, exploring the interplay between international and domestic factors in policymaking, and contemporary state–market relations, with a focus on energy policy dynamics in Russia and Central Asia. She is currently working on a manuscript that examines how energy firms have shaped the energy relationship between Russia and Europe and the energy strategies of the former Soviet states.

www.ingramcontent.com/pod-product-compliance
Lightning Source LLC
Chambersburg PA
CBHW040820280326
41926CB00093B/4634